D1644756

Making Sense
of Competition
Policy

Making Sense of Competition Policy

Frank Fishwick

KOGAN
PAGE

First published in 1993

Apart from any fair dealing for the purposes of research or private study, or criticism or review, as permitted under the Copyright, Designs and Patents Act, 1988, this publication may only be reproduced, stored or transmitted, in any form or by any means, with the prior permission in writing of the publishers, or in the case of reprographic reproduction in accordance with the terms of licences issued by the Copyright Licensing Agency. Enquiries concerning reproduction outside those terms should be sent to the publishers at the undermentioned address:

Kogan Page Limited
120 Pentonville Road
London N1 9JN

© Frank Fishwick, 1993

British Library Cataloguing in Publication Data

A CIP record for this book is available from the British Library.

ISBN 0 7494 1035 3

Typeset by Books Unlimited (Nottm), Sutton-in-Ashfield NG17 1AL
Printed and bound in Great Britain by Biddles Ltd, Guildford and Kings Lynn

CONTENTS

List of Figures 7

List of Tables 8

The Cranfield Management Research Series 9

1 Introduction and Overview **11**

Objectives and outline of this book 11
Conflicting views on competition policy 15
Conclusions 26

2 Underlying Economic Principles **27**

Outline of chapter 27
Perfect competition and comparison with monopoly 28
Market contestability 40
Oligopoly — competition among the few 47
Basic economic principles and norms of competition policy 55
Conclusion 62

3 Definition of Dominance or Market Power **63**

Introduction 63
Definition of dominance and the relevant market concept 64
Market definition and potential competition 78
Indices of market concentration 83
The analytical framework of the CEC and the MMC for
  assessment of dominance 88
Conclusion 91

4 Competition Policy in the European Economic Community   **92**

Introduction: the basic conflict of views   *92*
Restrictive agreements   *94*
Abuse of a dominant position   *103*
Mergers and acquistions   *115*

5 UK Competition Policy in Relation to that of the EEC   **136**

Introduction   *136*
Historical and political background   *138*
Policy on restrictive agreements   *145*
Market power and its abuse   *150*
Policy on mergers   *163*

6 Some Major Issues and General Conclusions   **175**

Introduction   *175*
Five specific issues   *176*
Conclusions   *194*

Appendix — Tables of cases   **197**

Bibliography   **200**

Index   **207**

LIST OF FIGURES

2.1   Monopoly v perfect competition — same short-run marginal
       costs   30

2.2   The individual firm in perfect competition   32

2.3(a) Perfect competition — short- and long-run pricing   34

2.3(b) Monopoly — pricing with very low marginal cost   34

2.4   Demand under oligopoly   48

2.5   Price stability under oligopoly   50

4.1   The Merger Control Regulation — how it works   125

LIST OF TABLES

3.1	Two market structures to illustrate indices	85
4.1	Mergers and acquisitions affecting EC companies	116
4.2	Merger control regulation — thresholds for application	118

THE CRANFIELD MANAGEMENT RESEARCH SERIES

The Cranfield Management Research Series represents an exciting joint initiative between the Cranfield School of Management and Kogan Page.

As one of Europe's leading post-graduate business schools, Cranfield is renowned for its applied research activities, which cover a wide range of issues relating to the practice of management.

Each title in the Series is based on current research and authored by Cranfield faculty or their associates. Many of the research projects have been undertaken with the sponsorship and active assistance of organisations from the industrial, commercial or public sectors. The aim of the Series is to make the findings of direct relevance to managers through texts which are academically sound, accessible and practical.

For managers and academics alike, the Cranfield Management Research Series will provide access to up-to-date management thinking from some of Europe's leading academics and practitioners. The series represents both Cranfield's and Kogan Page's commitment to furthering the improvement of management practice in all types of organisations.

THE SERIES EDITORS

Frank Fishwick
Reader in Managerial Economics
Director of Admissions at Cranfield School of Management

Frank joined Cranfield from Aston University in 1966, having previously worked in textiles, electronics and local government (town and country planning). Recent research and consultancy interests have been focused on business concentration, competition policy and the book publishing industry. He has been directing a series of research studies for the Commission of the European Communities, working in collaboration with business economists in France and Germany. Frank is permanent economic adviser to the Publishers Association in the UK and is a regular consultant to other public and private sector organisations in the UK, continental Europe and the US.

Gerry Johnson
Professor of Strategic Management
Director of the Centre for Strategic Management and Organisational Change
Director of Research at Cranfield School of Management

After graduating from University College London, Gerry worked for several years in management positions in Unilever and Reed International before becoming a Management Consultant. Since 1976, he has taught at Aston University Management Centre, Manchester Business School, and from 1988 at Cranfield School of Management. His research work is primarily concerned with processes of strategic decision making and strategic change in organisations. He also works as a consultant on issues of strategy formulation change at a senior level with a number of UK and international firms.

Shaun Tyson
Professor of Human Resource Management
Director of the Human Resource Research Centre
Dean of the Faculty of Management and Administration at Cranfield School of Management

Shaun studied at London University and spent eleven years in senior positions in industry within engineering and electronic companies.

For four years he was a lecturer in personnel management at the Civil Service College, and joined Cranfield in 1979. He has acted as a consultant and researched widely into human resource strategies, policies and the evaluation of the function. He has published ten books.

1

Introduction and Overview

OBJECTIVES AND OUTLINE OF THIS BOOK

Competition or 'antitrust' policy is a term used broadly to describe intervention by public authorities to ensure competition in the markets for goods and services. It covers prevention or control of agreements between firms to limit competition (explicit cartels or tacit collusion), control over monopoly power and its abuse, and the process of business concentration through mergers and acquisitions.

There is a vast literature on competition policy but most of it has been written by specialists, lawyers or economists, for other specialists in the same discipline. In particular, antitrust economists seem to have written very little which seeks to explain for those outside their own specialism the principles underlying different forms of competition policy and the controversies about them. The treatment of the subject in general textbooks on applied economics tends to be descriptive and quite divorced from related economic theory. The objective of this book is to try to fill this gap, for the benefit of the many people other than antitrust economists who may have an interest in competition policy — other economists, legal specialists and managers of businesses who may become involved. By exploring the different economic and political arguments influencing both the design of policy and decisions in particular cases, it is hoped to give readers an insight that they can apply to any cases arising in future.

The author has worked in the area of competition policy for 20 years, mainly in relation to European Economic Community (EEC) policies. Much of this work has been financed by the Commission of the European Communities (CEC), some of it undertaken by research teams at Cranfield. Some has been financed by firms or trade associations in dispute with the CEC. Throughout, the objective has been the application of basic economic principles to particular cases, within the context of the legislation. Although one cannot write a book about competition policy without describing the legal framework and also the political influences, what follows is not intended as a reference work on the legislation but as an explanation and critique of the underlying economics.

The rest of this first chapter outlines the basic purposes of competition policy, which is seen by most of its supporters as a necessary condition for the efficient allocation of resources through market forces. The need for such policies is questioned by economists and politicians on the 'right' who appear to see them as an intervention in the market mechanism itself and even as a slur on that mechanism. There is also criticism from the 'left', from those who emphasise weaknesses of the market mechanism. For them, competition policies are not only insufficient as a means of correcting problems of 'market failure' but may indeed aggravate such problems by preventing interventionist solutions. As unemployment has increased in Europe, so this conflict between competition and 'industrial' policies has tended to intensify. Finally, some supporters of policies to maintain competition and prevent business concentration see these as objectives in themselves, not merely as necessary to ensure economic efficiency. This philosophy is concerned mainly with prevention of concentration of economic power; those who hold to it would sacrifice some of the advantages of business concentration for the purpose of ensuring freedom for individual enterprise. These conflicting ideas are important because they are reflected not only in the design of competition legislation but also in its practical enforcement.

Some of the basic economic concepts are introduced in the general overview which forms the rest of this chapter. Chapter 2 examines in greater detail the theoretical basis for intervention by government to maintain effective competition, covering the conventional theories of perfect competition, monopoly and oligopoly and discusses in greater detail the principle of contestability. Those with a solid grounding in economics will find it possible to skip much of this chapter; those whose interest is primarily in the practical application of the principles may prefer to 'skim-read' much of the material; it is deliberately structured to facilitate this. As may be expected, the point is made that perfect competition, on which much of the conceptual framework of antitrust economics still remains based (albeit implicitly), is an inadequate foundation in the real world.

Chapter 3 examines the different approaches adopted by antitrust authorities to analyse the impact of restrictive agreements; of mergers, abuse of monopoly power or anti-competitive practices. For example, must a 'dominant position' be measured by share of a 'market' and, if so, is potential competition in that market considered separately from market share, or included in its computation? How is concentration in a market measured and what is the significance of the use of different concentration indices? Chapter 3 is concerned essentially with the practical derivation and application of the concepts described in Chapter 2. Because much of the literature about competition policy is of American origin, this chapter explains several aspects of US policy.

Chapter 4 examines policies in the European Community. These include general prohibition of:

1. agreements which have as their objective or effect the restriction of competition, provided they affect trade between member states (Article 85 of the EEC Treaty — the Treaty of Rome);
2. abuse of a dominant position, again provided this affects inter-state trade (Article 86);
3. only since September 1990, large-scale mergers of firms based in two or more member states, where these would create or reinforce a dominant position (Council Regulation 4064/89 of December 1989).

EEC cases provide interesting evidence of the conflicting philosophies about competition policy. Within the Community, there has been strong support for the corporatist and interventionist notions of industrial policy (reflected in the absence of control over mergers before 1990). There has also been contradictory current of support for small and medium-sized firms reflected in pronouncements directed more towards protection of competitors rather than the process of competition. In more recent years, the Commission, in particular, has tried to focus attention on the purely economic considerations set out in Chapters 2 and 3.

Chapter 5 describes and discusses policies applied in the UK. The placing of this discussion after that of EC policies may seem strange, because UK competition policy predated even the existence of the European Economic Community. The main reason for this sequence is the current debate, encouraged by the publication of government discussion documents about the desirability of alignment of UK policies towards those applied at Community level. Current UK laws provide for:

1. registration and judicial consideration of agreements which restrict competition, with a presumption that these will operate against the public interest unless justified by one or more specified criteria or 'gateways' (Restrictive Trade Practices Act 1976, based mainly on the corresponding Act of 1956);
2. investigation into the possible existence and consequences of monopoly in the supply or purchase of specified goods or services and government powers to deal with these if they harm public interest (Fair Trading Act 1973, consolidating legislation dating from 1948);
3. investigation into alleged anti-competitive practices, not necessarily

associated with monopoly, and powers to deal with these if they operate against the public interest (Competition Act 1980);

4. consideration of mergers which exceed a certain threshold size and possible prohibition if these would be contrary to the public interest (Fair Trading Act 1973, the control on mergers dating from 1965);
5. prohibition, unless specifically exempted, of any agreements to apply fixed resale prices (Resale Prices Act 1964).

The main difference between UK competition policy and that of the EEC is a more equivocal attitude towards the effects of monopoly power. In neither jurisprudence is there a presumption that monopoly power is necessarily bad for economic welfare but Article 86 *prohibits* abuse of such power and provides for imposition of retrospective penalties. The UK government has power to prevent the continuation of abuse of monopoly power or other anti-competitive practice but there are no penalties for past conduct. If an abuse is an inevitable consequence of a monopoly with beneficial as well as adverse effects it may be permitted to continue. There is a similar difference with restrictive trade practices and agreements — unlike the EEC, the UK has no *retrospective* penalties. In the case of mergers, there is an explicit presumption in the UK that these are generally in the public interest, unless proved otherwise.

Chapter 6 discusses some issues reflecting the controversies described later in this chapter using material from Chapters 2 to 5. Attention is focused on certain elements in competition policy which are not always consistent with the basic economic principle of maximum aggregate welfare — a concept explained in Chapter 2. The specific topics examined are:

- 'vertical' agreements (between producers and distributors of the same product) with particular reference to resale price maintenance;
- the control of adverse effects of oligopoly, domination of the market by a small number of roughly equal competing firms;
- the market power versus efficiency argument with regard to mergers;
- definition of abuse of market power and of anti-competitive practices and whether this should depend on the size of the firm(s) accused;
- the related, but broader, question of whether competition policy should protect the process of competition, for the sake of society as a whole, or the rights of individual competitors.

Discussion of these issues provides an effective summary of earlier chapters, gives the author an opportunity for some provocative conclusions, but, most important, highlights arguments that will continue to dominate cases for the foreseeable future. A general conclusion is drawn: that those responsible for competition policies need to make the conceptual foundations clearer, with the objective of a consistent analytical framework. More controversial, perhaps, is the author's view that any objectives other than aggregate welfare should be made explicit.

CONFLICTING VIEWS ON COMPETITION POLICY

The role of competition in the market economy

Vickers and Hay (1987, p 2) provided a statement of the purpose of competition policy which has subsequently been widely quoted with approval:

> The prime purpose of competition policy is, in our view, to promote and maintain a process of effective competition so as to achieve a more efficient allocation of resources.

This view implies that competition is a necessary condition for the efficient allocation of resources through the market mechanism. The greater emphasis on competition policy in much of the world over the last few years results at least in part from a political move away from government planning and intervention towards reliance on the price mechanism. An almost religious respect for 'market forces' appears to have swept aside much of the socialism which seemed entrenched even 20 years ago. Although it may appear to be almost a truism that competition is essential to the working of markets, consideration of this statement introduces a number of conflicting factors which policy makers need to balance.

Let us leave aside, for the moment, benefits and costs which affect people or organisations outside trading transactions (externalities) and ignore any welfare effects related to distribution of income. Let us also assume that full employment can be achieved through adjustment of real wage rates to reflect the supply of and demand for labour in different occupations, industries and locations. (It may seem pedantic to present this long list of assumptions but what follows is a very strong statement which, in the view of some economists, tends to be accepted too readily.)

Given these assumptions, price provides an objective test of value for money in the use of resources. In general, a unit of a product will be supplied only if its price is at least equal to incremental variable cost or 'marginal cost'. In the short term, firms may sell some products at prices below marginal cost, perhaps to induce customers to buy them for the first time or to buy other products offered simultaneously, perhaps to gain or maintain a competitive position — there are many possible reasons. However, in the longer term a good or service will be produced only if the price is high enough to provide a profit. At the same time, customers will buy a product only if the price is less than or equal to its value to them. This key principle can be summarised in symbols:

$$\text{Value to customer} \geq \text{Price} \geq \text{Marginal cost}$$

This statement raises obvious questions. First, by how much does price exceed marginal cost? In the absence of competition, the demand for the product might not be sensitive ('elastic') to price, if this were set close to marginal cost. The supplier would then raise prices until sensitivity became evident, in principle until the decrease in sales turnover resulting from the increase in price were equal to the incremental cost of lost production. In other words, suppliers will find it profitable to increase prices until competition would make any further increase unprofitable. If price significantly exceeds marginal cost, this means that customers who would have been prepared to pay the cost of the supply of the product to them are denied the opportunity to do so.

This is the main argument emerging from conventional 'neoclassical' economic theory with regard to the disadvantages of monopoly, presented in greater detail in Chapter 2. Note that it is not just a question of transfer from consumers to producers. Producers make more profits at the expense of those consumers who buy the product at a higher price — this is a straight transfer of benefit (from 'consumer surplus' to 'producer surplus', terms to be explained in Chapter 2), but the loss of benefit from the units of output no longer sold is not compensated — it is a 'deadweight loss'.

Reverting to the above equation/inequality, we can see another possible problem, this time arising from lack of competition among buyers. A dominant buyer may use its bargaining power to push price appreciably below what it would have been prepared to pay for the product if it did not have that power. In this case, units may not be produced because incremental cost would be greater than the price, even though it would be less than the (competitive) market value of the product. This results in a deadweight loss for producers under conditions of *monopsony* (dominant buyer) which is a mirror image of that affecting consumers under monopoly. Monopsony gets less attention than monopoly, both in the economics literature and in competition policy, but is generally covered by the latter, and cases have occasionally arisen (eg that affecting joint purchasing by hypermarket chains in France in 1985).

Power to influence price — to raise it in the case of dominant producers and to depress it in that of dominant buyers — was traditionally the main focus of the economics of market structure. The net effect, the 'deadweight loss' has been described (eg in Ordover, 1990) as the *static* effect of market power, because it is based on given demand and cost conditions. In the way it is often presented, it involves a comparison with a notional situation of 'perfect competition', where a very large number of firms, producing identical products and unprotected from new entrants to the market, make just enough profit to survive. Unfortunately, conclusions drawn from comparison with this model still appear to pervade, perhaps subliminally, a lot of analysis in the area of competition policy.

The static effect of market power is unambiguous. It always implies unequivocally that, with any given demand and cost conditions, competition is good. However, economists have never been able to use this argument to justify outright condemnation of monopoly or the absence of competition, because the assumption of given demand and cost conditions is obviously unrealistic.

Let us first consider costs, or what Ordover calls the internal efficiency of the firm. On the one hand, competition may increase efficiency by forcing managers to pay constant attention to reducing costs and eliminating waste. The 'quiet life' effect of monopoly, often given the curious description of 'X-inefficiency', is regarded by some economists as more significant than exploitation of market power, especially as the latter is more likely to attract adverse attention. In a monopoly situation, managers may be satisfied to make just enough profit to keep shareholders happy, to transfer some of the proceeds of market power to employees in higher wages for less effort and to make their own lives enjoyable and comfortable. Criticism of this kind undoubtedly underlies much of the support for privatisation of public utilities in the UK and for subsequent rigorous regulation.

On the other hand, an activity may require large indivisible inputs which imply irrecoverable expenditure (sunk costs). Economies of scale, reflecting the spread of these indivisible costs over greater outputs, mean that in some activities it would be impossible for more than one firm to survive. In others, the practical alternative to monopoly could only be a small number of firms — oligopoly. Competition under oligopoly tends to focus on advertising and other promotion, rather than price. In the longer term such promotion expenditures may have little effect on market shares but may mean customers paying higher prices than they would if there were only one supplier.

So, with regard to the implications of competition for the costs of the firm ('internal efficiency'), economic theory is inconclusive. This inconclusiveness has long been recognised in UK competition policy and was also reflected in EEC policy as presented in Articles 85 and 86 of the Treaty of Rome.

The dynamic effects of competition are not confined to the internal efficiency of firms. In order to consider these effects, we need to remember the aim of each of the firms engaged in competition — to win. Any policy designed to prevent the development of monopoly power or to control its abuse must take into account the need to provide an incentive for firms to compete. One US law professor (R B Shapiro) has described enforcement of US antitrust laws as 'winner-bashing'.

The acquisition of market power by explicit or tacit collusion may be presumed bad for economic welfare in most cases, a principle usually reflected in competition policies. Acquisition of power by merger or takeover is generally judged by comparison of any harmful effects on competition with any gains in internal efficiency, though the relative emphasis varies both between different régimes and over time. The main dilemma for those drafting competition policy is how it should deal with market power gained by what was described in a 1945 US judgement (*Alcoa*) as 'skill, foresight and industry'. In particular, how should it deal with practices aimed at eliminating actual or potential competitors? After all, that is what competition is all about — putting your competitor out of business.

Solution of this dilemma for competition policy is not greatly helped by conventional 'neoclassical' economic theory, particularly the model of perfect competition. In this model there are many firms selling identical products to perfectly informed consumers. There is no scope for product differentiation or for persuasive advertising. In the real world, a major form of competition consists of developing different products and persuading customers of the value of the differences. Again in the model of perfect competition there are no barriers to entry: a new entrant can compete on equal terms with those firms already in the market, selling at the same price and with the same costs. In the real world, competition implies action by existing firms to create barriers to entry and to devise and employ *competitive* strategies to repel any would-be entrant. Discriminatory pricing, brand proliferation, exclusive dealing arrangements with suppliers or distributors, loyalty rebates — all tend to be regarded in principle as anti-competitive devices but, from the point of view of the firms employing them, they are competitive weapons.

Although some general rules can be established, such as the principle that agreements to restrict competition are generally harmful unless shown otherwise, present day economics is inconclusive about the net advantages of competition in business for society as a whole. While, in principle, the existence of competition may be expected to produce a better outcome than that which would have occurred in its absence, this principle does not hold universally. Moreover, implementation of this principle in competition policy is fraught with problems — first, the problems caused by economies of scale and the consequent inefficiency of fragmented business and, second, the simple truth that, by denying any firm the fruits of market power, competition policies may be removing the prize of the competitive process. What competition can exist without a prize?

Chapter 2 explains these principles more technically. It is concerned entirely with the (inconclusive) economic arguments about competition.

Criticism of competition policy from new laissez-faire economics

Since economic theory, once it is adapted towards greater realism, can provide few general conclusions about the desirability of particular market structures or of particular business practices or strategies, competition policy tends to be applied on a case-by-case basis. This is slow and expensive, in terms not just of administrative costs but also of the value of time and effort of business managers involved and of the distorting effects on business which may result. For example, the reference of a proposed hostile takeover to the UK Monopolies and Mergers Commission (MMC) or for full investigation by the Commission of the European Communities (CEC) may imply a delay of five or six months, a long period of uncertainty for all parties concerned.

The case-by-case approach also makes the detailed application of competition policy unpredictable, with allegations of inconsistency, of lack of transparency and of political influence. There are demands for general rules, particularly from lawyers (eg Merkin and Williams (1984) on UK policy). However, since no two cases are identical and the issues are not black-and-white, these demands are difficult to meet. This case-by-case approach by competition authorities leads to what could be considered major intervention in the practical affairs of management.

In the US there has since 1980 been a general tendency towards less enforcement of antitrust (competition) policies. In particular, there has been a more permissive attitude towards mergers and towards vertical agreements (exclusive dealing, product tie-ins and similar non-price arrangements between producers and distributors), together with the introduction of de-regulation in such activities as telecommunications and airline operation. What some observers (eg Hay, 1985; Comanor, 1990) see as a politically motivated retreat has been accompanied by support from economists, eager to champion the case for leaving everything to market forces. These advocates of 'new laissez-faire economics' suggest that imperfections of the market mechanism have been grossly exaggerated in analysis of market structure based on departures from the unrealistic concept of perfect competition. They argue that, with very few exceptions, the evolution of business concentration itself can and should be left to market forces. (An excellent and amusing exposition of this view is presented by Adams and Brock, 1991.)

The main plank of criticisms of antitrust policies from this 'right-wing' stance is the general existence of potential competition. Economists and lawyers from the 'Chicago School' (a major source of this philosophy) argue, for example, that market shares should be based not on current sales within a defined market but on the total capacity available to all firms with any current sales at all in that market. This principle has been formally introduced into the Department of Justice's guidelines for evaluation of mergers (see Chapter 3). As the denominator for the computation of market shares, the guidelines suggest the aggregate of sales which would be supplied to the market within one year of a 5 per cent increase in price. In practice, this principle implies widening of the market to include world-wide sales of any current supplier to the market.

If concentration remains significant even in this widely defined 'market', consideration must be given to the degree of 'contestability' — the ease with which firms not currently present within it could enter. Market 'contestability' depends primarily on absence of sunk costs of entry — costs which could not be recovered if the new entrant decided to withdraw. If there were no sunk costs, then incumbent firms could not exploit market dominance (individual or collective), either to realise high profits or to enjoy a quiet or wasteful existence. Outside firms could indulge in 'hit and run' competition, ultimately forcing incumbents to keep costs low and profits close to the minimum level required to retain funds.

Contestability is more fully explained and discussed further in Chapter 2, but the essence of the concept is probably quite clear. Indeed, the reader may wonder why contestability is presented as a novelty, as a creation of the 1980s. Surely, it is common sense which should have been recognised by economists from the earliest days of competition policy? Well it was, but it was not given this name. Potential competition from firms not present in the market was critical to a number of decisions both in UK and EEC policy administration in the 1970s and was analysed by reference to sunk costs. The main criticism of contestability theory is not directed at its internal logic. If there were no sunk costs of entry to a market then one would not expect prices to continue for long periods above the level required to cover minimum attainable costs — but how many markets exist with zero sunk costs of entry?

A final argument put forward by those who favour less active competition policy is that dominant positions tend to decay with time, unless they are bolstered by continuing increases in efficiency (and are therefore to be commended). Changes in the external environment, affecting both costs and demand, require constant changes in strategy and operating methods. A 'sleeping giant' which did not react to these changes would in due course lose its dominant position. The history of several formerly dominant firms illustrates this argument but counter-examples can also be found. The giant firm does not need to remain more efficient or innovative than potential competitors. It can maintain its dominant position by exploiting 'first user advantages' (Schmalensee, 1987a) to build an impregnable defensive wall around it and also by predatory tactics, selective attacks on smaller new entrants. Such attacks can be cross-subsidised by other market segments.

Reading through the articles produced by exponents of the new laissez-faire economics, it is difficult to find much that is new in principle. Potential competition and the specific concept of contestability, the natural decay of dominant positions not protected by government regulation, predatory conduct or greater efficiency — these are all notions long familiar to economists. In the author's view, the main contribution of those who champion this attack on competition policy from the 'right' has been to formalise the concepts and thereby to give them greater emphasis. They have certainly succeeded in getting antitrust/competition authorities to pay more regard to potential competition, an element which has not always been given enough attention. However, they have also provided ammunition for those whose attack on competition policy was primarily political.

Competition policy and interventionist policies

Before considering the role of competition policy in the market economy, we explicitly left aside a number of factors which may be used to justify intervention in the market mechanism. These include external costs and benefits, distributional effects and unemployment. Elements of 'market failure' arising from these welfare considerations are not generally corrected by competition policies — indeed such policies may aggravate them.

Consider the case of an external cost. Research undertaken at Cranfield during the 1970s when driver-only buses were first being introduced to urban routes in the UK showed that these imposed a significant cost on other road users. This can be substantially reduced by fare simplification or by off-vehicle sale of tickets or travel passes. With one licensed operator on each route or with common fares it is possible for the relevant public authority to insist on an appropriate rapid fare-collection system. In a competitive environment such intervention, indeed any similar regulation, is much more difficult.

External benefits may in principle be compensated by subsidies, a prospect much discussed in relation to the operation of 'socially desirable' railway lines after the proposed fragmentation of British Rail into private companies. Subsidies in some senses contradict the aims of competition policy, because they may give unfair advantages to the recipient company. If an inefficient railway operator claims that the subsidy it receives is not enough to enable it to keep a particular service going, there is often public pressure for an increase in subsidy.

Some practices dependent on the existence of market imperfections have a 'favourable' effect on the distribution of welfare, yielding benefits to lower income groups at the expense of the better off. Advertising by companies engaged in oligopolistic competition is condemned as 'wasteful' by many specialists in antitrust economics (eg Vickers and Hay p 8) but it finances commercial television, a major source of pleasure for people in low income groups, especially pensioners and other housebound people. A less obvious and less contentious example is price discrimination. Only a monopoly operator (or a cartel of operators jointly fixing price) can exploit the inelasticity of demand in one market segment and then set prices much closer to marginal cost in another price-elastic segment. Quite often (though obviously not always) the high price segment will represent people in higher income groups, so that the net effect of price discrimination will be redistributive.

Perhaps of greatest importance at the time of writing are arguments about market failure based on the existence of unemployment. Let us return to the equation/inequality:

$$\text{Value to customer} \geq \text{Price} \geq \text{Marginal cost}$$

If marginal cost includes the use of resources (including labour) which would otherwise be unemployed, then it may overstate the cost to society of supplying the product. Unemployment may result from structural problems in the economy — a mismatch between the composition of demand and that of the capacity to supply. Unemployed specialists cannot immediately take up other occupations in other geographical areas. When unemployment is more general, the argument that the cost to society of employing someone who would otherwise be unemployed is only the value of that person's lost leisure is even harder to refute. Provided the cost of subsidies is less than the benefits paid to the unemployed plus the taxes they would pay when back at work, they also look good for public finances.

Of course, the pro-market economist will argue that the price mechanism, if not hindered by misguided employment protection and social welfare provision, would resolve the problem of unemployment. The theoretical debate about this view is irrelevant: in practice, voters may demand that government 'does something about unemployment'. Such action may take the form of outright protection or subsidy but these policies run against the tide of pro-competitive philosophy which has advanced over the last 20 years and also run the risk of retaliation by foreign governments, viewing them as 'beggar-my-neighbour' tactics. More likely are 'industrial' policies, designed to make entire industries more competitive, not within themselves but in relation to industries in other countries and continents.

One of the reasons why the Treaty of Rome did not provide for control of mergers was that the founders of the EEC envisaged the emergence of giant industrial champions able to compete with similar firms from the US, Japan and anywhere else (see references in Chapter 4). Until 1965 there was no control over mergers in the UK and even after this control was introduced, the Industrial Reconstruction Corporation (a government body) was organising the 'rationalisation' of British industries, including computing, electrical engineering, aircraft production — all affected by the 'white heat of technology'. In the 1970s the National Enterprise Board had a similar objective.

Business concentration facilitates industrial policy and the kind of 'indicative planning' introduced in the UK and France in the 1960s and 1970s — in the UK a tripartite arrangement involving government, the trade unions and (normally big) employers. A revival of interest in such policies to deal with growing unemployment appears to have affected many politicians, even in parties which were until recently firmly committed to faith in competitive markets.

It is perhaps a little ironic that these critics of competition policy from the left often adduce the same arguments for a benevolent attitude towards business concentration as those voiced by critics from the right whose laissez-faire views are diametrically opposite. Both parties emphasise economies of scale and internal efficiency; both emphasise the possibility of long-term contestability, though the enthusiasts for 'industrial policy' may wish to defer this until their fledgling or recuperating 'champions' are fit to fight.

Competition policy and liberalism

In contrast to the new laissez-faire philosophy on the right and the interventionist philosophy on the left, both of which regard competition policy as an irrelevance if not hindrance, there is a third philosophical stance which supports competition policy *per se,* because it hinders the concentration of economic power.

Jacquemin and de Jong (1977, pp 198–9) explained this view very clearly:

> 'A first eventual goal' (of European competition policy) is the *diffusion of economic power* and the protection of individual freedom... Private power can cross economic boundaries and poses the threat of an 'extra market' power which can change the rules of the game in favour of the dominant corporations. In such a situation, where relationships between firms and their socio-economic environment constitute a mixture of market and non-market bonds, the authorities aim at the dispersion of private power. Even if this entails some loss of economic efficiency, such a choice would not necessarily be irrational, because such costs may be outweighed by social or political advantages.
>
> (original authors' emphasis)

Note the phrase 'Even if this entails some loss of economic efficiency'. This argument is not concerned primarily with economic welfare but with freedom within society. Indeed economic efficiency comes only third in the goals for competition policy set out by Jacquemin and de Jong: 'The second goal may be to protect the *economic freedom of market participants,* specifically of small and medium-sized firms. Here the protection of competitors takes precedence over the defence of the competitive process as such' *(ibid)*. It should be emphasised that Jacquemin and de Jong, two of Europe's leading specialists in antitrust economics, were not so much stating their own beliefs about the purposes of competition policy but describing the philosophy underlying much of the support for that policy in the original EEC. They quote, for example, an affirmation by Cairncross et al (1974):

> Our concern for the maintenance of effective competition extends beyond purely economic considerations. Competition is one of the foundations of an open society ... It is therefore necessary to weigh against the gains from industrial concentration the socio-political consequences of concentrations of private power, which could discredit property owning democracy.

As long ago as 1961, Adelman commented (in the context of new US legislation extending control over mergers to take account of vertical effects): 'Legislators have never shown much interest in consumer welfare. Their chief concern has always been to protect some business firms against others, chiefly larger ones ...'

The argument that economic concentration is anti-democratic and restricts individual freedom and enterprise is obviously an additional consideration in the trade-off between possible economies of scale on the one hand, and the advantages of competition on the other. Its influence, however, is greater than this. The desire to protect competitors rather than the process of competition is apparent in a number of controversial elements of competition policy.

German competition law in particular reflects this political philosophy. As well as a tight control over cartels, mergers with anti-competitive effects and abuse of market power, German competition law (dating from 1957) prohibits abuse by one firm of the dependence (*Abhängikeit*) upon it of another. Exploitation of brand leadership, of financial difficulties of a supplier or distributor, of long-term commitment or of buyer power are all explicitly forbidden.

On the grounds of straight economic theory one might question this approach, unless it could be shown that consumers were adversely affected. For example, a manufacturing firm which decides to sell most of its production to one retailer for resale under the latter's own label may avoid many advertising and other promotion costs. Obviously there is a risk and the supplier must do what it can to tie in the retailer either by legal contracts or by creating significant barriers to switching. If, with the supplier in a dependent position, the retailer puts downward pressure on prices or decides to change its strategy and acquires its own manufacturing facilities for the relevant product, is this a proper matter for competition authorities?

There is no clear answer to this question as far as UK or EEC competition policies are concerned. However, the latter has produced a number of cases raising this question and creating widespread controversy — *Commercial Solvents v Zoja* (1972), *Hugin v Lipton* (1977) and *Eurofix and Bauco v Hilti* (1988) are all discussed in Chapter 4. Each of these cases concerned an alleged abuse of dominance, but EEC law does not make clear whether 'dominance' is over trading partners or competitors on the one hand, or ultimate consumers on the other.

French competition law was changed in 1986 to allow for legal action against abuse of dependence (explicitly '*un état de dépendance*'). This followed a case considered by the French Competition Commission (*Commission de la Concurrence*) in 1985, concerned with pooled purchasing activity by major retail chains (*supercentrales d'achat*). The Commission found that the retail groups concerned still held a relatively small share of most product markets and, anyway, were competing among themselves for final customers. Aggregate welfare was probably not affected — indeed final prices may have been lower as a result of the exploitation of joint buyer power. The Commission was therefore powerless to condemn the practice under the criteria then in place — hence a change in law to protect small and medium-size producers.

French economists and lawyers have expressed other concerns indicative of the 'liberal' objectives of competition policy. Glais and Laurent (1983) described the economic power which can result from conglomerate activities or from vertical integration, both of which tend to be viewed as more benign than horizontal expansion (growth within the same activity) by most Anglo-Saxon antitrust specialists. They and other French commentators expressed concern about the networks (*filières*) along which conglomerate and vertically integrated firms can extend their tentacles.

Of course, some French politicians with an inclination towards industrial policy, intervention or *planification* might welcome the very feature about which these authors were anxious. As pointed out earlier, it is easier to 'manage' a more concentrated economy. In the UK in the early post-war period, many Conservative politicians were unwilling to lumber big business with the interference of competition policy and Labour politicians were more interested in establishing a corporatist philosophy, involving government, business and trade unions. Until very recently, there was comparatively little support for the 'liberal' aims of competition policy outside Germany, where the problems caused by concentration of economic power had in the past been all too evident.

CONCLUSIONS

The focus of the next two chapters is essentially to explore the role of competition policy in promoting the efficiency of the market economy. However, the conflicting philosophies presented in this introductory chapter cannot be ignored at any stage. Support for particular contributions to the (ostensibly more technical) economic debate is often coloured by the general philosophy held by the individual concerned.

When we come to examine the origins and nature of competition policies legislated for the EEC and the UK, these different philosophies re-appear repeatedly. In the final chapter, which is an attempt to draw together the contents of the book through discussion of selected major issues, their significance is once again emphasised.

Underlying Economic Principles

OUTLINE OF CHAPTER

This chapter is aimed primarily at readers unfamiliar with the economic theories relating business conduct to market structure. It is on these theories that most of the logic underlying competition policy is based. In order to explain them it is necessary to explain also some of the elementary concepts of 'micro-economics', so called because it is concerned with analysis of individual markets — small parts of the aggregate ('macro') economy. Readers with a solid grounding in microeconomics will be able to skip or skim-read some parts of the presentation.

The word 'monopoly' is derived from the Greek words for 'single seller'. The derivation does not help much with definition, because the word 'monopoly' also has a connotation of power, of 'dominance' — the term used instead of 'monopoly' in EEC competition policy and in the national policies of France and Germany. Monopoly implies power when it describes a single seller of a product with no existing or potential substitutes. If monopoly is defined in this way, the opposite extreme or zero point of monopoly power would be a market with a very large number of existing sellers of perfectly substitutable products, combined with complete freedom of entry for new potential competitors. This opposite extreme is represented in microeconomics by the theoretical model of 'perfect competition'.

In the author's view it is impossible to understand the logic used in analysis of monopoly and restrictive practices without a grasp of the model of perfect competition. Many economists specialising in this field may disagree with this starting-point, arguing that comparison with perfect competition as an attainable alternative to a real-world, highly concentrated market has long been abandoned as unrealistic. However, this hypothetical extreme is still included in much of the background analysis as a theoretical limit from which the consequences of market power or restrictive agreements can be evaluated. This model and its relevance are studied on pp 28–40.

In recent years, some leading economists have given great emphasis to the argument that the threat of competition from potential substitutes is sufficient to prevent monopoly power. They propose that, instead of the hypothetical situation of perfect competition, a more realistic zero-point from which to measure such power is the 'perfectly contestable' market. This is defined as a market into which potential competitors may enter without incurring any investment costs which could not be recovered if they subsequently withdrew ('sunk costs'). Provided that such potential competition were possible, a firm with no existing competitors could not exploit this position, so it could not be described as a monopoly or being in a dominant position. The model of market contestability and its practical relevance are examined on pp 40–7.

In activities with substantial economies of scale there is no possibility of anything approaching perfect competition and there may be little threat of entry by new firms. In these circumstances, the only practical alternative to single-firm monopoly may be the presence of two or three large firms. A market dominated by a few suppliers, termed an *oligopoly*, requires a different analytical approach from that applied to monopoly and perfect (or reasonably 'workable') competition. It can fairly be argued that no fully satisfactory model to predict business behaviour under conditions of oligopoly has yet been developed. The pattern of behaviour may indeed be unpredictable. From observation of competition under oligopoly, it is clear that, from the standpoint of general welfare, oligopoly may be less satisfactory than monopoly of a market, see pp 47–55.

The final section of the chapter considers how economic analysis can be applied to the major concerns of competition policy — restrictive agreements and trade practices, the existence of monopoly power and its abuse, anti-competitive practices more generally and control over mergers. In this final section we are primarily concerned with how economic theory, with its attendant ambiguities, can be applied in the broad design of antitrust policies and their implementation in individual cases, see pp 55–62.

PERFECT COMPETITION AND COMPARISON WITH MONOPOLY

If monopoly ('market power' or 'dominance' — the three terms are practically interchangeable) is defined by absence of actual or potential substitutes, then one of its manifestations will be ability of the firm in this position to apply and maintain a higher price than if such substitutes (or the threat of them) existed. Much of the theory underlying competition (antitrust) policy starts from this concept and in the US in particular market power has been defined by this ability. 'The term "market power" refers to the ability of a firm (or group of firms, acting jointly) to raise price above the competitive level without losing so many sales so rapidly that the price increase is unprofitable' (Landes and Posner (1981) p 937); 'Market power to a seller is the ability profitably to maintain prices above competitive levels for a significant period of time' (US Department of Justice, Merger Guidelines, p 4). One may argue that this ability is a consequence of market power, which can be exploited in other ways, but these quotations reflect the emphasis in traditional economic theory. This concentrates on comparison of the price of a product sold by a hypothetical monopolist with the price which would apply if the same product were supplied under conditions of (even more hypothetical) perfect competition.

Price determination under perfect competition

Etymologically, the word 'perfect' derives from the Latin for 'complete' and it is in this sense that the adjective applies to perfect competition. It does not necessarily signify a desirable ideal. The alternative, but little used, term 'atomistic competition' avoids the apparent commendation and also reminds us of the key feature of the model — the presence of a very large number of small firms all producing identical products, recognised as such by each of a very large number of customers. There is no collusion of any kind either among the suppliers or among customers. Entry to and exit from this atomistically structured market are assumed costless and incumbent firms have no advantages over new entrants.

It is worth noting at this point the key assumption about substitutability of products. The perfect competition model assumes that all products *within* the market are perfectly substitutable but that there is a discrete gap in substitutability between these products and others *outside* the market. In reality, there are few perfect substitutes and when this assumption is dropped there may be a problem of finding a gap in a continuum of substitution. In other words, where can one define a market? We return to this point, one of the greatest concerns in competition policy, in Chapter 3.

If a perfectly competitive market were to exist, price would be determined by the interaction of demand (the quantity which customers are willing and able to buy) and supply (the quantity that sellers are prepared to offer for sale). As price increases, demand falls and supply rises; there will be one price which clears the market, where demand and supply are equal.

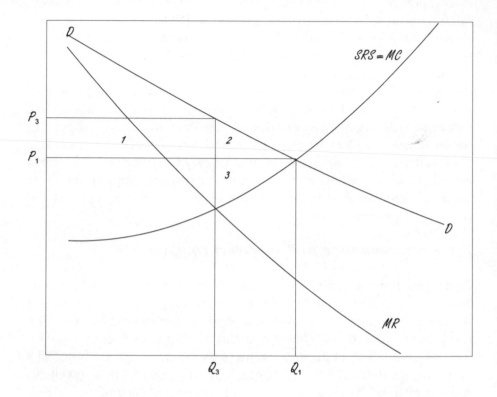

Figure 2.1 Monopoly v perfect competition — same short-run marginal costs

Figure 2.1 represents the market for a given product, with quantity demanded or supplied (Q) on the horizontal axis and price (P) on the vertical. This product (X) is defined so that all units within the definition are perfectly substitutable from the standpoint of purchasers — they are both physically identical and recognised as such. However, there is limited opportunity for substitution between X and other products. The relationships between a) price and quantity demanded and b) price and quantity supplied are based on the assumption that all other factors which may influence quantities demanded and supplied remain constant, including the prices of all other products. (This *ceteris paribus* assumption makes it very difficult to try to estimate these relationships in practice.)

Demand

The relationship between quantity demanded and price, the 'demand curve' (DD), has a negative slope — as the price of X falls the quantity demanded rises. (This is equivalent to saying that the greater the quantity to be sold on the market, the lower the price that each unit will fetch.) There are two reasons for this. First, at lower prices, X represents comparatively better value for money than other products; secondly, customers can afford more. The closer the substitutes available from outside the market and the greater the sensitivity of consumer demand to changes in real income, the flatter the demand curve will be at any given price (and with the same scale on each axis).

The sensitivity of quantity demanded (Q) to changes in price (P) plays an important part in discussion about market power. It is normally termed 'price-elasticity of demand'. ('Price-sensitivity' is equally correct and would be more widely understood!) It is defined as the proportionate change in quantity demanded divided by the proportionate change in price:

$$\frac{\delta Q}{Q} \div \frac{\delta P}{P} = \frac{\delta Q}{\delta P} \cdot \frac{P}{Q}$$

Because the changes in price and quantity will normally be in opposite directions, price-elasticity of demand is usually negative but it is often quoted as a positive value. Economists talk about demand being 'price-elastic' or having 'price-elasticity greater than unity' which means that the response of demand is proportionately greater than the change in price — a decrease in price then leads to an increase in total sales revenue (price × quantity) and an increase in price leads to a loss of revenue. Similarly, when demand is 'price-inelastic' or has 'price-elasticity less than unity' the response of demand is proportionately less than the change in price — if price goes down revenue falls and if price rises so does revenue.

It is important to recognise that price-elasticity will normally vary along the demand curve (its absolute value), increasing with price. This is evident from the formula above — the further left on the demand curve the greater the value of (P ÷ Q). A practical illustration of this was presented by the decline in the demand for petroleum products after the big price increases in the 1970s. At much lower price levels demand had been very price-inelastic. Because price-elasticity will normally increase with price, it follows that the response to a price change from any given level will depend on the direction and size of the change.

Although the price that the total market will bear for X usually decreases as the total quantity offered on the market is increased, the individual firm under conditions of total competition is so small that the volume of X which it decides to place on the market does not significantly affect price.

The individual firm is a 'price-taker'. It has no control over the price of its product, which is determined by total demand and supply on the market.

Supply

The model of perfect competition requires that the most efficient level of output by the individual firm (at which average cost per unit is minimised) is very small in relation to the total market. This implies not only that there are no large indivisible inputs, which would lead to economies of large-scale operation ('economies of scale'), but also that there are some smaller fixed inputs which cannot be expanded, such as the time and effort of the proprietor of a one-person business and the fixed equipment that he or she operates. Increases in production to levels beyond the normal capacity of the fixed inputs, eg by working longer hours or sub-contracting, will tend to lead to diminishing returns (per extra pound

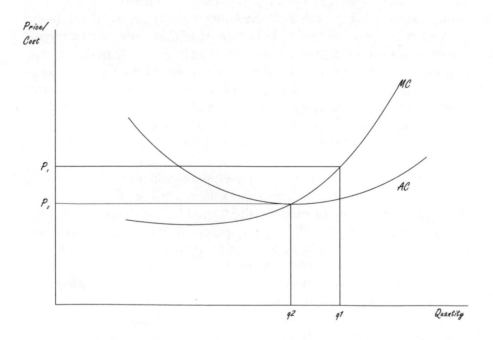

Figure 2.2 The individual firm in perfect competition

of cost). This means that the cost of the incremental unit produced at the margin ('marginal cost') will increase at an accelerating rate.

Figure 2.2 represents the price—output decision of the individual firm under conditions of perfect competition. Its inability to influence market price is reflected in the horizontal price line (P_1). The marginal cost line (MC) depicts the relationship between marginal cost and output (q) described in the last paragraph. The firm will add to profits by producing a marginal unit provided that the selling price (P_1) exceeds the increment of cost (marginal cost). The quantity supplied by this individual firm is where price just covers marginal cost (q_1).

Note that the conclusion that price equals marginal cost implies that marginal cost is equal for all firms. This does not mean that all must have the same cost-output relationships, ie that they are all equally efficient. In the *Woodpulp* case (1984) the Commission of the EC decided that there had been concertation on prices by producers of identical grades of woodpulp. One of the elements of circumstantial evidence produced in support of this decision (para 95 of the Decision document) was the existence of substantial differences in average costs. In presenting observations to the Court of Justice hearing of the appeal against the *Woodpulp* Decision, several economists pointed out that this reasoning was invalid: identical products can only sell at identical prices; each profit-maximising firm will sell the quantity at which this (identical) price is equal to *marginal* cost. Both the variable costs of 'intra-marginal' units and fixed costs may vary. There may be differences in output levels, average costs and profits but price and the incremental cost of the marginal unit will be the same (see Cockram and Fishwick, 1991).

In the short-term, the combined quantity of the product which will be supplied at any given price by all firms currently supplying the market will be the sum of the outputs determined by the marginal cost for each firm, the sum of the quantities given by q_1 for the individual firm. The short-run supply-curve (SRS) in Figure 2.1 shows the quantity which would be supplied by existing firms in the market at each of a range of prices. As an alternative presentation of the same concept, one could state that it shows the price which would be required to induce existing firms to supply each of a range of quantities.

At the level of output where average cost is at a minimum, marginal cost and average cost are equal. This is intuitively obvious: if marginal cost were less than average cost, the firm could reduce average cost by increasing output; if marginal cost exceeded average cost, the latter could be reduced by a decrease in supply. For the individual firm under perfect competition, price is equal to marginal cost at a level of output where

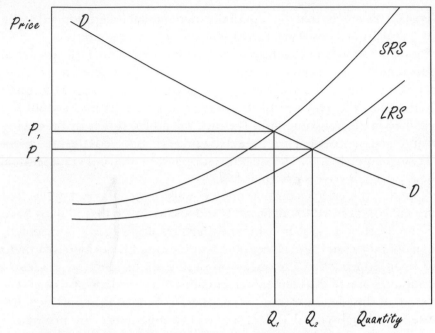

Figure 2.3(a) Perfect competition — short- and long-run pricing

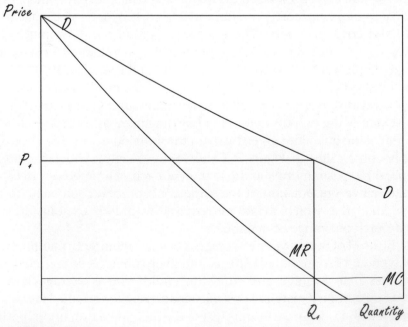

Figure 2.3(b) Monopoly — pricing with very low marginal cost

marginal cost is rising. This implies that price must exceed the variable costs of units of output below the marginal unit, so that the sale of these 'intra-marginal' units makes a contribution to fixed costs. If this contribution exceeds fixed costs the firm is said to be making 'abnormal' profits and this attracts new entrants into the market, depressing market price. So long as some firms are making abnormal profits, this entry process will continue. Existing firms can maintain or increase their profits only by reducing their costs, but, because the model assumes no advantages for the individual firm (and hence complete freedom of access to technology and resources), such cost reductions can immediately be matched by all existing firms and new entrants.

The cumulative effect of free entry and competition through cost reduction is to force price down towards minimum attainable average cost (P_2 in Figure 2.2). This effect is represented in Figure 2.3(a) by the long-run supply curve (LRS), showing a fall in market price to P_2 and a rise in market quantity to Q_2. (Although the quantity supplied by each individual firm has decreased there are now many more such individual firms.) The movement of the supply curve to LRS and of price to P_2 is not, however, the end of the process: the quest for profits is assumed to encourage firms to achieve further reductions in costs, which will in turn be passed on to customers.

The welfare benefits of perfect competition

1. Price is equal to the incremental cost to every firm of supplying the marginal unit. This means that no customer who is prepared to pay the cost of production and delivery of a unit of the product is denied access to it.
2. There is constant downward pressure on costs, because cost-reduction is the only means whereby firms can stay in business and increase profits. Because of competition from both existing firms and new entrants, such cost reductions are always passed on in lower prices to customers.

Comparison with monopoly

Let us return to Figure 2.1. Even today, exposition of the effects of market power usually begins from this diagram. Let us assume that all the firms/productive units were combined into a single group operating them with the marginal costs as before. Let us assume also that this group could prevent completely the entry of new competitors to the market. Finally, let us assume that there would still be a very large number of consumers, none of whom would have any significant bargaining power and that there were no regulation or other form of government control on the group's ability to exploit its monopoly power. The only restraint on such exploitation would be possible competition from products *outside* the market. The price which the monopoly group would set would be determined by marginal cost on the one hand and the price-elasticity of total market demand on the other.

In terms of economic jargon, profit would be maximised where 'marginal revenue' were equal to marginal cost. Marginal revenue is the increase in total revenue resulting from the sale of the marginal unit. With a downward sloping demand curve, the sale of the marginal (n th) unit requires a reduction in price (δP) and marginal revenue is equal to the new price (P) minus the loss of revenue on units now sold at a lower price: $P - (n - 1)\ \delta P$. In principle, the term should be defined in terms of differential calculus and it can be shown that $MR = P(1 + 1/e)$, where P is price (assumed uniform for all units sold) and e is the elasticity of the demand curve at that price.

The marginal revenue curve has been added to Figure 2.1. This diagram shows that, if the demand curve is known (the relationship between price and quantity demanded) and the relationship between marginal cost and quantity supplied, the profit-maximising monopolist would sell output Q_3 at price P_3, in contrast to the higher output (Q_1) and lower price (P_1) which would have occurred under conditions of perfect competition in the short run.

From the diagram it is obvious that consumers would lose because of the exploitation by the monopoly group of any inelasticity of demand for the product. The rectangle marked 1 depicts a transfer of benefit from consumers to producers. Under competition, the consumers of the Q_3 units sold at P_3 were getting them at price P_1. This means that they were gaining from the supplying firms' inability to extract this 'consumer surplus' from them, because competition was forcing price down to marginal cost. US authors in particular (eg Ordover) have argued and persuaded most other commentators that this transfer of consumer surplus into profits for monopoly firms does not of itself concern competition/antitrust authorities. A social preference for consumers' over producers' welfare may have no valid basis in terms of income distribution — take the case of an employee-owned firm supplying rich consumers (*ibid*, p 14). The welfare losses from monopoly power are represented by areas 2 and 3 in Figure 2.1, which are known as 'deadweight losses' and reflect a misallocation of resources.

Area 2 — the loss of consumer surplus which is not turned into profits for producers — amounts to a loss of benefit by people who would have been prepared to pay more than the opportunity costs (marginal costs) for the lost output $Q_1 - Q_3$. Area 3 represents a sacrifice of profits by the monopolist on intra-marginal units no longer produced. The reason it does not produce them is that the increase in price resulting from restricted supply to the market adds more to profit.

This comparison of perfect competition with profit-maximising monopoly, with identical production methods and marginal costs, shows unambiguously that the latter will supply a lower quantity to the market in order to enforce a higher price. This result implies not only a transfer of benefit from consumers to producer but also a significant misallocation of resources, by preventing the supply of units of output which would provide benefits in excess of resource costs (marginal costs to the firm).

The second obvious difference between monopoly and perfect competition is the absence of pressure from competition to reduce costs. A leading Oxford economist of the 1930–50s period, Sir John Hicks, has been quoted as saying that the greatest monopoly profit is the quiet life. Leibenstein (1966) argued that what he called X-inefficiency within firms caused greater welfare loss to society than the resource misallocation on which we have concentrated so far. Perfect competition with its essential assumption of free entry is inconsistent with the quiet life.

Criticisms of perfect competition and their implications

While comparison of monopoly with perfect competition may appear to produce unambiguous conclusions, these are of little relevance to competition policy if perfect competition is not a practical alternative. Moreover, the model of perfect competition, in which none of the large number of small firms can ever gain an advantage over the others, may be questioned on more fundamental grounds — does it assume many forms of competition away?

Incompatibility of perfect competition with major economies of scale

Under perfect competition price is equal to marginal cost. The model assumes that at the profit-maximising output marginal cost will be greater than the variable cost of intra-marginal units, so that there is an excess of sales revenue over variable costs at least equal to fixed costs. Where an activity requires a large inescapable and indivisible fixed input, so that fixed costs are very high in relation to marginal costs, perfect competition is impossible. Fixed costs may be so great that only a limited number of suppliers, possibly only one, could break even — that is could achieve enough revenue to recover fixed plus variable costs.

In the course of lecturing on this particular point over the last 30 years, the author has often used the historical development of British railways as an example. In retrospect it seemed to have been folly on the part of Victorian parliaments to have rejected proposals for amalgamation of railway companies, which would have prevented the construction of competing routes between major cities. The opening of new, duplicating services often meant that neither those nor the original services earned enough profit to finance replacement and improvement, so that by the early 1920s Britain had a dilapidated railway service. It is remarkable that the planned privatisation of the railways is reviving a call for competition between services, though the decision to retain a single Track Authority may imply (belated) recognition of this anomaly.

The notion that monopoly may be more efficient than competition in the presence of substantial economies of scale has long been recognised in competition policy. This recognition is reflected in the investigative approach of UK policy established in the 1948 Monopolies and Restrictive Practices (Inquiry and Control) Act and in the focus of EEC policy on abuse of dominance rather than its existence.

The impact of economies of scale in the static welfare comparison between monopoly and perfect competition can be seen diagrammatically. Figure 2.3(a) replicates the market equilibrium model of perfect competition and includes the trend towards lower prices through increasing supply over time. In Figure 2.3(b) the demand curve is the same but monopoly is assumed so that price and output are determined by equality of marginal cost with marginal revenue. However, marginal cost is also assumed to be much lower and constant because of economies of scale. Although the monopolist is assumed to be maximising profits by restricting supply to keep price up, this price is still lower than it would have been under perfect competition. The explanation for this is simply that fragmentation of supply would prevent the realisation of the economies of scale. The total of consumers' surplus and producers' surplus over marginal costs is considerably greater than in the perfectly competitive situation — unless fixed costs are very high, the aggregate welfare benefit from output may be greater under monopoly than under competition.

The perfect competition model assumes away much real-world competition

In a published synopsis of earlier criticisms of the perfect competition concept, Kirzner (1973) stated that 'Perfect competition denotes for the price theorist the situation in which every market participant does exactly what everyone else is doing, in which it is utterly pointless to try to achieve something in any way better than what is being done already by others.' Hayek (1945) declared that perfect competition symbolised complete absence of competition.

The point of these critics is that the model assumes that no firm can gain any advantage from competing. By assuming perfect knowledge on the part of consumers and identical products, the model excludes any competition for market share other than through price reduction, which is immediately followed. There are no opportunities for product differentiation or development, for tying in customers through loyalty ('fidelity') rebates or offering of inducements, for doing anything which would give the individual firm any power to vary the price of its product.

Firms are assumed to compete on costs but again any cost reductions are assumed to be available to all. There is no secrecy, no element of property right on any innovation — no possibility that one firm can 'steal a march' on its competitors. In which case, why be the first mover?

It has been argued that it is the prospect of a competitive advantage, which will not rapidly be eliminated, that provides the motivation for innovation and improvement in the effectiveness, design or marketing of products and in methods of producing them. This argument is particularly associated with Schumpeter (1947) who regarded short-term monopolies as necessary for innovation and part of a process of destructive competition. This principle has long been implemented in laws granting patents and/or copyright protection for innovations in products and production methods, as well as scientific, literary, musical and artistic works. The existence of a highly competitive environment within industry has, in the view of some economists, tended to retard innovation. For example, Galbraith (1957) stated 'Industries which are distinguished by a close approach to the competitive model are, one can say almost without exception, marked by a near absence of research and technical development' (*op cit*, p 105 of 1973 reprint)

Most empirical research in fact produces no simple conclusion. Once a firm has established a dominant position founded on a particular product range or technology into which it has sunk resources, its incentive to introduce new products and processes might be expected to be low.

There is a dilemma here for competition policy, neatly summarised in Vickers and Hay: the prospect of a monopoly position acts as a stimulus to innovation but the existence of monopoly may, at least in the short term, discourage it. Adherents of the Austrian and Chicago schools of economics (to which Schumpeter and Kirzner, but not Galbraith, would be classified) would argue that if the monopoly undertaking abused its position — if only by lapsing into inertia — opportunities for potential competitors would inevitably develop. The world is not static — patterns of consumption and investment change, new needs and ideas emerge.

Another form of competition which is assumed away in the perfect competition model is the construction of barriers against the entry of new competitors. Many writers have used the analogy of military warfare to describe real-world competition in industry. An objective of competition may be to gain a commanding position and then to secure it against attack. If competition laws were effective in preventing any defence of a dominant position — through devices such as loyalty rebates, exclusive dealing, predatory pricing, brand establishment or brand proliferation — would such a position be worth gaining?

Some readers may be becoming perplexed at this point. How can we describe as an element of competition practices which are widely viewed as 'anti-competitive' or 'unfair'? The ultimate answer must be 'It's all a matter of degree'. There should be no general condemnation of the existence of monopoly, nor of the 'things done' (the 1948 Act in the UK) to maintain or exploit it. Abandonment of the naïve assumptions of perfect competition points towards a case-by-case approach to control over monopoly.

MARKET CONTESTABILITY

Given that economies of scale make anything approaching perfect competition impossible in many industries, the prevalent market structure tends to be one where a small number of large sellers (perhaps only one) faces a large number of small buyers. Traditional economic thinking suggests that some form of intervention may be required in such markets to prevent or control abuse of dominance — effective competition (antitrust) policies, regulation or public ownership. Those who champion the supremacy of market forces tend to regard all three with dismay and have been quick to embrace the theory of market contestability, which appears to offer a different view of this dilemma.

Outline of theory and implications

Contestability theory starts from the principle that the favourable welfare implications of perfect competition may be realised if only one of its premises is fulfilled — freedom of entry to the market. Whatever the existing structure of the market, freedom of entry by new suppliers is sufficient to ensure that incumbent firms *a)* cannot abuse monopoly power at the expense of customers (eg in high prices) and *b)* will be forced into maintaining and indeed increasing efficiency.

This principle is, of course, fairly obvious and has long been recognised. However, most of the articles about barriers to entry published before 1980 appear to have implied that it was irrelevant. Since economies of scale, or rather the inescapable and indivisible fixed inputs which cause them, are themselves a barrier to entry, activities in which they occur are protected from the entry of new firms. As they recognise this protection, the behaviour of existing firms will not be restrained by any perceived threat of potential competition.

The essential contribution of contestability theory is to emphasise another relevant aspect of the inescapable and indivisible costs which lead to economies of scale — can they be recovered in the event of withdrawal from the market?

For example, one of the major costs of operating an air route is the cost of the aircraft itself. A service from, say, London to Melbourne requires a big aircraft and will be uneconomic unless that aircraft can be filled. Given a finite number of passengers between London and Melbourne, with limited price-elasticity of demand, one might expect this route to be served by a small number of airlines, who might profitably cooperate in pricing policy. However, this could be seen as a contestable market because if the existing airlines did collude on price to maximise joint profits, this would create an opportunity for a company not part of this informal cartel to offer a less expensive but still profitable service. It might expect to fill its aircraft quite easily, especially if it had a good reputation earned on services elsewhere. The end result would probably be a reduction of price by the previous incumbents, perhaps making it unprofitable for all of them (plus the new firm) to remain on this route. The essential point now is that whichever firm leaves can take its aircraft somewhere else, or dispose of it: the fixed cost is not irrecoverable or 'sunk'.

This example to emphasise the significance of sunk costs also demonstrates the key feature of contestable markets — vulnerability to 'hit-and-run' entry. If, on considering entry to a market, a firm can be reasonably confident that necessary initial investment costs could be recovered in the event of enforced exit, then this will greatly increase the expected value of returns.

If a market were perfectly contestable (hit-and-run entry is possible with no sunk costs) and this were recognised by the existing firm, then the threat would force them to pursue policies which would remove any incentive for a new entrant. Prices would be kept close to the minimum required to make business worthwhile and there would be constant pressure to reduce costs, to forestall entry by a more efficient potential competitor.

Critique of contestability theory

There are two main criticisms of contestability theory, one concerned with the unrealistic nature of the implied assumption about the price reactions of existing firms, the other more fundamental, regarding the likelihood of absence of sunk costs.

First, the point about price reactions of existing firms. Schwartz (1986) points out that entry into a contestable market will take place only if price is currently above minimum attainable average cost (or marginal cost plus the required return on fixed cost). If a monopolist were exploiting the inelasticity of market demand (that is a captive market) this might be the case. However, if the existing firm(s) reduced price to match that of the new entrant, it would be impossible for all to break even. One firm would have to leave the market. The opportunities for profit from 'hit-and-run' entry depend upon a delay in reaction by existing firms. In the real world, few markets will be perfectly contestable — there are bound to be some sunk costs or delays before an entrant can compete on equal terms with previous incumbents. In a moderately, rather than perfectly, contestable market, the ability of existing firms to respond quickly to new competition — by general or (in the case of narrowly focused entry) selective price-cutting — may deter entry.

If the threat of entry is very strong, then the incumbent firm(s) is (are) more likely to take preventive measures to defend a dominant position than to forgo all the advantages which that position might provide. Devices such as the bundling or tying of products to prevent entry into a single element of the range, fidelity rebates and brand proliferation are examples of constructed barriers discussed below. If no barrier of this kind is effective, each existing firm need promise only to match prices offered by any other supplier. This promise may be enough to deter any of the incumbents from breaking ranks and abandoning tacit collusion on price; it may also dissuade any potential entrant from attempting hit-and-run entry. If the customer has no benchmark with which to compare prevailing prices, exploitation of market dominance in this situation can continue without too much public protest. The fact that entry would involve little sunk cost is of no consequence.

▷ The second, more general and widely voiced, criticism is that the conditions described by the assumptions of market contestability rarely exist. There are few markets which can be entered without significant expenditure on sunk costs. To demonstrate this point, we may divide barriers to entry into two groups — the purchase of physical assets and expenditures to overcome what Schmalensee (1987a) called the 'first-mover advantages' of incumbent firms, the latter comprising several different elements.

It should be noted that entry into a market need not imply entry into an industry. Such a move may be what Koutsoyiannis (1979) described as 'cross-entry' — a firm producing product X and selling it in country A may see an opportunity to supply to country B (the widening of geographical markets is one benefit expected from the European Single Market — see Fishwick and Denison, 1992). Another form of cross-entry would be switching of transferable machinery and specialist labour to a product physically similar to X but serving a completely different need. The author once worked in a textile weaving mill where a major product line was mattress coverings or 'tickings'; diversification into the market for stage curtains required no investment in physical assets. In general, expenditure on physical assets is likely to be a less common barrier to entry than the need to overcome the advantages of firms already in the market.

Where entry does require major investment in physical assets, there may be an advantage for the new entrant in being able to install the latest available 'state-of-the-art' equipment, which may offer higher quality and/or reduced production costs. This advantage will be even greater when, as in many electronic applications, prices of more sophisticated equipment have fallen.

Whether expenditure on new physical assets represents a sunk cost depends upon their flexibility, that is the ease with which they can be transferred to other markets in the event of aborted or short-lived entry. Transport vehicles which can be transferred to other routes are one, much quoted, flexible asset — taxi-cabs, buses, aircraft and ships are all examples. Transfer to other routes may be effected by the same operator or via sale to another operator. Computer hardware (but not necessarily all software), flexible manufacturing systems and many modern machine tools and most office equipment are other examples. Most buildings used for industry or other business are multi-purpose and therefore disposable. Sunk costs are associated with capital projects designed for a specific purpose — deep mines and transport 'infrastructures' (railways, roads, airports) are good examples. If the Channel Tunnel succeeds in eliminating competition from ferries and short-haul airlines, then its monopoly position would be uncontestable — expenditure on the 40 kilometre tunnel is an archetypical sunk cost.

Since entry to a market may often involve little expenditure on fixed assets and, as the above examples show, comparatively few fixed assets involve sunk costs, the main limit on contestability will be the competitive advantages of entrenched firms. The literature on barriers to entry is very extensive and cannot be summarised systematically in a few paragraphs. Bain (1956) grouped entry barriers into the following broad categories: product differentiation, absolute cost advantages and economies of scale.

We have already considered the importance of economies of scale associated with indivisible fixed assets and concluded that these are likely to deter hit-and-run entry to a market only if the assets concerned are not transferable to other markets. Other economies of scale, described by Bain as 'pecuniary', are the lower input prices which may be obtained by large firms with effective buying power. This may be a barrier to entry on a small scale. Product differentiation, particularly the ability of firms established in the market to persuade customers to remain loyal to them, was regarded by Bain as the most effective barrier to entry, a view confirmed by empirical work. Where preferences for existing brands are deeply entrenched, new entrants must either incur much higher promotional costs than existing firms or must offer some other persuasive inducement, such as lower prices. The view has been expressed by some enthusiasts for the contestability hypothesis that incumbent firms must have incurred equivalent entry costs earlier, so they have no net advantage (a view tentatively presented by Salop, 1986). This ignores a number of advantages derived from early presence in the market and attainment of scale economies in marketing.

First, expenditure on advertising is an investment; existing firms may have built up reputations for their brands over many years. Matching of current expenditure in absolute terms would not give a new entrant equivalent influence. Nor is it even a matter of matching the sum of current promotion by existing firms plus the 'present value' of their previous promotional spend discounted by some rate of decay. While such mathematically nice expressions attract economists, this approach ignores the point that existing firms (or at least one of them) would have launched their products without the 'noise' of competitors' advertising and other promotion. Moreover, existing brands may have been established when the market was expanding, so there was less resistance by incumbents concerned about loss of sales.

Secondly, there is substantial evidence of scale economies in advertising — the level required to maintain market share increases less than proportionately to that share. Entry to a market on a small scale requires disproportionately heavy advertising (see Fishwick and Denison).

Thirdly, empirical research has also shown that brands with smaller market share generally attract less loyalty than the market leaders. Because of this 'double jeopardy' effect combined with disproportionate advertising, a minor market share may not be an attractive proposition economically.

Obviously, the influence of advertising varies between products. The marketing literature refers to products which purchasers use as a 'sign' to others or to themselves — as part of their image. This factor is most evidently associated with cars, but also extends to certain 'ostentatious' non-durables such as trendy drinks, some cosmetics and even holidays. A related but psychologically distinct factor is described as the 'hedonic' role of certain products. Much advertising is intended to surround a mundane product with connotations relating to consumers' idiosyncrasies, memories or even fantasies. Chocolates, perfumes and beer are products regarded as susceptible to such advertising (McWilliam, 1992).

Although our marketing colleagues tend to stress the 'image' and 'hedonic' aspects of product promotion, they generally acknowledge the key importance of the combination stressed in the economics literature — risk to the purchaser combined with lack of information. Bain suggested that risk and therefore brand preference would increase with the durability and complexity of the product. While this seems intuitively correct and has been echoed in the economics literature many times, it does not explain the observed high rates of repurchases of many branded consumer non-durables. Why do people so rarely switch between rival brands of detergents, shoe polish, breakfast cereals or disposable razors — none of which have much image, hedonism, risk or complexity? One explanation of this (Hoyer, 1984) is minimisation of effort on the part of the shopper — even if risk is low, provided the last purchase was acceptable, why change? If the shopper is buying for others (eg the family) he or she is particularly likely to play safe.

Even with those products not particularly affected by brand loyalty, existing firms can still force extra advertising costs on new entrants, by brand proliferation. If a large incumbent offers multiple brands, each appealing (either in design or content or perhaps mainly in method of promotion) to a different market segment, the impact of a new brand is likely to be diluted.

Product differentiation has been treated at some length here because some specialists in antitrust economics tend to play it down. The most important point about barriers to entry which result from product differentiation is that expenditures to overcome them are not generally recoverable on subsequent exit from a market. Such expenditures would be sunk costs. Where brand preferences are strong, entry to a market may be possible only by acquisition of existing brands — which does not generally lead to a more competitive market structure.

Returning to Bain's classification of entry barriers, we have yet to discuss absolute advantages of existing firms, other than the product differentiation which they may have achieved. Schmalensee (1987a) outlined some of the strategies available to incumbent 'first mover' firms, to deter entry of new competitors. Apart from brand advertising and proliferation, these include *a*) creation of excess capacity, which poses a threat of retaliation ('predatory pricing') and reduces the potential disposal value of any capacity created by a new entrant and *b*) imposition of switching costs by devices such as loyalty rebates, limited technical compatibility and product bundling.

Defensive reaction by existing firms may take the form of price reductions or increased advertising aimed at the particular market segment occupied by the new entrant. The mere threat of predatory action of this kind may deter entry.

The final category of advantages which may be available to existing firms comprises what are generally described as vertical links, either backwards to suppliers or forwards to downstream customers, particularly distributors. Vertical integration, eg ownership of a source of supply of an input with limited availability or ownership of outlets, is an obvious advantage over new entrants, provided that there is adequate 'synergy' between the stages. (Sometimes vertical integration can be a disadvantage, for example if the upstream subsidiary is not the least-cost source of some materials produced in combination, or if the downstream distributor needs to offer a wide range of choice.) Ownership is, however, not always necessary. If an existing firm buys a range of inputs from a supplier, it may be able to impose exclusive dealing — 'if you sell product X to firm A, then we'll buy neither X nor Y from you'. It may use a similar strategy to tie-in distributors. With the changing structure of distribution in many countries, the greater power of major retailers may have made such 'full-line forcing' impossible. However, there is now a new problem for new entrants — the tendency for most retail groups to offer fewer brands.

Although this list of criticisms of contestability theory may appear formidable, there have been cases, both in UK and EEC enforcement of competition policy, where the investigators have found markets to be so contestable that actual or potential monopoly did not give rise to concern. Particularly with intermediate industrial products and materials, or with products sold to well-informed customers (perhaps with their own testing equipment), marketing-type barriers are often less important. With the development of flexible manufacturing systems, computer-aided manufacture and similar developments, capacity has become more widely transferable. This reduces the proportion of technical entry costs which would be regarded as sunk. Contestability is not a general justification for allowing antitrust vigilance to decline; but neither should it be dismissed as an academic eccentricity.

OLIGOPOLY — COMPETITION AMONG THE FEW

Given economies of scale and effective barriers to contestability, the alternative to monopoly in many markets is not perfect (atomistic) competition or anything vaguely approaching it — only a small number of firms may be able to survive. *Oligopoly*, a word formed from Greek to mean simply 'few sellers', has always posed problems for economic theory because it is difficult to model behaviour of firms under such conditions. On the basis of observed behaviour, it is by no means obvious that oligopoly is better for overall welfare than monopoly.

The key feature of oligopoly is the interdependence between the firms in performance and strategy. The marketing decisions of any one firm will affect the sales of the others to the extent that they will react, if they can. Every firm will recognise this interdependence and take it into account before implementing any marketing decision. In theory, as we conclude below, this should lead to a lack of competition, to what is described as *oligopolistic détente*. In practice, competition may occur, but take particular forms which may result in 'wasteful' expenditures. Models of oligopoly do not provide much help in the design of general rules for application in competition policy and we are left again with the conclusion that only a case-by-case approach is valid.

Oligopolistic interdependence — the kinked demand curve

Some economists (eg Koutsoyiannis, p 232) deplore the emphasis in most economics textbooks on the kinked demand curve as a tool for analysis of oligopoly. They point out that this approach does not explain how price and other elements of marketing mix are determined under conditions of oligopoly, only why they tend to stay unchanged for long periods. While this point is valid, the conclusions which can be drawn from the kinked demand analysis are very important. Moreover, the theoretical models sometimes used in attempts to derive a predictive model of price–output decisions in oligopoly rest on very dubious assumptions. The kinked demand curve is usually helpful in analysis of individual cases.

Let us consider an archetypical near-pure oligopoly situation. There is a very small number of firms (perhaps only two) of roughly equal size and resources. Each firm is selling an almost identical product for which there is very little competition from outside the market, either actual (substitute products) or potential (the market is not contestable). There are

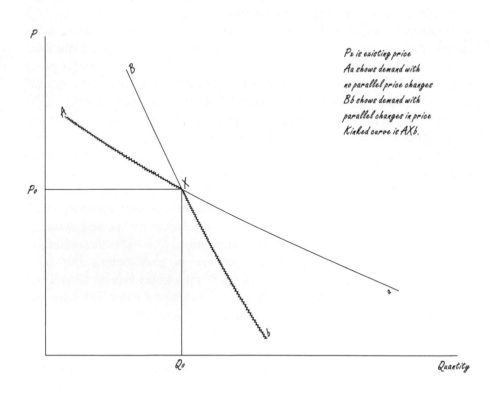

Po is existing price
Aa shows demand with
no parallel price changes
Bb shows demand with
parallel changes in price
Kinked curve is AXb.

Figure 2.4 Demand under oligopoly

substantial economies of scale and for every firm marginal cost is below average cost per unit of output, a condition which we can describe as 'excess capacity'.

Figure 2.4 represents the price–output decision of one firm in this situation. P_o is the existing price — how it came to be established is irrelevant at this stage — Q_o is the existing volume of sales. We can draw two demand curves through $^X(P_oQ_o)$, each representing the belief of the managers of the firm about the response of quantity demanded to a change in price from P_o. Aa shows what they believe would happen if the other firms in the oligopoly left their prices unchanged, Bb reflects the assumption that any price changes would be fully matched by these other firms. Aa shows demand to be very price sensitive (elastic): this reflects the near-homogeneity of the product — a good example would be petrol (gasolene) subject to regularly enforced legal standards; the only differentiation between rival filling stations may be convenience of location. On the other hand Bb shows demand insensitive to changes from the existing price (inelastic). This is because the market product has no close external substitute. If all firms changed their prices simultaneously and uniformly, each firm's share of the relatively constant market would (all other things equal) remain unchanged.

Since all firms have excess capacity, the managers of the firm shown in Figure 2.4 fear that if they were to increase price their competitors might leave their own prices unchanged. Obviously, they would all gain by a collective price increase but, in the absence of a binding agreement, there is a danger that one firm would reap a large short-term benefit from not following suit. Similarly, the managers believe that if they were to reduce price the impact on competitors' sales would be so great that they would be obliged to match the price cut. The demand 'curve' which represents these views of probable response to price changes is the 'kinked' line AXb — hence the kinked demand curve theory.

The most obvious implication of the kinked demand curve is that in the archetypical situation described firms will be reluctant to vary price either up or down. This stability in prices would continue even if there were significant changes in marginal costs. This can be explained by further development of the kinked demand curve model, shown in Figure 2.5. A marginal revenue curve, derived from the two price-quantity relationships which constitute the kinked curve, will have a discontinuity at the prevailing price/quantity. Assuming no collusion (and therefore the continuing validity of the line AXb), the firm would raise prices only if the increase in marginal cost were so large that it would be more profitable to lose considerable business than to leave price unchanged. Price would be reduced after a fall in marginal costs only if management believed that other firms could not achieve an equivalent cost reduction and so would be unable to match the price cut. Given the assumption built into the kinked demand curve, that any price cut would be fully matched, the individual firm would not pass on any cost reduction in a price-inelastic market.

Another implication of the kinked demand curve theory is that if, by some exceptional circumstance, a collective price change did occur, then (given the continued existence of excess capacity for all sellers) the kink would shift to the new price. This consequence is particularly important as a deterrent against any action to precipitate a short-term price war. One firm may consider the overall market to be more price sensitive than its competitors believe and may, therefore, think of testing this view. The risk of being wrong is, however, quite high, because once price has been forced down, who will feel confident enough to lead a price increase?

Because the mutual gains from collective price increases are so large, collusion may be an attractive proposition to all oligopolists. This may take the form of a tacit arrangement for price leadership (though here the

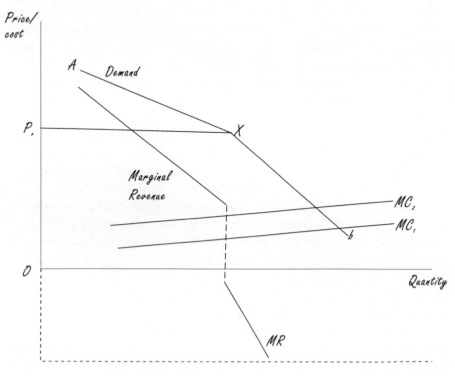

Figure 2.5 Price stability under oligopoly

price leader may feel constrained by the looseness of such an arrangement) or for 'barometric pricing', a tacit agreement to follow some
external indicator, where this would at least safeguard collective interests.

Although, from the point of view of competition authorities, collusion
is an obvious threat in an oligopolisitic market, it may be difficult to prove
because independent conduct by individual firms may lead to results
identical with those of collusion. Particularly when aggregate demand
varies cyclically, there will be periods when excess capacity is eliminated.
Under these conditions, the individual firm will feel able to raise price,
knowing that its competitors have no capacity to supply the extra demand
that they would gain by leaving prices unchanged. In other words, there
would be an upward ratchet effect increase in market price until excess
capacity reappeared (either because of a cyclical downturn or because of
the price increase itself). A new kink would now be established at the
higher price and, even if there were now a substantial cyclical decline in
demand, this higher price would tend to persist.

In the European market for woodpulp between 1975 and 1977, prices
stayed at the same level despite a recession, large stocks and excess
capacity. Between 1978 and 1980 they rose in parallel in response to
growth of demand combined with supply constraints and then in the next
recession stuck again at the recently established high level. In the
Woodpulp case, the Commission of the European Communities (CEC)
decided that the manufacturers concerned had concerted on prices. Since
the structure of supply of any single grade of woodpulp was oligopolistic,
the Commission had great difficulty in the subsequent hearing in the
Court of Justice in proving collusion, except where there was direct
evidence of it. The main counter-argument to the Commission's case was
that independent profit-maximising behaviour by each oligopoly supplier
would have produced the same results. (This case is discussed in more
detail in Chapter 6.)

The kinked demand curve principle applies in theory to forms of
competition other than price. For example, the aggregate market for a
product may be insensitive to total advertising or other forms of
promotion. Does advertising have much effect on *aggregate* sales of
petrol (gasolene), detergents, toilet paper or toothpaste — all products
heavily advertised in the popular media? Probably not, but the market
share of each individual oligopolist supplier may be very sensitive indeed.
In principle, no one supplier will risk reduction of advertising lest
competitors do not follow suit (equivalent to a rise in price on a kinked
demand curve). Equally, suppliers may be reluctant to increase advertising because competitors may be expected to follow, leaving everyone's

sales little changed but profits reduced by the advertising costs. A new, higher, 'equilibrium' level of advertising would then be established.

So, the kinked demand curve theory predicts that firms in oligopoly markets will refrain from competition, because each knows that cost which it incurs in an attempt to increase sales will rapidly be incurred also by competitors. The net result will be sales little changed but profits (for all firms) reduced. Collusion — collective action to raise prices, reduce promotional expenditures or to reduce the quality of the product (in its broadest sense) — might be in every firm's interest. There remains, however, the danger (inherent in any cartel) that one firm may 'cheat' and gain considerably. It is this danger that diminishes the risk of exploitative cartels in oligopoly markets. Mutual recognition of interdependence may be reflected more generally in *détente* from competition rather than joint profit maximisation.

A good example of oligopolistic détente was immediate pre-nationalisation railway service between British cities. Trains operated by the 'rival' Great Western and London Midland and Scottish Railways between London and Birmingham (GWR service from Paddington to Snow Hill, LMS from Euston to New Street) ran to identical timetables, both for departure and arrival times; fares and fare-structures were identical and facilities on trains were very similar. This lack of competition was the result of earlier competition which had come to be recognised as 'destructive'.

Oligopolistic competition in practice

Rail services in the 1930s are an example of the oligopolistic détente which is a consequence implied by the kinked demand curve theory. However, this was an obviously unusual case — a mature industry with significant financial problems and limited opportunities (at that time) for the application of new ideas. An evident weakness of the kinked demand hypothesis is that competition does occur under conditions of oligopoly. The model is essentially one of comparative statics — Firm A does not reduce price, improve quality or increase advertising because, if this tactic succeeds in raising sales, competitors will be obliged to follow suit. Then, because the *total* market is insensitive to these variables, all firms will lose. This logic ignores the time dimension. During the time between the initial move (often a closely guarded secret until it occurs) and the recognition by customers of the effective response, Firm A may gain significant market share. To regain ground lost, competitors may have to offer something even better.

Knickerbocker (1973) suggested that the predominant form of competition in oligopolistic markets was 'aggressive action followed by defensive reaction'. He used this argument to explain clustering of US direct overseas investment — up to that date most production units established overseas by US firms were in clusters of one country and one industry within the same three-year period. An interesting general observation about Knickerbocker's findings is that most of the defensive reaction to aggressive action by one oligopolist is identical to that initial action. One producer of razor blades in the UK in the 1970s decided to sponsor a knock-out cup competition in cricket — its arch-rival sponsored another cricket cup! One producer of breakfast cereals introduced plastic models of spacecraft to interest children; its arch-rival did almost exactly the same thing. The reader can no doubt add his or her own list.

Of all the aggressive actions open to an oligopolist, a price-cut is likely to give the advantage of shortest duration. Unless the initiator of a price war has a particular cost advantage, his/her competitors can respond quickly. We can contrast this with a well-planned and designed advertising campaign, a product improvement based on both technical and consumer research or a promotional idea (free gifts, charity spin-offs, sponsorship, customer competitions etc). It takes time to emulate more complex moves of this kind. Competition under oligopoly often appears to take the form of exploitation of marketing or design 'ideas', to which competitors' response may be slow. Oligopolistic markets, particularly those supplying goods to household consumers, more likely to be influenced by promotional publicity, tend to be characterised by intense non-price competition.

What are the implications of such non-price competition for welfare? With regard to advertising, Vickers and Hay cite empirical research by other authors in support of their view that this can be wasteful and, in this regard, intense non-price competition in oligopoly may be less satisfactory for welfare than monopoly. The UK MMC report on *Household Detergents* (1966) concluded that promotional expenditures by the two dominant producers, amounting to around 30 per cent of the retail value of sales, did little to influence their respective market shares and were against the public interest. Such expenditures may, of course, maintain barriers to entry to the market and therefore be in the joint interests of the oligopolists, though in the case of detergents this was at least debatable, because of economies of scale in production. In extreme cases, the only gainers from such balanced (and therefore ineffective) advertising expenditures may be owners of advertising media. Consumers and producers both lose.

Product innovation may also lead to 'wasteful' expenditures (a view again supported by Vickers and Hay). Attempts at product differentiation are a common feature of oligopoly — they may be viewed as another way of a stealing a march on competitors. They may, alternatively or additionally, form part of a different strategy, of brand proliferation intended to make it more difficult for new competitors to enter the market. These tactics may lead to duplication of research effort, to comparatively trivial changes in product design or composition accompanied by loss of economies of scale.

On the other hand, oligopolistic competition can lead to product improvements which would not have occurred under monopoly. A prime example is vehicle tyres: the launch by Michelin of radial tyres in the late 1960s was followed by a period of continuous product improvement so that the average life-distance of the typical car tyre was trebled. Attempts by a (weak) cartel to halt this process failed, but show what might have happened under monopoly — it would not be in the interests of any dominant firm to implement a policy which would reduce potential sales so substantially (see Fishwick, 1977 for further discussion of this example).

Oligopoly — generalisations and implications for policy

The kinked demand curve analysis does not explain how output and price are determined under oligopoly, nor (as we have seen) does it produce realistic predictions of non-price competition. It remains useful as a guide to changes in price.

What about more general models? First, we might briefly consider the application of games theory. The discussion of 'aggressive action followed by defensive reaction' may have reminded chess-players of certain strategies applied in that game; other readers may have perceived a more military analogy — several authors have applied military strategy analysis to oligopoly (eg Rothschild, 1947; Linda, 1972). While games theory can be used to model competition in conditions of oligopoly, it may be viewed ultimately as an extension of the approach set out above. It does not produce a general theory of oligopoly behaviour.

Attempts to produce more general theories require assumptions about how one firm in an oligopoly expects the others to react to any competitive move on its own part. The simplest theories, developed as long ago as 1833 and 1883 by the French economists Cournot and Bertrand respectively, were based on the premise that one firm would assume that its competitor would always react by keeping output

(Cournot) or price (Bertrand) unchanged. Both models have been substantially extended and developed to provide mathematical determination of output and prices under conditions of oligopoly. Little use has been made of this more advanced microeconomic theory in the practical application of competition policy, but see Phlips (1987) for a strong plea that such use ought to be made. The complexity of the mathematics contrasts uncomfortably with the relative simplicity of the basic assumptions about decision-making under uncertainty.

In conclusion, the consequences of oligopoly, in terms of the conduct of firms and the effect of that conduct on general welfare cannot generally be predicted. The enforcement of competition/antitrust policy to markets characterised by this structure requires analysis of the conditions in each individual case.

One of the unresolved issues of competition policy concerns comparison of markets dominated by two or three firms of equal size with those in which one firm has a much larger market share than the other oligopolists. For example, should competition authorities prefer a market in which shares (in percentages) are 35, 35 and 30, to one where they are 50 plus 5×10? Both structures could be described as 'oligopolistic' in the sense that action by any one firm would provoke reaction by its competitors. In the second case, the largest firm may appear to have a more dominant position and it may seem that this situation would raise more concern. On the other hand, interdependence in the first case may be so high that collusion would be inevitable. Again we can reach no general conclusions — we return to this specific question in Chapters 3, 4 and 6.

BASIC ECONOMIC PRINCIPLES AND NORMS OF COMPETITION POLICY

In Chapter 3 we examine some of the problems and controversies arising from attempts to apply economic analysis to the enforcement of competition policy. At different stages of this current chapter, discussion of underlying economic principles has led to the conclusion that enforcement must be on a case-by-case basis. Economic theory suggests few hard and fast rules: the implications of market structure and conduct depend on conditions in each case. There is often a trade-off between competitive pressures on the one hand and economies of scale on the other; under different conditions the same business conduct may be viewed as pro- or anti-competitive; the implications of market structure for innovation are ambiguous ... the list goes on. Are there any general conclusions at all to be drawn? Before looking in greater detail at problems of enforcement case by case, we need to consider this question.

Agreements between firms to restrict competition

It is important to distinguish between horizontal and vertical agreements. A *horizontal* agreement is one between two or more firms at the same stage of a production or value-added chain. Such firms may agree to fix the same prices for their products, to limit length of product life, not to offer ancillary services — in other words not to try to compete for sales at each other's expense. Long-standing laws against agreements of this kind mean that they are often tacit rather than explicit. Other apparently innocuous agreements, such as one to exchange sales information, may raise opposition from competition authorities, because they facilitate the operation and enforcement of clandestine, tacit or passive collusion.

Economic theory supports general condemnation of horizontal agreements. When two or more firms merge into one to form a single decision-making unit, this may create or reinforce dominance over a market, but there may be offsetting benefits to consumers and aggregate welfare because of economies of scale, greater efficiency or more effective use of innovation. An agreement between firms to exploit a captive market collectively, with no 'rationalisation' of activities, offers less prospect of compensating welfare benefits. There are always exceptions. There are potential benefits from agreements to pool research and development activities, particularly when the parties concerned represent only part of the market or when the joint activity is restricted to basic research, at a much earlier stage than product design. Such research agreements may avoid unnecessary duplicate use and dilution of scarce research resources. Economies of scale may follow from agreements between firms to specialise in different areas of production; these would be a benefit to set against any diminution of competition. Competition policies do allow for such exceptions, under stringent conditions, but as a general principle horizontal agreements are presumed to be bad or actually prohibited. This negative view is consistent with economic theory.

Economists are more equivocal about vertical agreements, between firms at different stages of the value-added chain. One example is exclusive dealing under which a producer supplies a distributor only if the latter agrees not to distribute competing products, and/or the distributor requires the manufacturer not to supply competing outlets. At first sight, this may appear to be a simple anti-competitive arrangement designed to bar entry to the market. While this may be the case, it may also be viewed as pro-competitive. For example certain small manufacturers of specialist audio equipment challenge the supremacy of their bigger rivals by aiming at extra quality and reliability, supported by a high standard of pre- and after-sales service by distributors. As part of their competitive strategy, they may wish to supply only those distributors with a necessary level of technical competence and also with commitment to their product. The distributor concerned may justly argue that he/she needs to invest in the expertise relevant to the particular product range and may require a guarantee that such investment will not be undermined by its availability at other outlets 'free-riding' on his/her services.

The net welfare consequences of vertical agreements to restrict competition depend on the relative importance of their *intra-* and *inter-*brand effects. *Intra-*brand competition is that between downstream producers or distributors in further processing or resale of given brand X. Obviously, an exclusive distribution arrangement or imposition of a minimum resale price will prevent, distort or reduce intra-brand competition. However, if such an arrangement enables brand X to compete more effectively with other brands, it clearly increases *inter-*brand competition.

The treatment of vertical restrictions has been one of the most controversial issues affecting competition policy in recent years. Economic theory does not support a general condemnation of such vertical arrangements, requiring a case-by-case evaluation. As well as limiting intra-brand competition, vertical restrictions may form part of a wider arrangement to restrict competition between brands. For example, resale price maintenance increases transparency and may assist 'policing' of tacit collusion on prices. Exclusive dealing could form part of a collective strategy (formal or informal) to limit entry to a market, particularly when the exclusivity is reciprocal: producer X will supply only distributor Y and Y will buy exclusively from X.

If a vertical restriction is imposed collectively by a group of producers, it is (obviously) unlikely to be a device which encourages competition between them. Indeed it is more likely to be part of an anti-competitive strategy.

Imagine that a group of firms supplying substitutable products imposes a collective exclusive dealing arrangement on distributors, so that any distributor stocking products from suppliers outside the group would be subject to collective boycott. *A priori*, one would expect this agreement to be a device to exclude existing or potential competition from outside the group and probably to be part of an arrangement for exploitation of collective market power — for example, price-fixing, quality limitation or depression of distributors' margins. There may be a more benign motive. For example, the group of suppliers may provide collective technical support to distributors, and wish to deny non-contributors the opportunity to 'free-ride' on this service. Another possibility, also partly related to 'free-riding', is that the group agree to attain a common minimum quality standard and do not wish confidence in their products to be eroded by outsiders supplying inferior substitutes via the same outlets.

Competition laws normally allow for consideration of such benign motives for collectively imposed vertical restrictions, but they would be regarded as exceptions to a general presumption that such restrictions are anti-competitive. UK legislation provides 'gateways' for exemption of agreements with specified (not very precisely) beneficial effects — see Chapter 5. EEC law also provides for exemption but only when the restriction on competition is indispensable to the securing of the beneficial effects — see Chapter 4. In the above example, it is possible that neither of the suggested beneficial effects would require exclusive dealing. Technical support could be sold to distributors at a fee; any producer could then decide if he or she wished to limit supplies to distributors who were receiving this support. The problem of quality assurance might be overcome by use of an externally accredited standard.

As a general principle, both national and Community policies in Europe presume collectively imposed vertical restrictions to be harmful, unless proved otherwise, while vertical restrictions imposed by individual producers (except those relating to resale price) receive more favourable consideration.

This general European attitude reflects that of US courts. Since the mid–1970s, when vertical restraints of any kind had effectively become illegal, there has been a progressive movement in the application of US law away from the presumption that all such restraints are harmful. Only vertical price restraints (resale price maintenance) remain *per se* illegal and this exception has been widely challenged (Comanor, 1990, pp 68–9).

The existence of monopoly power and its abuse

We have explored at some length the reasons why economists, if they can leave aside political preferences, cannot make a general statement that monopoly is better or worse than competition. While competition among a large number of independent sellers ensures that the captive nature of the total market is not exploited and requires each firm to remain efficient to survive, economies of scale may make a fragmented structure inefficient or indeed impossible. It certainly cannot be concluded from economic principles that oligopoly, competition among a few large firms, is better for welfare than monopoly. Such competition may be wasteful. If a market were perfectly contestable then its structure would be of little long-term consequence, but contestability is in practice a matter of degree and detailed investigation may be required to assess it.

So, economic theory is inconclusive about the relative merits of different degrees of competition. For the most part, this lack of generalisation is reflected in competition policies but, because the design of these policies is influenced also by political philosophies, there are notable exceptions.

There are even greater analytical problems about 'abusive' or 'anti-competitive' conduct. Earlier in this chapter, we saw that some business practices may be regarded, in different circumstances, as pro- or anti-competitive. One example would be a loyalty rebate — introduced by a small company trying to establish a niche clientèle, it might be regarded benignly by competition authorities. Applied by an established monopoly, particularly one enjoying economies of scope (a wide product range), it could be viewed as an abuse designed to keep out new entrants. In the discussion of vertical agreements (on pp 56–8), it was suggested that exclusive dealing arrangements could be pro- or anti-competitive.

There is a logical difficulty here for competition/antitrust policy which rarely receives explicit treatment in the literature. The small firm seeking to establish itself in the market and the large firm concerned to defend or strengthen a dominant position may employ the same competitive weapons. Are these to be tolerated when used in its own interests by the small firm but to be condemned as 'unfair' when used by the near-mo-nopolist?

This question does not arise in every case. The European Commission's Memorandum on Concentration (1965) defined an abuse of a dominant position as exploitation of ability to acquire advantages which would not be obtainable under effective competition. Such abuses might include high prices, low quality or other exploitation of the captive position of the customer. The definition of abuse becomes much less clear-cut when the 'victim' is a competitor.

Vickers and Hay (pp 38–9) discuss this problem and conclude that competition/antitrust authorities should not condemn particular business practices as such but '… insist that dominance be established before abuse can be found. The latter view is consistent with the firm's conduct providing evidence of dominance as long as there is independent reason to think that *the conduct could be practised only by a dominant firm*' (our emphasis). In the author's view, the words emphasised in this quotation are important. There is an occasional tendency for competition authorities to penalise companies for seeking to defend their own interests by legitimate means, simply because this implies perpetuation of monopoly. If, when a company emerges as victor of a competitive process its hands are then going to be tied, other companies may wonder about trying to win in the first place. It is arguments like these which encourage protagonists of market contestability to urge that the adverse conse- quences of dominance be remedied by ensuring that markets are open to entry rather than by control or regulation of conduct. Unfortunately this is not always possible.

The 1992 discussion paper 'Abuse of Power' published by the UK government (DTI, 1992) questioned this principle of insistence on proof of a dominant position before any intervention by competition authorities to control conduct. Some of the forms of competition which might predominate under oligopoly conditions might be wasteful or might create barriers to entry, protecting inefficiency. Existing law in the UK (the 1980 Competition Act) provides for control of 'anti-competitive' practices even in the absence of dominance. It may be argued that certain of the less desirable consequences of oligopoly could not be controlled if it were always necessary first to provide the existence of 'dominance'.

The inconclusive nature of this discussion demonstrates again the need for a case-by-case approach, with very little scope for presumptions based on economic theory. We return to the subject in Chapter 6.

Mergers

Given that a firm has significant power, a policy of controlling abuse of that power may imply continual surveillance and interference. Some economists (notably Hay and Vickers; Jacquemin and de Jong) argue strongly that 'prevention is better than cure' as a treatment for abuse of monopoly power and therefore emphasise the need for strict control over mergers.

Under this heading are included acquisitions and other forms of what the new Community law, translating directly from French, calls 'concentrations'. These are defined as changes which lead to unification of decision making within the two or more firms involved. As with agreements, these may be classified into horizontal and vertical, with a third category, conglomerate, involving firms with no product overlap.

In general, economic theory (certainly that based on departures from perfect competition) has little to say about *conglomerate mergers*, which do not lead to any greater concentration of power in any single 'market'. This is reflected in a generally tolerant attitude towards them in competition policy though certain economists, eg Glais and Laurent (1983), express concern about the advantages of large conglomerate firms in terms of capacity for discriminatory or predatory behaviour (by cross-subsidisation) and spreading of risk. Mergers between companies in different markets (defined either in product or geographical terms) may also reduce potential competition by eliminating the threat of entry by each firm into the other's market. Examples of this consequence of conglomerate mergers, which may bypass merger control policies, are given in Chapters 3 and 4.

Vertical mergers between firms at different stages of the value chain of production raise concern about possible foreclosure. Acquisition by a company producing product B of a supplier of essential component A may lead to restriction of supplies to other manufacturers of B. Similarly, acquisition of a distributor may make it difficult for competitors to secure the distribution of their products. In both cases, much depends on the degree of concentration at each level of the product chain. These 'foreclosure' effects of vertical mergers will be important only when there is limited competition, both actual and potential, in the level of activity where the merger occurs.

The main focus of merger control is on *horizontal mergers*, between firms selling similar products to the same group of customers. Such a merger may have adverse welfare effects if it creates or reinforces a position of dominance in the market which can then be exploited at the ultimate expense of customers or suppliers. However, such negative effects may be balanced by gains in efficiency, for example through economies of scale or greater capability for innovation. Moreover, very rigid control of mergers might remove or greatly reduce the perceived threat of takeover, as viewed by management, and thereby diminish an effective discipline on managerial behaviour.

It may be argued that, where reduction of competition would evidently result from a merger, the burden of proof that this would be offset by efficiency gains or other benefits should lie with the firm(s) proposing the merger. Vickers and Hay present reasons for this. First, efficiency gains would initially benefit the merged undertaking; there must be concern about absence of pressure to pass this benefit to customers. Secondly, empirical evidence on efficiency consequences of mergers is generally negative. Thirdly, the firm(s) will have much more information available than the competition authorities, giving them an advantage in arguing their case. While one may sympathise with the general tenor of this view, it hardly points to a hard and fast rule and suggests yet again that policy enforcement must depend on appraisal of individual cases.

CONCLUSION

This discussion of economic principles in relation to the major elements of competition policy has shown that in most applications it is difficult to lay down general rules and presumptions; each case must be considered on its merits. Recognition of this in the design and practical enforcement of policy provides flexibility, normally allowing business managers to put forward their own case about restrictive agreements, allegations about monopoly or its abuse, or proposed mergers or acquisitions.

However, flexibility can lead to apparent arbitrariness and uncertainty unless there are clear and consistent criteria for assessment. It is not easy to rely on precedents as a guide to probable enforcement decisions. No two cases are identical, the external competitive environment evolves and there are changes, sometimes gradual, in the emphasis of policy enforcement.

There are two other problems adding to the uncertainty. First, the design of policies and their enforcement may reflect not only the comparatively objective, if rather ambiguous, economic criteria set out in this chapter but also the broad philosophical priorities described in Chapter 1. Secondly, there may at least occasionally be a wide gulf between the complex, often inconclusive, reasoning of academic economics and the need for comprehensible guidelines for practical application.

Definition of Dominance or Market Power

INTRODUCTION

For the most part, competition policy is concerned with the creation, existence or abuse of power or 'dominance', on the part of sellers or buyers. Such power may be in the hands of an individual firm or of a group of firms. It can be argued, though the argument leads to some problems of legal definition, that the effectiveness of horizontal agreements to restrict competition depends on the collective dominance of the parties to them. If a group of suppliers agree to fix prices (and production quotas) this agreement would have little effect if there were other substantial sources of supply, either actual or potential.

While aggregate concentration and the strength of conglomerates with widely diverse activities attract occasional interest, the main focus of attention is on dominance of the sale or purchase of specific products within specific geographical areas. There is still a lot of controversy about definition and measurement of dominance within a 'market'. Lawyers involved in the enforcement of antitrust/competition policy have generally wanted to measure dominance by share of a 'relevant market' and this approach has been imposed by the courts, at least in US and EEC policy enforcement. Also in EEC policy, certain statutory regulations require market definition. Some economists consider that the need to define the relevant market complicates analysis rather than simplifying it. The definition and measurement of dominance are examined in the next section (pp 64–78).

Measurement of dominance or market power by market share may be a misleading oversimplification. Even if a market can be clearly delineated, power within it will depend not only on the relative shares of existing suppliers but also on potential competition. Shares of a market with low barriers to entry are of little relevance. Likewise, if buying in a market is strongly concentrated, this will lead to little power if sellers have other potential outlets. In the US, the federal authorities responsible for antitrust policies have since 1982 recommended inclusion of potential competition in the calculation of market shares. This is because of the need to include potential competition in the assessment of market power combined with a desire to describe such power in terms of market share. The 'market shares' which result are largely hypothetical. European practice, including that in the UK, has generally been to consider current market shares and potential competition separately, but the issue is still hotly debated (pp 78–88).

Given the problems of market definition and the unresolved issue about the inclusion of potential competition in the computation of market shares, it is perhaps strange that so much attention is devoted to alternative indices of concentration based on these shares. Comparison of the different indices used does make evident some possible anomalies in competition policy, raising some interesting points of principle (pp 83–8).

Study of UK and EEC competition policies in practice shows that both the Directorate General for Competition (DGIV) of the Commission of the European Communities (CEC) and the UK Monopolies and Mergers Commission (MMC) have almost consistently used the same logical framework for analysis of market dominance. This framework, which has not been set out formally and is used only implicitly, comprises three stages: market definition (explicit in EEC cases, not in the UK), analysis of potential competition and finally consideration of whether market power may be constrained by competition in downstream or wider product markets. The use of this framework is consistent with economic welfare principles, but appears to be challenged by certain decisions in the Court of Justice of the European Communities (CJEC), so that issues of principle remain unresolved (pp 88–91).

DEFINITION OF DOMINANCE AND THE RELEVANT MARKET CONCEPT

The notion of dominance or market power

In the US the Sherman Antitrust Act of 1890, on which US antitrust policy is still based, made it illegal to 'monopolize or attempt to monopolize'. Article 86 of the Treaty of Rome (1957) prohibits the abuse of a 'dominant position', insofar as this affects interstate trade within the European common market. Neither statute defines the key terms, 'monopolize' and 'dominant position' respectively. Meanwhile in the UK, the 1973 Fair Trading Act uses the term 'monopoly' to describe the condition where one firm or group of firms accounts for at least 25 per cent of the sale or purchase of any product defined in a reference to the MMC. Since this product may have ben quite arbitrarily defined, there is no presumption that the statutory 'monopoly' implies market power.

Absence of statutory definition has led to emergence of definitions through administration of the policies and through court decisions. The interpretation of 'dominant position' by the Court of Justice of the European Communities (CJEC) and by the CEC comprises:

(a)   ability to act independently, with freedom from restraints of competition, and

(b)   dependence of customers, suppliers or other firms in the market, for whom the dominant firm is an obligatory trading partner.

The dependence element, formally presented in the CJEC Judgement on the *Vitamins* case in 1979, is disputable. Freedom of conduct, (a) above, may normally be expected to imply that customers (or suppliers) had no alternative to trading with the firm(s) in question, so the addition of (b) as a separate criterion may be unnecessary if (a) is proven. On the other hand, it is possible for firms with trading partners dependent on them to be constrained by competition. For example a major retailer may have established 'dominance' over a small supplier for whom it is the major customer. If the retailer itself is facing intense competition for sales, is this 'dominant position' over the supplier the situation envisaged by those who drafted Article 86 of the Treaty of Rome? The answer to this key question has unfortunately not yet been fully clarified by cases arising from Article 86; the controversy about it is discussed further on p 90 and in Chapter 4.

There is more widespread agreement about criterion (a) — freedom of conduct unrestrained by competition. For example in its 1992 Green Paper on Abuse of Market Power, para 3.2, the UK Department of Trade and Industry stated quite simply that 'A dominant position has been defined as the ability to operate substantially independently of competitors.'

In US antitrust enforcement this independent conduct has generally been considered with regard to pricing. In a famous 1956 decision (*Du pont*), the Supreme Court defined monopoly power as 'the power to control prices or exclude rivals'. Most of the literature about market power and its abuse has emanated from the US and has reflected this emphasis on price, which accords well with the normal emphasis of economists.

Conduct as evidence of dominance or market power

Since there is widespread agreement that dominance or market power ('monopoly' in US legislation) may be defined as the ability to act independently without the restraints of competition, it may be argued that such conduct is the best evidence of its existence. This view is widely expressed in the French-language literature including a recent paper by an assistant director-general of DGIV of the CEC (Gyselen, 1992), who described the fact of abuse as 'the best measure of dominance'. The US economist Schmalensee (1982, p 108), wrote as long ago as 1982 that 'Depending on the facts of the case at hand, data on profits or on patterns of conduct may be more informative than are market shares'. Obviously, abnormally high profits or other evidence of exploitation of market power can be used only retrospectively as proof of its existence. Such an approach would be of no use in the control of mergers, or other preventive antitrust policies. It may be possible to use information on profits or abusive conduct to assess the degree of market power at a time up to the present, but this is unlikely to be conclusive without the support of other evidence.

Under the model of perfect competition, price will be equal to marginal cost. Given the several dimensions of monopoly power starting from the zero point of competition, Lerner (1934) proposed that it be measured in terms of its effect, by the difference between price (P) and marginal cost (MC) as a proportion of price: $L = (P - MC)/P$. In a perfectly contestable market, price would also tend to be close to long-run marginal cost (technically, output would be at a level where marginal and average cost were equal, on a horizontal segment of the average cost curve).

Readers who have only skim-read Chapter 2 may find the previous paragraph gobbledegook. Rather than read it again more closely or (much worse) abandon the book at this stage, they may find it useful to think of the simple argument that, on the basis of the Lerner index, market power can be measured by the gross profit margin (sales minus variable costs as a proportion of sales).

At a more practical level, the Lerner index will require two major modifications before it can even be considered in this way. First, it is necessary to allow for different degrees of vertical integration — a clothing manufacturer buying all textile fabrics from outside sources would have a much smaller gross profit margin than a completely integrated textiles and clothing concern. This problem can be overcome by substituting value added for sales and labour costs for variable costs. Secondly, there must be an adjustment for capital intensity: a highly automated factory would require a much higher gross profit margin than a business employing little capital. We can deduct from the gross margin a capital charge, which according to Qualls (1972), should be derived by applying the national average return on equity for all business (r) to the equity capital of the firm concerned. Our practical modification of the Lerner index therefore becomes

$$L_m = \frac{\text{Value added} - \text{labour costs} - r\,(\text{Equity capital})}{\text{Value added}}$$

In the 1970s especially, there were numerous attempts to compute modified Lerner indices of this kind, usually at industry level (using an aggregate L_m for all firms) and to correlate these with measures of concentration in the industry. In the main, the degree of correlation in such structure-performance models was very weak, indeed often insignificant (see Fishwick, 1979). This is not surprising. Quite apart from problems of market definition affecting the concentration measures (see later sections), the profit margin, even in its much modified form, is an unreliable indication of market power.

First, we cannot conclude that a firm or group of firms reporting only modest profits does not possess or abuse market power. Protection from competition may enable management to charge prices considerably in excess of minimum attainable costs but they may dissipate these *a*) in inefficiency or discretionary expenditures (a quiet life of luxury for themselves) and/or *b*) in high labour costs. Wages tend to be higher in concentrated industries, because the related capital-intensity leads not only to greater productivity but also to greater bargaining power. It may justifiably be argued that the sharing of the fruits of monopoly between management and employees is an abuse of dominance. It will not be reflected in high profits.

Secondly, while high profits may be a sign of market power, investigating authorities must make sure that they cannot be explained by other causes. For example, they may reflect an unusually high level of risk in the activity concerned. The use of long-term average returns cannot eliminate this possible distortion from inter-industry comparisons. Because investors tend to be risk-averse, they generally require a higher average return over time from activities with abnormally high variance in returns. Efficiency is another factor which may produce a high profit margin. True, in a contestable market, abnormally high profits would be whittled away by competition, whatever their origin, but antitrust/competition authorities should not take action against firms which continue to earn them because they manage to remain one step ahead of the competition.

The point that high profits can be taken as evidence of abuse of market power only if they cannot be explained otherwise may be applied to conclusions about dominance drawn from other evidence of 'abusive conduct.' Such conduct can be accepted as evidence of dominance only if it could not occur in the presence of competition, a point already emphasised in Chapter 2.

As a general rule, an observation of apparent abuse of dominance will be a useful starting point for identification of the source of that power. For example, one practice considered abusive under certain circumstances is 'product bundling.' An EEC Article 86 case (*Eurofix and Bauco v Hilti*, 1988) concerned the joint sale of nails and cartridge strips by Hilti AG, one of Europe's largest producers of nail-guns. This denied a market in nails compatible with Hilti guns to other nail manufacturers, because Hilti had a monopoly protected by patent on cartridge strips. The source of power to abuse could be traced from the abuse itself.

The importance of substitution in determining dominance

Although the evidence of abuse may provide useful indications of the existence of dominance or market power, we have seen that such evidence will not normally be conclusive. Moreover, the approach of tracing the source of power from observed abuse is applicable only to cases of alleged exploitation of market power or of collusive practices up to the present time. Antitrust/competition authorities need some other method to determine whether a merger 'will create or strengthen a dominant position' (the words of the EEC Merger Control Regulation) or to assess the effects of a notified agreement limiting competition among a group of firms. In such cases it is necessary to define the conditions for dominance in principle and to see whether a merger would create a dominant position defined by these conditions, or whether the parties to an agreement would collectively enjoy such a position.

Dominance implies freedom from competition from existing or potential substitutes. Buyer dominance, *monopsony*, implies that suppliers are unable or unwilling to switch to substitute customers, either existing or potential, and may therefore be forced to accept conditions of trade which they would not accept if they had wider customer base. Its welfare implications are uncertain, unless the dominant buyer or group of buyers also dominates the market in which it sells, ie has monopoly power.

Seller dominance, *monopoly*, to which most attention is directed, implies that if the product concerned were sold at a price reflecting cost (marginal cost plus enough contribution to cover fixed costs) customers would be unable or unwilling to switch to substitute products ('demand-substitution') in response to a small price increase. Dominance also implies that under the same conditions a small price increase would not induce other sellers to supply new substitutes or greater quantities of existing ones ('supply-substitution'). Given these conditions, the dominant firm(s) would raise prices, or in some other way offer less value for money, up to the point where either demand- or supply-substitution became a constraint.

Note that the existence of demand- and/or supply-substitution at current price levels does not imply the absence of dominance. A village store with a local monopoly may be able to raise prices to the point where these are equal to those in a neighbouring town (with greater competition) plus cost of travel to the town and a bit extra for customer convenience.

In the US the Merger Guidelines issued by the Department of Justice state that the test of whether a merger would have serious consequences for competition should be based on the response of both demand- and supply-substitution to a 5 per cent increase in price above the current level. This has been criticised on the grounds that it incorporates the so-called 'Cellophane fallacy', so named after the 1956 case in which the US Supreme Court decided that Du Pont did not have monopoly power from being the sole supplier of Cellophane, because there were many substitutes. This overlooked the logic that a monopoly will increase profits by raising prices until substitution is encountered.

There is much dispute among US economists about whether the Cellophane fallacy invalidates assessment of mergers on the basis of possible increases in prices from current levels. The justification for this approach, implicitly accepting and ignoring the possible existence of dominance already, is that 'merger policy is preventive, designed to keep matters from getting worse' (Fisher, 1987, p 29). While this may be conceded, the method whereby the hypothetical price increase is introduced into US antitrust policy (described below) appears flawed and may conceal the existence and exploitation of market power. (See Schmalensee (1987b), p 48 for support of this view.)

Having noted the danger of the Cellophane fallacy, let us now consider in greater detail what is meant by demand- and supply-substitution.

Demand-substitution depends not only on substitutability of products in end-use but also on customers' recognition of that substitutability. In jargon, we can refer to 'functional interchangeability' in end-use and 'reactive interchangeability' from the viewpoint of customer demand. (To what degree will customers react to a rise in the price of product A by changing to product B?) Even when customers do regard products as substitutes there may be significant barriers or switching costs, some of them functional (for example, changes between gas and electricity for cooking or heating depend on investments in equipment), others created by company strategies — loyalty rebates, product-bundling. Much marketing is aimed at reduction of substitution, both by blurring customers' perceptions of functional interchangeability and creating barriers to switching.

Although we have so far considered substitution in terms of switching between products, it also has a geographical dimension. Larger customers in particular might be able to transfer their demand to suppliers further afield if local suppliers were to try to exploit an apparent monopoly. Where these wider geographical substitution opportunities exist, a local 'monopoly' does not confer much dominance or market power, since the more distant competition restrains freedom of conduct.

In most cases arising under antitrust/competition policies, the firms accused of enjoying, exploiting or seeking to create or reinforce dominance usually argue that they face a much wider range of substitutes, defined in both product and geographical terms, than the enforcement authorities are prepared to concede. Empirical investigation of substitutability is expensive and time consuming and so reference is often made to statistical measures. These include 'cross- (price) elasticity of demand', the percentage change in the quantity sold of product A divided by the percentage change in the price of product B, with the assumption that all other influences on demand for A are unchanged. This measure, originally suggested by Triffin (1940), is of very limited practical value, mainly because of problems in fulfilling the assumption that all other factors are equal. Cross-elasticity of demand would be very difficult to isolate if price changes were followed by sellers of different products (quite a likely situation if the degree of substitution is high). Yet another objection is that substitutability will change over time, as new products evolve and incomes and tastes change.

The conceptual difficulties surrounding cross-elasticity of demand manifest themselves in technical deficiencies in attempts to derive it econometrically, by multiple regression. These are not discussed here (see Fishwick, 1986, Appendix 1 for outline presentation) but readers should be cautious about using any estimates of cross-elasticity of demand without checking that the equation from which they are derived is fully specified and is free of the typical pitfalls of time-series regression analysis.

Because of the difficulties in deriving and interpreting cross-elasticity of demand, a direct measure of substitution, some US authors have suggested indirect measures. One of the most widely quoted is that developed by Stigler and Sherwin (1985). They proposed that the degree of substitution between two products, or the same product in two geographical areas, could be measured by the coefficient of correlation between proportionate changes in their prices over time (strictly between changes in the logarithms of their prices). This measure has intuitive appeal but there are several potential problems: correlation may reflect common cost components; common percentage changes may conceal wide absolute price differences, which may reflect market power in the case of a premium product (example below); a deliberate price strategy on the part of the producer of A not to follow the price of close substitute B could dramatically reduce the correlation, and finally positive correlation could reflect a common external factor rather than substitutability: on hot days we might expect both soft drinks and ice cream to become more expensive. Are they substitutes or complements?

Like the cross-elasticity of demand, the Stigler-Sherwin measure of correlation between price movements is valid only if factors influencing demand for the two or more products have a constant effect on each of them. In the real world the degree of substitution changes. Another problem about the use of such measures is that they do not avoid the Cellophane fallacy. There may be quite a high cross-elasticity of demand between branded and unbranded analgesics. If the price of all branded items rose by 17.5 per cent (say because VAT were extended to them) but unbranded generics remained at the same price, demand for the latter might rise more than proportionately. However, this does not mean that the manufacturers of the branded items are not exploiting market power — it simply means that they have exploited it to the limit. In this same example, one would also expect to find strong correlation between relative price changes.

This extended criticism does not mean that cross-elasticities of demand or parallel movements in prices are not useful evidence in assessing substitution. Both measures can be applied to variables other than price — heavy advertising of one product may reduce demand for substitutes, and parallel changes in the scale and/or form of promotion of two products also suggest a degree of substitution between them. The key point is that, in practice, attempts to measure substitution statistically by one of these devices are rarely successful. In fact, they rarely appear in practical enforcement of policy.

Elementary theory gives much less emphasis to *supply-substitution*, the willingness of sellers of other products to switch to the supply of the relevant product in the event of an increase in its price, relative to those of other products. Supply-substitution is one element in the elasticity of the total supply of a product. Firm A with 100 per cent of current sales of product X which had no close substitute in the demand sense (that is nothing else would fulfil the same need) could not exploit its monopoly if other firms could easily switch production to X and sell it in A's market. Note that if supply-substitution were very significant, the prices of products between which suppliers could switch would tend to be similar, or at least to move in parallel. This means that the Stigler-Sherwin test should pick up both demand- and supply-substitution, without necessarily distinguishing between them.

Direct measurement of price-elasticity

Another statistic which in theory would capture both demand- and supply-substitution is the price-elasticity of demand faced by the individual firm or group of firms. This brings us back to the Lerner index, $L = (P - MC)/P$. For a profit maximising firm, marginal revenue (MR) is equal to marginal cost (MC) and by substituting MR for MC in the Lerner index, one can show that $L = 1/\varepsilon$ where ε is the (positively expressed) price-elasticity of demand, showing the percentage fall in quantity demanded in response to a 1 per cent rise in price from the current level.

Every profit-maximising firm with positive marginal cost (only nuisance by-products would be an exception) will fix price at a level where demand is elastic. To avoid the Cellophane fallacy, we would ideally wish to know the price-elasticity at the hypothetical point $P = MC$, where no monopoly power is exploited. The reciprocal of this price-elasticity would be an ideal measure of monopoly power. (Note that it would no longer be equal to the Lerner index, which assumes profit maximisation, and would have no upper limit.)

This excursion into theory may have puzzled some readers but direct estimation of price-elasticity from factual evidence of the ability to pass on price increases has been attempted by US antitrust authorities and the more widespread application of the technique has been urged. Technically, the key value ε is not the normal price-elasticity of demand of the standard textbooks, which is based on the assumption of all other prices remaining unchanged. Instead, it measures the proportionate change in quantity demanded of the product of firm A divided by the percentage change in A's price, after allowing for consequent changes in the prices and quantities supplied by all other firms.

For example, if the price of wine rose in the UK by 20 per cent (because of devaluation) there would be an increase in demand for beer. However, beer producers may not find it profitable to expand sales at current prices, because of capacity constraints. They may therefore raise prices by, say, 5 per cent after which they can meet the extra demand profitably. The coefficient ε represents the percentage change in the quantity of wine demand divided by the (20 per cent) change in price, after all these consequent changes have taken place in the prices and quantities supplied of substitute products. It is termed the *residual demand elasticity*.

The statistical derivation of residual demand elasticity is complex — Fishwick and Denison (1992) attempted a gentle introduction to the more specialist literature. Moreover, the technique, even when feasible, may be criticised in principle.

First there are problems in interpretation of results which are not statistically significant: if the direct estimate of monopoly power (b in the expression $P = aQ^b$...) is not significantly different from zero, this does not imply necessarily that there is no dominance. Given the complexity of the statistical estimation, it may merely reflect inadequate data or a technical weakness in the computation procedure (one can never prove a null hypothesis).

Secondly, there are problems arising from the need to extrapolate. Elasticity changes with price, ie along the demand curve, and the constant-elasticity model normally used provides a reliable estimate only for observations close to the mean values of the sample data. This estimate may be invalid even at current price levels and cannot validly be extrapolated to assess the consequences of a merger which might lead to big price increases. Nor can it be extrapolated to assess the potential for price increases above the 'competitive level' (long-run marginal cost), the ideal measure of monopoly power.

Finally, like other statistical measures of substitution derived from analysis of past time series, residual demand elasticity cannot be a reliable indicator in a changing environment. The estimate itself will only be an average of a value which may have changed over time. For example, progress towards completion of the Single Market has increased competition within the EC in recent years, so that the degree of both demand- and supply-substitution has undoubtedly increased. Several years of data are required for statistically significant results but an average value over a period of rapid change is meaningless. Even more open to question is the use of that average value to assess the significance of mergers or notified agreements for future competition, given the prospect of full realisation of the Single Market.

This discussion of residual demand elasticity has, like that of other statistical measures of substitution, been rather negative. This is perhaps unfortunate: such measures are particularly useful for background analysis, helping to focus the logic of assessment of dominance. There is little prospect that dominance (market power or whatever other words are used to describe it) can ever be quantified in a single index. The continuing search for such an index, still revealed in the literature, is remarkable in view of the comment by J P Miller (1955, p 119):

> It is a sign of the immaturity of the science of economics that the notion should persist that the competitiveness of the economy or a sector of the economy can ultimately be characterized by some single number of set of numbers.

The relevant market concept

The last quotation applies not only to the various more complex indices of market power examined in the last sub-section but, perhaps even more so, to the widespread desire to describe it by market share. Perhaps this is understandable: in trying to design and apply consistent rules for application to many cases, antitrust/competition authorities need some kind of comprehensible measure if only as a preliminary indication of possible dominance. Economic theorists have spent a lot of time and effort in designing and then criticising other measures of market power. The antitrust/competition authorities have a job to do. Their predilection for market shares is understandable.

Certainly, this predilection is obvious. Although US statutory law makes no specific reference to market share as a measure of monopoly, the courts have consistently over the years required and relied upon this measure. Holley (1977, pp 180–1) asserted: 'In virtually all of the US cases the market share percentage is the starting point for an examination of the possible existence of monopoly power, even if specific acts consistent with monopoly power are alleged.' Comanor also describes, and criticises, this emphasis. In France, the *Commission* (now *Conseil*) *de la Concurrence*, a body very similar to the British MMC, decided in its first report (1978) that in order to identify a dominant position, it must ask itself two main questions: what is the relevant market and what is the concentration of power on that market (computed from market shares)? In UK policy, the term 'market share' is often applied to a share of sales of a product defined in a reference to the MMC, which may not necessarily be a market in the economic sense. It is interesting to note, however, that in the Green Paper on Abuse of Market Power (1992), the DTI refers to a market share of 40 per cent as a criterion of a dominant position as defined by Article 86 of the Treaty of Rome (paras 3.2 and 4.9).

In the administration of EEC legislation, shares of the relevant market have been accorded great emphasis. Although Article 86 itself makes no reference to markets, interpretation by the Court of Justice and (perhaps in consequence) by the Commission makes a high market share a necessary and (if it is very high) a sufficient condition for a dominant position. In its famous judgement in the *Continental Can* case in 1973 the Court made it clear that proof of dominance required definition of the relevant market — 'the determination of the relevant market is of essential importance'. In its 1979 judgement on the *Hoffman-Laroche* case, the Court implied that market shares above 40 per cent might lead to dominance if other companies had much smaller shares. In commenting on shares of 80 per cent and over, the Court declared:

> ... the view may legitimately be taken that very large shares in themselves, and save in exceptional circumstances, are evidence of the existence of a dominant position.
>
> (Judgement *Hoffman-Laroche v Commission,*
> *para 41, ECR 1979*)

There has been less emphasis on market definition in relation to Article 85 relating to restrictive agreements. This may be because the Article itself refers neither to the market nor to collective dominance, which is not a *de jure* condition for enforcement of the prohibition of agreements. (In Chapter 4, it is argued that it is a *de facto* condition of its relevance). Paragraph (b) of Section 3 of Article 85, dealing with possible exemptions from the general prohibition, precludes exemption of any agreements which 'afford the possibility of eliminating competition in respect of a substantial part of the *products in question*' (our emphasis). While this suggests a possible requirement for product market definition, this has not been made a formal requirement by the Court as in Article 86 cases.

The relevant market concept has, however, been formally introduced into the application of Article 85 by six of the regulations providing for block exemptions under Section 3. These refer to agreements on exclusive distribution, patent licensing, motor vehicle distribution and servicing, 'specialisation' and research and development. Each regulation contains conditions to ensure that effective competition remains in the supply of the relevant product, defined in a very similar way in each of the regulations, for example: 'Identical products or services, or products of services considered by users as equivalent in view of their characteristics, price and intended use' (Regulation 2349/84 relating to patent licensing). With regard to the geographical dimension of the market, the regulations on exclusive dealings, exclusive purchasing and patent licensing explicitly refer to the 'contract' or 'licensed' territory. The other three regulations refer to the competition in the 'common market or a substantial part thereof' and so require definition of the relevant geographical area to make possible computation of market shares. The regulations relating to specialisation and research and development allow exemptions only when the combined market share of the parties to the agreement in question do not exceed 20 per cent. (For fuller explanation see Fishwick, 1986; or Jacobs and Stewart-Clark, 1991).

The Merger Control Regulation (MCR) is concerned with the creation or reinforcement of a dominant position. Gyselen (1992) makes it explicit that the definition is consistent with that set out for Article 86 cases by the Court of Justice — the main criterion will be the capacity of the merged undertakings for conduct unrestrained by competition even in the long term. In principle, this capacity can be assessed without the notion of a 'market'. Ability to behave independently depends upon freedom from actual or potential competition from substitutes. Economic analysis does not require these to be grouped into those within a market and the rest. However, the formal application of the MCR does. The preamble states the presumption that concentration is unlikely to impede effective competition where 'the *market share* of the undertakings concerned does not exceed 25 per cent either in the common market or in a substantial part of it'. The Commission has been able to avoid formal definition in about one-third of the cases considered in the first two years, by showing that under any combination of the narrowest reasonable definitions of product and geographical markets the 25 per cent threshold would not be reached. However, the formal requirement is there and market definition has been a major issue in several cases.

The first objection to the requirement for market definition is that it is often unnecessary. The analysis of existing dominance can begin from identification of the source of power which has been abused. In assessment of the effects of agreements, it is possible to begin the analysis from the product range and territory over which these are effective and to consider existing and potential substitutes. Anti-competitive effects of mergers may be measured by reference to any overlapping products and/or territories supplied and again to existing or potential substitutes. There is no need (and indeed it may be distorting) to divide these substitutes on an 'all-or-nothing' basis into those within the market and those outside. Secondly, markets can rarely be delineated unambiguously. The principle of market definition was set out by Joan Robinson in 1933 (p 5). She defined a monopoly as the single seller of a product 'bounded on all sides by a market *gap* in the chain of substitutes. Such a gap in nature provides us with a rough-and-ready definition of a single commodity ... which is congenial to common sense and causes no trouble' (our emphasis). Many years later Joan Robinson herself observed that things were not so simple (1969). The impracticality of the 'marked gap' was emphasised by Schmalensee (1982), leading him to conclude that market shares were unreliable indicators. In Europe, Vogel (1990) and Glais (1992) are among European economists who regard insistence on market definition as the 'Achilles' heel' of Community competition policy.

A third problem in market definition is the issue of vertical independence. A monopolist of an essential component A of another product B, which is its only application, has little ultimate power if the cost of A is an important element in the price of B and if B faces intense competition. Normal practice in Europe, both at EEC and national levels, has been to define markets at one horizontal stage of the value chain — at level A — but to consider interdependence separately. This last stage may be important, as shown on p 90–1.

The final objection to reliance upon market shares concerns the treatment of potential competition. If shares are based only on current sales by existing suppliers of the relevant product within the relevant geographical market, they may overstate market power. In a perfectly contestable market even a 100 per cent share confers no long-term power. On the other hand, if potential competition is in some way incorporated into the computation of market shares, these become hypothetical and also rather difficult to interpret.

The reference product in many monopoly and merger cases considered by the UK MMC is only a starting point for analysis and is not intended as a market in the economic sense of an area surrounded by a 'marked gap' in substitution. This means that UK competition policy makes no formal use of the economic market concept. Some specialists, while accepting the limitations of the concept, have expressed regret about this absence of formal market definition, on the grounds that it reduces transparency and consistency of MMC and OFT decisions. Among such critics is Professor K D George, a part-time member of the MMC (see George (1985); also Merkin and Williams (1984)). A research paper recently published by the OFT (Ridyard et al (1992)) examines market definition in UK competition policy and observes that many MMC reports do not deal explicitly with the concept and that there is little consistency in the way in which it is used in analysis of individual cases.

In contrast, our own research suggests that the MMC and DGIV of the CEC have in fact used a consistent and logically sound framework for decisions, in which market definition is the first stage (implicit in MMC cases, explicit in those arising from EEC policy). There is much to be gained from the formal and overt adoption of this framework, examined on p 88–91. Transparency would do much to ensure consistent application of the law.

MARKET DEFINITION AND POTENTIAL COMPETITION

This topic merits a section on its own because it is a major focus of controversy. In the US before about 1980, monopoly power (equivalent to 'dominance' in EEC parlance) was measured almost entirely by market share. It is quite true that the Merger Guidelines issued by the Department of Justice in 1968 urged consideration of potential competition as an additional factor which might moderate monopoly power, but the courts generally preferred a single measure of that power — market share.

After the publication of articles by economists and lawyers criticising the existing policy, including some from the Chicago School with its strong philosophical attachment to 'free-market' economics, the US policy was changed with new Merger Guidelines in 1982, revised further in 1984 and 1992. These changes introduced the principle that both demand- and supply-substitution be incorporated in calculation of market shares. Much of the literature about antitrust economics now emanating from the US presumes that markets will be defined in this way, which may cause confusion when the arguments are transferred to the European environment.

Current US practice in relation to theoretical background

Much of the logic underlying the current US Guidelines appeared in a major and much quoted paper by Landes and Posner (1982). They proposed that the computation of market share be widened to include all demand-side substitutes and the potential output of existing suppliers of those substitutes. They showed that, provided the market is defined in this way, the firm's own price-elasticity of demand can be analysed in terms of its market share (S_i), combined price-elasticity for all market products (E_x) and the elasticity of supply of all other firms in the market (e_j) in response to a small increase in price.

$$E_i = \frac{1}{S_i} (E_x + e_j (1 - S_i))$$

The authors themselves note that E_i is not the normal price-elasticity of demand presented in the textbooks, because it is not based on the assumption that the prices of all firms other than i remain unchanged. If firm i increased prices by (say) 10 per cent, then other firms may increase prices to a lesser degree and increase market share at i's expense. This price response of supply by other firms is measured notionally by e_j. E_i is therefore the residual demand-elasticity for firm i, which we earlier described by the symbol ε. The reciprocal of this measure shows the power of the firm concerned to raise prices above the current level.

From 1982 onwards, the US Merger Guidelines have defined a 'market' to denote a combination of product range and geographical area in which a hypothetical monopolist would apply and maintain a higher price. The 1992 Guidelines (p 7) express this as follows:

> A market is defined as a product or group of products and a geographic area in which it is produced or sold such that a hypothetical profit-maximising firm ... that was the only present and future producer or seller of these products in that area likely would impose at least a 'small but non-transitory' increase in pricing, assuming the terms of sale of all other products are held constant.

A 'small but non-transitory' price increase is defined subsequently (*ibid*, p 14) as an increase of 5 per cent which could be maintained for the foreseeable future. The inclusion of supply-substitution is made quite explicit in the definition of participants in the relevant market:

> Participants (in the relevant market) include firms currently producing or selling the market's products in the market's geographical area. In addition, participants may include other firms depending on their likely supply responses to a 'small but significant and non-transitory' price increase. A firm is viewed as a participant if, in response to a 'small but significant and non-transitory' price increase, it likely would enter rapidly into production or sale of a market product in the market's area, without incurring significant sunk costs of entry and exit.

A sunk cost is '... one that would not be recouped within one year of commencement of the supply response' (*ibid*, p 21). Finally, as though to emphasise again the inclusion of supply-substitution in market participation, the Guidelines define the denominator for the computation of market shares as 'total sales or capacity currently devoted to the relevant market together with that which likely would be devoted to the relevant market in response to a "small but non-transitory price increase" ' (*ibid,* p 25). The Guidelines base definition implicitly on the term E_x in the Landes-Posner formula, the price-elasticity of demand for the aggregate market output. By basing market shares on existing and potential suppliers (within 12 months of a 5 per cent price increase), they implicitly define residual demand elasticity in accordance with the Landes-Posner formula. The reciprocal of this coefficient is the Lerner index of monopoly power. Once a market has been defined in this way, the effect of a merger on concentration is examined. If this would cause an increase in concentration above permitted levels, measured by the Herfindahl-Herschman index described in the next section, a decision not to allow it may be modified by further considerations. These include longer-term entry possibilities and any offsetting gains in efficiency.

Non-economists, in particular, who have stuck with the last few paragraphs may have become rather perplexed. They are not alone. Most of the criticism of the US Guidelines is directed at their complexity and impracticality. Some US economists have suggested that this complexity, which dates from the 1982 version, is part of a broader policy to lessen the impact of antitrust laws (Hay; Fox).

Criticism is not confined to the problem that the US Guidelines are so difficult to understand and to apply. One defect has been explained earlier in the discussion of the Lerner index, the reciprocal of the price-elasticity of demand at the current price, on which the Guidelines formula is based. This is the so-called Cellophane fallacy: if one or more dominant sellers were already exploiting monopoly power to the point where competition from other products had become a restraint, the market definition would be widened to include these other products. This problem is evident in national markets affected by monopoly or cartel pricing, where prices may be raised to the point where imports become competitive, despite transport and transaction costs. The Merger Guidelines state that wherever imports to the US are significant, the entire world-wide capacity of the source of the imports should be included in the denominator for computation of US market share.

We have already examined the implications of this fallacy — and whether it matters in the case of merger control (see above). The other main criticism of principle which may be levelled at the US approach is that the integration of potential competition into the definition of market participants and market size conceals some important elements in the assessment of market power.

The advantages of treating actual and potential competition separately

Market definition has always included supply-substitution where this is perfect. An example, originating in the *Brown Shoe* case in the US, is a product, ie shoes, made in different sizes and styles in the same factory and distributed via the same outlets. A pair of size eight shoes is not a demand-substitute for a pair of size ten shoes, even in the same style and colour. A commonsense approach groups such perfect supply-substitutes into one product market. Apart from such self-evident cases, market definition in the US as elsewhere, was based exclusively on demand substitution until the early 1980s.

Most US economists welcomed the inclusion of short-term potential competitors within the relevant market, mainly because potential competition received too little attention before the 1982 Guidelines. Some US observers (notably Kaplov, 1982; Pitofsky, 1990) have expressed a preference for a two-stage process–definition of the market and of market shares on the basis of current competition followed by consideration of potential increases in sales by existing suppliers and new entrants as one of the factors diminishing dominance. The latter approach has been generally adopted within Europe and this has received wide support from both economists and lawyers. (An opposing view supporting the application of the US principles to Europe is expressed by Venit (1991), and also Ridyard et al).

The main arguments for separating supply-substitution from definition of market shares may be summarised as follows:

1. Assessment of competition through expansion of supply, by existing suppliers to the market or by new entrants, requires consideration of the hypothetical question: *could* and *would* these undertakings respond to a rise in price in the relevant market by increasing their supply to it? The *could* part of the question requires consideration of the capacity available to potential suppliers. Could idle capacity easily be brought into production? How much capacity devoted to other products could be transferred? Could sales of the relevant product be switched from other geographical markets? Then, one must ask whether such transfers *would* occur — if supplies to other markets (in both product and geographical terms) were reduced, this would raise prices in those other markets. The supply response to a hypothetical price increase depends therefore on conditions outside the market in question. Another possible barrier to potential competition is what is sometimes called collusive détente — 'you stay out of my market and I'll stay out of yours'. The hypothetical question about supply response to a price increase needs to be considered but, as Kaplov pointed out, it calls for judgement and cannot be answered on an 'all-or-nothing' basis — do we add into the market all the sales (or capacity) of a possible short-term entrant or do we exclude them completely?

2. The prospect of entry must be qualified by a time dimension. Time

must elapse before firms decide to transfer capacity to sales of the relevant product within the relevant geographical area. Before these potential suppliers incur the necessary costs, they must be confident that the market opportunity created by the hypothetical price increase will continue. Once the decision has been taken there will be further delay while it is put into effect. This time factor is uncertain, which is why the German *Monopolkommission* recommended that supply-side substitution be omitted from the definition of the relevant market and included within what is called the 'near-market' (*Marktnähebereich*). Kaplov points out that the use of an arbitrary criterion period for easy entry (one year) is another example of an unsatisfactory 'all-or-nothing' formula.

3. Use of actual sales of the relevant product within the relevant geographical area also has significant advantages for administration. If current market shares are low, this implies absence of a dominant position and there is no need for further investigation. This saves time and expense both for the competition authorities and for firms required to provide information and/or waiting for decisions. As we shall see later, both EEC and UK policies for merger control involve a two-stage procedure with arrangements for rapid clearance of proposed mergers with no significant anti-competitive effects. Use of current market shares facilitates this rapid clearance.

4. Separation of actual from potential competition has another advantage particular to control of mergers, acquisitions and joint ventures. The main concern about a merger is whether it will create or reinforce a dominant position. A merger may combine two or more enterprises each of which is dominant in a market, but may have no 'horizontal effect', in the sense that these markets do not overlap. An example is the proposed merger between Renault and Volvo. Because of past procurement policies, the Commission of the EC, CEC, decided that the markets for buses remained national markets in 1990 but would become more Community-wide as the Single Market developed. In 1989 Volvo supplied 64 per cent of buses sold in the UK, Renault supplied 70 per cent of those produced in France. Applying the American criterion (response within one year to 5 per cent price increase), one would still define national markets and overlook a possible anti-competitive effect of this merger — the elimination of potential competition between Renault and Volvo in the more integrated Single Market. This could be interpreted as a reinforcement of their dominant position in each of the two national markets. (In the event the Commission did consider this possibility but decided that

there would remain sufficient competition from other potential suppliers in the Community. This case, which may have political significance, is examined in more detail in Chapter 4).

The US Merger Guidelines of 1984 Section 4.1, p 24, describe this problem which may occur with a non-horizontal merger and is not detected by analysis of shares of a relevant market:

> By eliminating the possibility of entry by the acquiring firm in a more procompetitive manner, the merger could result in a lost opportunity for improvement in market performance resulting from the addition of a significant competitor. The more procompetitive alternatives include both new entry and entry through a 'toehold acquisition of a present small competitor.

It is interesting to note that the 1992 Guidelines make no reference to this point — a further indication of a more favourable attitude towards mergers?

5. Even when potential competition is included in the definition of the relevant market, as indicated in the US Guidelines, the resulting market shares are still insufficient as indicators of market power. It is still necessary to consider factors such as longer term entry (Section 3 of the 1992 Guidelines) and the effects of countervailing buyer power, not specifically discussed in US Guidelines but introduced into certain of the Commission's decisions under the MCR (for example, those relating to motor vehicle components supplied to manufacturers).

The integration of supply-substitution into the computation of market shares results partly from the desire to summarise market power (or dominance) in a single coefficient, particularly one easy to understand, as it may superficially appear. In fact once it has been modified to include responses to a hypothetical price increase, market share becomes a concept far removed from the normal interpretation of the term. Moreover, this modification confuses, rather than clarifying, the practical analysis of market power.

INDICES OF MARKET CONCENTRATION

Having read so much about the inadequacies of market share as an indicator of dominance, the reader may wonder why a section is now devoted to statistical measures of concentration derived from these market shares. There are two reasons for this. First there is frequent reference to certain indices in practical policy enforcement — in some Court cases both in the US and in the EEC the discussion sometimes becomes a little too academic for many. It is therefore difficult to understand some of the arguments without any knowledge of the terms. Secondly, the properties of the indices and the ways in which they are used highlight some interesting issues and possible inconsistencies in policy.

The basic principles of concentration indices

The summary presented here focuses on those indices most often used in practice and is not intended as a comprehensive reference source. (The author's own PhD thesis was devoted largely to a full technical exposition — see Fishwick, 1979).

There are two elements in business concentration which are reflected in varying degrees by the numerous index numbers which have been proposed: *a*) the number of firms and their absolute size, and *b*) the inequality between the size of firms. The index numbers which most simply describe the first feature are absolute concentration ratios, for example the share of market sales obtained by the four largest firms. A measure of inequality easy to understand is the combined share of market sales obtained by (say) the top 20 per cent of firms ranked in order of market share. More comprehensive, if less comprehensible, measures of inequality would be the coefficient of variation of market shares (standard deviation as percentage of mean) or the standard deviation of their logarithms.

Indices based exclusively on inequality are little used in practical enforcement of competition policy, though they have appeared frequently in the literature, especially in the 1970s. Statistically minded readers may be interested by the theory, backed by some empirical investigation, that the distribution of company sizes tends over time towards a log-normal pattern. This means that the standard deviation of logarithms and coefficients mathematically related to it, notably the Gini coefficient, are unambiguous indicators of inequality. While this feature has intrigued academics, who have written about it at length (see Fishwick for literature review), its practical interest is questionable. The inequality between the 31st and 32nd largest firms, which contributes to the standard deviation of logarithms just as much as that between the first and second, is of little importance. Attention must focus on those firms who may, singly or in combination, possibly enjoy market power.

The main objection to purely absolute indices is that they give no information about inequality within the group of firms selected — for example, a four-firm concentration ratio of 60 per cent for newspaper circulation in the UK in 1985 tells us nothing about the relative size within the group of four. Secondly, how do we choose the relevant number of firms? Even if we have data for all firms, how can we define a summary statistic which can be used as guidance for policy?

Table 3.1 highlights the two problems:

Table 3.1 Two market structures to illustrate indices

Firm (in descending order of share)	Market 1 %	Market 2 %
1	40	32
2	20	24
3	15	19
4	10	11
5	3	10
6	3	3
7	2	1
8	1	1
9–20 (each)	0.5	—

The four-firm concentration ratio for each market is 85 per cent but the largest firm in Market 1 is twice the size of its next competitor, whereas in Market 2 there is no similar inequality. Secondly, the concern in Market 2 should be focused on the top three firms or the top five; there is no reason for an arbitrary break at Firm 4.

Measures have been devised, eg by R Linda (formerly of DGIV of the Commission), to identify the 'oligopolistic arena' in each market and to summarise inequality within that arena (see Linda, 1976; Fishwick, 1979). Unfortunately such indices tend to be mathematically complex and are little used in practical enforcement.

One measure which has been more widely adopted in practice is the Herfindahl-Hirschman index, the sum of the squares of market shares. This index was named after two researchers who separately but concurrently identified its significance in the late 1940s. The measure reflects both the number of firms and the inequality between them. If V represents the coefficient of variation of market shares (S_i for each firm i) and h is the number of firms, then:

$$HH = \Sigma \, S_i{}^2 = (V^2 + 1)/_n$$

The maximum value is 1 if the shares are expressed as proportions of the total market and 10,000 (100^2) if they are expressed as percentages. The minimum value is 1/n (or 100/n) for n firms of equal size, which would tend to 0 under conditions of perfect competition, where the number of firms is very large. So, the HH index has a number of desirable properties — it takes into account both the number of firms and the inequality among them, it has a scale from 0 to 1 and it is relatively easy to understand. However, the HH index, because of the squaring procedure, is dominated by large firms and tends to be greater for a fairly evenly split oligopoly than for a market dominated by a single firm. Consider the following two market structures.

	Market A			Market B	
Firm	Share (%)	HH	Firm	Share (%)	HH
1	50	2500	1	40	1600
2	10	100	2	30	900
3–42	40 x 1	40	3	30	900
	100	2640		100	3400

In Market A the leading firm with 50 per cent of the market, five times as much as its largest competitor, would be expected to have substantial freedom of manoeuvre, whereas in Market B everything would depend on the effectiveness of collusion between the only three players.

A second problem, which is possibly evident already, is that the same HH value may describe very different distributions. For example:

	Market A			Market B	
Firm	Share (%)	HH	Firm	Share (%)	HH
1	50	2500	1	40	1600
2	20	400	2	35	1225
3	15	225	3	20	400
4	10	100	4	5	25
5	5	25	—	—	—
	100	3250		100	3250

Concentration indices used in practice

US antitrust policy makes most formal use of concentration indices. Until 1982, the Merger Guidelines referred to critical levels of four-firm concentration ratios but from 1982 onwards these have been replaced by the Herfindahl-Hirschman (HH) index. The 1992 Guidelines specify that if after a merger the HH index for the relevant market would be less than 1000 then there should be no concern about adverse effects. When the post-merger HH index would be between 1000 and 1800 the market would become 'moderately concentrated'; any merger raising HH by more than 100 may cause concern. Finally, if the post-merger HH index would exceed 1800, the market is defined as 'highly concentrated'. Any merger raising HH by more than 50 points may raise concern; any which would increase it by more than 100 may be presumed to create or enhance market power. This set of precise quantitative criteria should, of course, be considered in the context of the difficulties of market definition, based on presumed responses to a hypothetical price increase.

The application of the US rules might create an interesting and inequitable situation. If firms A and B, two market leaders, merge and this increases the HH to a value just below the threshold of 1800, a subsequent merger between two smaller firms C and D would be subject to stricter scrutiny. C and D might argue that their merger was necessary as a defence against the combined strength of A and B, a legitimate argument overlooked by the formal guidelines.

EEC competition policy has been through a series of phases with regard to concentration indices. In the 1970s the Commission of the European Communities (CEC) published an extensive series of studies of concentration in different national markets throughout the Community. These included a wide range of indices including purely absolute measures, measures of inequality (coefficients of variation and Gini), coefficients of oligopoly delimitation (Linda) and alternative composite measures (HH and entropy indices). After this statistical overkill, which did not (fortunately?) extend into case law, the CEC sought a more selective approach. A close mathematical scrutiny of the various indices undertaken for the CEC in 1983 by Professors Piesch and Schmidt recommended use of the HH index, mainly because this reflects the importance of the largest firms (Piesch and Schmidt, 1983, p 84). The two German professors did, however, go on to discuss (inconclusively) the fact that the HH index does not distinguish adequately between single-firm dominance and tight oligopoly.

An example above has shown that HH may yield a lower value for a market with one single leader and a large number of fringe suppliers than for one shared comparatively equally by a very small number of competitors. The relative importance of the number of players in a market and the inequality between them remains an unresolved issue in EEC policy enforcement. The problem is illustrated by the CEC's decisions that certain mergers (eg *Varta/Bosch* and *Nestlé/Perrier*, both discussed in Chapter 4) could proceed only if there were some additional concentration among other firms in each relevant market, to provide a substantial effective competitor for the merged firm. Such additional concentration would, of course, increase the HH index and would be subject to even stricter scrutiny under the principles of the US Merger Guidelines.

The CEC's decision in these cases can be supported by the argument that a dominant firm may be more effectively checked by a single powerful competitor than by a multitude of 'fringe' firms. The counter-argument is that the dominant firm may be able to reach a tacit agreement or détente more easily with one (or two) such big competitors than with a lot of small firms, including uncooperative 'mavericks'. This is one of the oldest disputes in antitrust economics. The Landes-Posner formula has been criticised as giving too much emphasis to the 'fringe' firms in the relevant market, dividing market participants into the leading firm i with market share S_i and including as a restraint on its conduct the elasticity of supply of all the rest (e_j). The influence of this restraint is measured by $(1-S_i) e_j$. This formula ignores whether the market share $(1-S_i)$ represents the combined shares of many small firms or whether it consists mainly or even entirely of the share of one other large competitor. The Merger Guidelines since 1982 have been based substantially on the Landes-Posner formula. It is disputable practice.

The main objection to the adoption of a different approach by the CEC is that no reasons or explanation of this change have been published, or even made explicit. The reasoning contradicts the logic and conclusions of the Piesch-Schmidt report published by the Commission, placing emphasis on the HH index as a critical factor in EEC policy.

The debate about which it would be more correct to emphasise in competition policy, the number of major players or the inequality between them, gets less attention in UK policy, which tends to be administered pragmatically rather than dogmatically. Lest this should raise a patriotic cheer in the British reader's soul, it must be pointed out again that there are many complaints about lack of transparency and consequent inconsistency in UK practice. There is a dilemma here: formal rules are difficult to apply because there are conflicting arguments, which have different weight according to the circumstances of each case. If there are no rules at all or if (as in the EEC merger examples) the rules are not always transparent, policy can appear arbitrary.

THE ANALYTICAL FRAMEWORK OF THE CEC AND THE MMC FOR ASSESSMENT OF DOMINANCE

Despite the widespread criticism from both economists and lawyers that UK policy relies excessively on an *ad hoc* approach with lack of transparency and consistency, our own analysis of cases referred to the MMC shows that it has followed one analytical framework remarkably consistently. This implicit framework is very similar to that also adopted by the CEC in cases arising under Article 86 of the EEC treaty, referring to abuse of dominance. The MMC has applied a related logic to appraisal of merger proposals and a similar pattern appears to be emerging from cases so far considered by the CEC under the Merger Control Regulation.

Before proceeding in the next two chapters to examine EEC and UK competition policies in greater detail, it seems useful to present in outline what the author considers to be this common, implicit framework. A more detailed, technical explanation appears in earlier papers produced for specialist publications (Fishwick, 1986, 1989a).

The procedure can be divided into three stages, the first of which could itself be divided into three. The stages are:

1. Analysis of current market structure

(a) Consideration of substitute products available and acceptable to customers (or substitute outlets in the rare analysis of monopsony), proceeding formally in EEC cases to definition of the relevant product market.

(b) Consideration of the geographical dimension of the market, again proceeding formally in EEC cases to definition of the relevant geographical market.

(c) In EEC cases only, computation of shares of the market defined by (a) and (b). The MMC does not need formally to define markets and quantify shares. In the case of a product referred to it, it examines whether this product does 'form the relevant market for the purpose of assessing dominance.' (Merkin and Williams, 1984, p 136). In the case of a merger, the MMC examines, in effect, whether a range of products and geographical area in which the merged firms would have a combined share of at least 25 per cent constitutes a market relevant to monopoly power. In both cases, it goes through the same reasoning as that required of the CEC; the only difference is the absence of formal definitions and computed market shares.

2. Evaluation of potential competition — supply substitution

Both the MMC and the CEC have tended to distinguish between potential expansion of sales by firms already active within the relevant market (or the implicit equivalent in the MMC's analysis) and entry into that market by other firms. In the first case, the two bodies generally consider excess capacity and then the economics of transferring capacity to the relevant product or sales of that product to the relevant geographical market from elsewhere. For firms not currently active in the relevant market they consider barriers to entry, increasingly laying emphasis on market contestability, with the implied focus on sunk costs.

3. Product interdependence

This is a more controversial element in the assessment of dominance. If the adverse welfare effects of abuse of dominance are to be measured by the net loss of consumer and producer surplus — by adding benefits and losses to all parties affected, then actions which merely transfer benefits between firms are of no significance. If a company operating in a competitive market is the only customer of a supplier which has become dependent on it, then downward pressure on that supplier's prices may be seen as an abuse of dominance over it, but it does not produce any adverse welfare effect. Indeed, if the downstream producer passes on the reduced component cost to the customers, while maintaining its own profit margin, the net effect will be an increase in aggregate welfare. The component supplier's loss is equal to the downstream producer's gain, while the lower final price means an increase in consumer surplus.

Several cases have raised issues of this kind. The fundamental question to be answered is whether the market power of a company, as the seller of an intermediate product (or the buyer of it, as in the monopsony situation just described) is diminished by competition in a downstream or composite product market.

The MMC decided that the monopoly enjoyed by *Ford* in the supply of replacement panels for its own cars (to replace crash-damaged panels) could not be substantiated because high prices would be reflected in higher insurance premiums for Ford cars. Insurance represents a significant element in the cost of owning a car. The MMC largely accepted Ford's argument that any power derived form its near monopoly of the supply of replacement panels was substantially diminished by competition in the wider (or composite) market for new cars. Although the monopoly deprived other body panel manufacturers of business, this was not a matter of public interest.

In EEC jurisprudence, it has not yet been clearly resolved that abuse of power over another trading partner (or competitor) is prohibited only when aggregate welfare is affected. However, in a number of cases of this kind the CEC has been through the same logic as that applied by the MMC in the case of replacement panels for Ford cars, examining first what proportion of the price of a downstream, wider or composite product is represented by the product or service in which dominance exists. If this proportion is significant enough to affect price in this downstream or wider market then competition in that market may diminish the adverse effects of dominance on general welfare. So far, the final decision has been that this proportion was too small (*Hugin v Lipton*) or that there was insufficient competition in the downstream or under market (eg *Commercial Solvents v Zoja* and *Eurofix and Bauco v Hilti*).

CONCLUSION

This three- (or five-) stage procedure is fully consistent with the economic principles outlined in Chapter 2. There is much to be said for making it more explicit and setting it out in the form of guidelines. This would help all partners involved in antitrust/competition policy enforcement. One problem with this suggestion is that, while many agree upon the need for guidelines, not everyone would agree that this three-stage process is ideal. (See, for example, Ridyard et al). The author's own perception is that the three-stage procedure described here is what the MMC and CEC have been following, implicitly and even unconsciously, in the vast majority of cases. It is soundly based on widely recognised economic principles.

Competition Policy in the European Economic Community

INTRODUCTION: THE BASIC CONFLICT OF VIEWS

This Chapter, as its title indicates, will deal with the application of competition law derived mainly from the Treaty of Rome 1957 and applying to the European Economic Community and not that relating to the coterminous European Coal and Steel Community, set up by the Treaty of Paris 1951. The economic and political environment of the coal and steel industries are quite different from that of most other business in Western Europe. ECSC competition rules are therefore of minor relevance to people not directly involved in these two basic industries.

Throughout its history, the application of EEC competition law has been affected by a conflict between two general philosophies described in Chapter 1. The first of these reflects the view held by some of those responsible for the foundation of the European Communities, with the ideal of a European common market and ultimate political union, a United States of Europe. This view foresaw that economic nationalism within the member states of a European Community would be replaced by what Jacquemin and de Jong (p 251), called 'European nationalism':

> Through mergers and the constitution of 'Eurogiants', the idea is to limit intra-European competitive forces and to unite European competitive strength to fend off foreign giants and penetrate foreign shores.

Those imbued with this philosophy emphasise competitiveness, in relation to rivals outside the Community, rather than competition within it. In English (unlike French, which uses two quite distinct words — *competitivité* and *concurrence*) the two terms are easily confused. Two politicians may agree that 'Europe needs competitive industries' and mean quite different things!

The second broad philosophy is directly opposed. This emphasises the desirability of fragmented market structures *per se*. This is partly because competition is seen as the best way to ensure increasing efficiency and innovation and therefore to ensure competitiveness. The risk that the European mega-producer might become a 'sleepy giant' is emphasised in this philosophy. However, like the opposing emphasis on Community-wide economies of scale, this structuralist creed has political overtones, stressing the social and political consequences of concentrations of private power (see the quotation from Cairncross *et al* in Chapter 1).

These two philosophies remain powerful influences within EEC competition policy, both on its formal instruments and on practical implementation. The relative emphasis changes over time and between different institutions: our analysis of cases will suggest that the Court of Justice of the European Communities ('Court' or CJCE in the rest of this chapter) has tended towards a structuralist view more than the Commission of the European Communities ('Commission' or CEC). However, the Commission has also in recent years demonstrated concern for maintenance of competitive structure by its support for small and medium-sized enterprises. In its 1988 Report on Competition Policy the CEC expressed its concern:

> ... to strengthen and preserve small and medium-sized enterprises (SMEs) as an essential element in a healthy environment ... because of the contribution they make to the competitive structure of the market, their flexibility and their dynamism.
>
> (*op cit*, p 29, cited by George and Jacquemin)

The presence and the varying influence of these two conflicting philosophies means that EEC competition policy cannot be analysed purely in terms of the economic concepts set out in Chapters 2 and 3. The basic principle, close to the heart of most US specialists in antitrust economics, is that competition policy must ultimately be concerned with the maximisation of the sum of consumer and producer surpluses. This principle implies consideration of trade-off between the consequences for welfare of lack of competition on the one hand and possible improvements to efficiency, resulting from scale or greater predictability, on the other. There would be widespread agreement among those concerned with the administration of EEC policies that such a trade-off must be considered. However, it would not be true to say that this assessment or indeed the more general principle of total welfare maximisation (producer plus consumer surpluses) is the only factor in their interpretation of the various policy instruments.

In the rest of this chapter, the influence of these two broad philosophies will be discussed in relation to three elements of policy: restrictive agreements, covered by Article 85 of the Treaty of Rome, p 94–103; abuse of a dominant position, p 103–14 and control over mergers, p 115–35. A fourth element in competition policy, the prohibition of state aids under Article 92 has not been included here, for four reasons:

- it involves economic concepts different from those relevant to the other three elements and set out in Chapters 2 and 3;
- its effects mainly concern government and public authorities, whose subventions to national business might distort inter-state competition;
- with the implementation of the Single Market, state aids to national industries ought to become less significant;
- the general drift away from interventionist individual policies on the part of governments worldwide means that this will be a less topical issue at least for the next few years.

In the discussion of the other three aspects of policy, the objective is not to explain every legal nicety. There are plenty of good texts written by lawyers who have specialised in this area. The aim is directed more at explanation of how the different policy instruments may be (and have been) variously interpreted in different circumstances. One conclusion of the analysis is that, in spite of the conflicting influences, the CEC (if not the CJEC) has generally but implicitly followed a logical framework appropriate to the aggregate-welfare criterion which 'objective' economists would prefer.

RESTRICTIVE AGREEMENTS

Horizontal collusion

As was pointed out in Chapter 2, economic theory supports a general condemnation of agreements between firms to limit competition between them, especially where the firms are at the same horizontal level of activity. Whereas combination into a single monopoly may yield advantages to offset the exploitation of market power, such as economies of scale or greater resources for innovation, a similar case is harder to make for cartels or other agreements which limit competition. There may be exceptions, such as joint funding of basic research to avoid unproductive duplication, but a general norm, based on Adam Smith's concern about meetings between business competitors, remains.

National government policies have not always been hostile towards restrictive agreements. Democracy does not always give greater power to consumers — groups representing both 'sides' of business (employers and employees, rather than producers and customers) have often wielded considerable political muscle, particularly in joint pleading. In the 1930s, for example, national governments including that of the UK introduced legislation to compel firms in many recession-hit staple industries to join agreements to fix prices and other terms of trading. Such policies, complemented by import restrictions, were intended to eliminate 'cut-throat' competition and to facilitate 'restructuring' of the industry concerned, often with government subsidies. In the recession of the 1980s policies of this kind have reappeared and have received a more favourable response from the CEC than might have been expected. (More about this later.)

Article 85 of the Treaty of Rome unequivocally prohibits restrictive agreements and limits exemptions to cases where the effects on competition are not significant. Paragraph (1) reads:

1. The following shall be prohibited as incompatible with the common market: all agreements between undertakings, decisions by associations of undertakings and concerted practices which may affect trade between Member States and which have as their object or effect the prevention, restriction or distortion of competition within the common market, and in particular those which:
    (a)   directly or indirectly fix purchase or selling prices or any other trading conditions;
    (b)   limit or control production, markets, technical development, or investment;
    (c)   share markets or sources of supply;
    (d)   apply dissimilar conditions to equivalent transactions with other trading parties, thereby placing them at a competitive disadvantage;
    (e)   make the conclusion of contracts subject to acceptance by the other parties of supplementary obligations which, by their nature or according to commercial usage, have no connection with the subject of such contracts.

The clause 'which may affect trade between Member States' is important. This is illustrated by the cases brought by the CEC against book publishers, first in Holland (*VBBB/VBVB* 1982) and then in the UK (*Publishers Association* 1989). Both related to the collective enforcement of fixed retail prices for books. The Dutch case (in which the Flemish Booksellers Association VBVB was also a defendant) concerned the application of fixed retail prices to books exported from the Netherlands to Belgium; the case against the UK Publishers Association concerned only books exported by them to the Republic of Ireland. In the Netherlands and the United Kingdom the arrangements for collective enforcement of resale price maintenance remain in operation for transactions within the respective countries and are not subject to prohibition under Article 85.

The list of particular forms of restriction seems to lack logical construction. For example, there is considerable interdependence between (a), (b) and (c). An agreement to fix prices can be effective only if the parties to it control all or most of the relevant market. This implies that, in order to avoid over-supply they must also agree upon a limit to the total amount offered to the market and also on quotas (or less formal sharing arrangements). This need for market sharing proves to be the demise of many cartels (the struggles of OPEC in this respect are well-known). In the *Woodpulp* case (1984) the Commission sought to prove 'concertation' on prices by Scandinavian and North American exporters of market pulp to the EEC mainly on the evidence of uniform prices, which were static at times of excess capacity and rose in parallel at boom times. As a number of economists appearing for the appellants against the CEC decision pointed out in the CJEC hearing, such price behaviour could easily be explained by the existence of non-collusive oligopoly. If the Commission had also been able to show stable market shares, its argument would have been more difficult to refute.

Paragraph (2) of Article 85 declares simply that agreements prohibited under 85(1) shall be automatically void. This would have the effect of making an affected agreement not specifically exempted from 85(1) or given clearance by the CEC (see below) unenforceable in courts within the Community.

Paragraph (3) deals with exemptions and states that the provisions of 85(1) may be declared inapplicable in the case of any agreement, collective decision or concerted practice:

> which contributes to improving the production or distribution of goods or to promoting technical or economic progress, while allowing consumers a fair share of the resulting benefit, and which does not:
> (a) impose on the undertakings concerned restrictions which are not indispensable to the attainment of those objectives;
> (b) afford such undertakings the possibility of eliminating competition in respect of a substantial part of the products in question.

The Commission is the exclusive enforcement agency of Article 85 (and also of Article 86). Procedures for enforcement were set out in Council Regulation 17, agreed in 1962. The Commission can initiate investigations, with wide powers to obtain evidence, either because of a complaint from an interested party or on its own observation of evidence of an agreement or concerted practice which might infringe Article 85. If it finds that such an agreement is or has been in force, that agreement is automatically void (under 85(2)) and it may impose fines of up to 10 per cent of turnover (under Article 15 of Regulation 17). This penalty arrangement is similar to, though more systematic than, US practice and contrasts with the position under UK law, which only prevents the continued enforcement of restrictive agreements and has no provision for retrospective penalties.

In order to avoid discovery and possible punitive action, the parties to an agreement may apply to the Commission either for 'negative clearance', confirming that it falls outside the scope of Article 85(1) or, recognising that it does fall within the scope of 85(1), seeking exemption under 85(3). Jacobs and Stewart-Clark state that an application in respect of an agreement which has been in force for some time does not remove the threat of incrimination and possible fines, unless it is granted. The legal problems posed by a notified agreement on which the Commission has made no formal decision are described more fully by Horspool and Korah (1992).

Because Article 85(1) refers to agreements which have as their anti-competitive objectives or *effects*, a 'letter of comfort' from the Commission saying that it does not intend to challenge an agreement notified to it does not imply immunity from legal action in future. If the agreement were subsequently found to have anti-competitive effects, aggrieved parties could still sue the firms involved in the agreement under Article 85. Even the Commission is not precluded from pursuing action against firms for concerted practices associated with an agreement which it has not formally exempted. In this sense, the 'negative clearance' procedure, which is applied to the vast majority of cases, is less satisfactory than the granting of exemptions. However, the latter would require detailed investigations on a scale beyond the current resources of DGIV of the CEC.

An agreement which contravenes Article 85(1) may have one or more different anti-competitive effects. It may serve to maintain or to increase the collective market power of the companies involved or, in the case of an agreement not to compete in particular market segments, may increase the power of each individual firm in its own segment. Agreements, such as those fixing prices or other trading conditions, may enable firms to *exploit* their collective market power. At first sight, Article 85(3) appears to give the Commission powers to examine the trade-off between these anti-competitive effects and possible efficiency gains.

This may seem surprising, first because economic theory provides a strong case for presuming horizontal collusion to be bad for general welfare, with only few exceptions, secondly because neither Article 85(3) nor Regulation 17 contains much guidance about the criteria to be applied in assessment of the case for exemption. George and Jacquemin (p 211) summarise the opportunity for political manoeuvring apparently offered by Article 85(3) as follows: 'The conditions of Article 85(3) ... do not rest on a strict and unambiguous welfare analysis and as a result there is a danger that decisions could be the outcome of political compromises between conflicting and incommensurable values.' As these authors point out, the danger is more apparent than real. First, the second condition of exemption, that the agreement does not enable the firms concerned 'to eliminate competition in respect of a substantial part of the products in question', effectively prevents exemption where the parties to the agreement enjoy (or would enjoy) collective dominance. True, the word 'substantial' is not defined but, if it is to be interpreted in terms of combined share of the relevant market, it is reasonable to assume consistency with the formal criterion levels established in the application of Article 86, dealing with abuse of dominance.

The logic that an agreement to restrict competition cannot have significant anti-competitive effects if the parties to it have an insignificant market share was reflected in a Notice providing for general derogation from the prohibition of Article 85 of 'agreements of minor importance'. This Notice was first issued by the Commission in 1970 and was last amended in 1986. An agreement 'of minor importance' is one where the parties' combined shares of any relevant market is less than 5 per cent and where their combined turnover does not exceed 200 million ecu. The inclusion of the turnover threshold, which has no foundation in conventional antitrust economics, may reflect the priority accorded to SMEs in the Commission's interpretation of policy.

There is a second reason why Article 85(3) does not, in practice, enable the CEC to sanction agreements with significant anti-competitive effects on grounds of offsetting 'efficiency' arguments. This is because this exemption clause has been implemented by means of block exemptions rather than consideration of individual cases. In the block exemption regulations, there is normally a condition that rules out automatic exemption if the parties to the agreement face little competition. For example, the regulations relating to agreements on specialisation and research and development allow exemptions only when the combined sales by all parties do not exceed 20 per cent of the relevant market defined in both product and geographical terms. In addition, the regulation on specialisation limits its application to firms with combined annual turnover not exceeding 1000m ecu (increased from 500m ecu in April 1993). (See Jacobs and Stewart-Clark, Chapter 5 for full presentation of block exemptions.)

With the exception of the more benign attitude to collusion between SMEs (which the text of the Notice on Agreements of Minor Importance terms 'cooperation'), the Commission and the Court have taken a firm line in prohibiting price-fixing and quota restrictions, both in the form of notified agreements and of 'concerted action' or tacit collusion. Information agreements apparently innocuous, have also been prohibited because they facilitate more obviously anti-competitive practices.

George and Jacquemin point out that during the 1980s, when major manufacturing activities across the Community experienced prolonged recession, the Commission adopted a tolerant attitude to agreements which provided for restructuring of the industries concerned, for example by the elimination of excess capacity. Many of these schemes included elements of state subsidy. While most of the agreements concerned affected SMEs in particular, there were some notable exceptions. Examples include an agreement between the ten largest European producers of synthetic fibres to rationalise output of synthetic textiles and a bilateral agreement between ICI and BP Chemicals to specialise rather than compete in the production of certain basic plastics. (This was allowed because effective competition would remain, so that neither firm would become dominant as a result of the agreement.)

The application of Article 85(3) has therefore demonstrated the willingness of the CEC to allow 'efficiency' grounds for exemption of horizontal agreements from the general prohibition of Article 85(1) when these do not create or exploit a position of collective market power. Officers of DGIV have objected when the author has used the term 'collective dominance' in this context in the past, because abuse of collective dominance should legally be pursued under Article 86. In practice, there has never been a 'collective dominance' case under Article 86 and, since this could not be exploited without an agreement between the firms concerned, an element of overlap seems inevitable. (Horspool and Korah suggest that the Court has been reluctant to see Article 86 applied to problems of oligopoly — ie collective dominance.)

The sanctioning of restructuring agreements, which must inevitably reduce competition between the firms concerned, raises concern about the vigour with which competition policy goals will be pursued during prolonged recession. In the UK the anti-competitive framework of cartels erected during the depression years of the 1930s was dismantled in the 1950s and 1960s, when supply constraints were the main impediment to growth. The test of political support for competition policy will be commitment to it in leaner years, when elimination of excess capacity through competition depends on the survival of the fittest. If the demise of the less fit is politically unacceptable, the objectives of competition policy may have to be compromised.

Vertical agreements

Article 85 deals with all agreements which have as their object or effect the prevention, restriction or distortion of competition and is not therefore confined to horizontal agreements. Vertical agreements which affect competition include those on selective or exclusive distribution, exclusive purchasing and resale price maintenance (an agreement between supplier and purchaser that the latter will not offer the product for resale at a price lower than that prescribed by the supplier). This list is not exhaustive: there are many other possible vertical arrangements which may be made the subject of an agreement between producers and/or distributors at different stages of the production-supply chain.

As explained in Chapter 2, economic theory is ambivalent about the net effects of vertical agreements, because limitation of intra-brand competition may form part of an inter-brand competitive strategy. In interpreting and enforcing Article 85, the Commission and the Court have repeatedly been obliged to balance these two conflicting effects. From the case law established, reflected in some of the block exemption regulations, certain consistent principles have emerged.

First, the Commission has always opposed *collective* vertical agreements concluded between groups of suppliers and distributors. Such collectively imposed or enforced agreements are more likely to be anti- rather than pro-competitive (an argument expanded in Chapter 2).

For an example where this principle has led to widespread debate, we may return to resale price maintenance (rpm) on books. This subject, a focus of research at Cranfield since 1981, raises a number of interesting issues about competition policy, including the split between national and Community jurisdiction. It is examined as a 'case study' in Chapter 6.

Although in its VBBB/VBVB Decision of 1982 to prohibit the transnational application of fixed resale prices for Dutch language books, the Commission relied substantially on arguments against rpm in principle, it consistently used the words '*collective* resale price maintenance' in every critical comment. Without the crucial adjective, this Decision would have been difficult to reconcile with the strong support for rpm from the European Parliament and with the Commission's own subsequent (1985) Communication to Council expressing support for some system of minimum resale prices for books across the Community. (The latter emanated from DGX — the Directorate-General for Cultural Affairs, rather than DGIV, the Directorate-General for Competition.) In its 1982 Decision the Commission objected particularly strongly to the *obligation* imposed on signatories to the VBBB/VBVB to fix minimum resale prices for books supplied from Holland to Belgium or vice versa.

Again in its December 1988 Decision on *Publishers Association — Net Book Agreement* the Commission went to some length to make it explicit that prohibition under Article 85 referred only to the collective application of standard terms and conditions to 'net books' (books for which publishers fix retail prices), not the imposition of fixed retail prices *per se*. (It avoided stating any opinion on the acceptability of any agreement between individual publishers and retailers.)

Similarly the Commission has maintained a firm line against collective exclusive-dealing agreements and arrangements for collective rebates. The vertical dimension in such arrangements is generally ancillary to a horizontal restriction in competition, in these cases probably aimed at prevention of new entry to a market in which the fruits of collective dominance are shared.

A second principle consistently applied by the Commission is prohibition of vertical agreements which might lead to 'market foreclosure'. Suppose an individual producer A made it a condition of supply that a downstream producer or distributor B purchased all requirements from it, to the exclusion of competitors. The effect of this restriction would depend partly on whether A held any monopoly power (if not, then the arrangement could not be forced upon B but would be accepted as mutually beneficial). It would also depend on the accessibility of other existing or potential outlets to A's competitors (also existing or potential).

Horspool and Korah suggest that the Court has adopted a different line from that of the Commission with regard to vertical agreements and Article 85(1), in requiring a market analysis before finding an infringement. The emphasis in Regulation 1984/83 dealing with block exemption of exclusive purchasing arrangements links the problem of market foreclosure 'to the duration and scope of the exclusive-purchasing agreement and the commercial freedom accorded to the resellers' (George and Jacquemin). However, in *Stergios Delimitis v Henniger Bräu* (1991) the Court ruled that a contract whereby the tenant of a bar agreed to buy beer exclusively from its brewery landlord did not necessarily have the object of restricting competition. Nor did it have the effect of restricting competition unless the number of bars were limited and the brewer concerned had a substantial market share. Horspool and Korah implicitly criticise the Commission for prohibiting certain vertical agreements too readily, on the grounds of potential foreclosure, without analysing sufficiently the degree of actual and potential competition. (Market definition is not always explicit in Article 85 decisions.)

A third principle applied by the Commission to vertical agreements is the prohibition of any restriction on parallel imports. An early test case of an exclusive distribution agreement was *Grundig-Consten* (1964), by which the German manufacturer of consumer electronics gave a French dealer exclusive selling rights within France. Grundig also required its non-French dealers not to sell in France. The result was that prices in France were substantially higher (from 20 to 50 per cent) than those for the same products in West Germany. A fundamental criterion of market integration is a common price for any one product and the Commission's stand against strategies which lead to differential pricing can be understood in the context of the objective of a European common market. It is reflected in an explicit ban in the Regulation providing for block exemption of bilateral exclusive distribution agreements (1983/83) on any clauses prohibiting parallel imports.

One could argue (with Horspool and Korah) that the Commission's perspective in this case was too narrow and took insufficient account of the economic motives for certain forms of vertical restraint. Assume that a producer wishes a distributor to provide certain services to promote the product, perhaps at a loss initially. This may mean giving it a bigger gross margin, which must be reflected, at least to some degree, in the price of the product. Alternatively, in the case of a product with uncertain demand, it may be sufficient to guarantee a margin, so that the dealer who takes the risk in stocking and promoting it will receive the fruits of any success. If distributors who would incur costs of promotion or risk-bearing run the further risk of being undercut by others who 'free-ride' on their actions, then they are unlikely to incur the costs in the first place.

In considering the impact of vertical restraints on intra- and inter-brand competition, it is desirable to compare the situation which exists with the restraint, with what would have occurred in its absence (an *ex-ante* comparison), not with what would happen now if it were removed. Perhaps because of the promotional activities of Consten, France became a profitable market for Grundig products. However, if there had been no initial guarantee of these profits for Consten, would Grundig products have secured a significant demand in the French market? Similarly with resale price maintenance on books. When a new author gets his or her first best-seller, people may feel that the title is over-priced and also that outlets such as supermarkets and chain-stores should be able to sell it at discounted prices. The question which should be asked is whether the book would have become a best-seller if it had not secured exposure in many outlets. Given the risk in stocking titles with uncertain demand, would this exposure have been secured unless the outlets concerned had been assured of profits from success?

Some of the decisions at Community level suggest insufficient recognition of the *ex-ante* pro-competitive effects of vertical agreements. Insistence on continuous access for parallel imports and prohibition of collective enforcement of resale price maintenance are indicative of this.

ABUSE OF A DOMINANT POSITION

Outline

Article 86 of the Treaty of Rome begins as follows:

> Any abuse by one or more undertakings of a dominant position within the Common Market or in a substantial part of it shall be prohibited as incompatible with the Common Market, in so far as it may affect trade between member states.

This statement seems to imply a neutral stance towards the existence of a dominant position. In the French, German and Italian versions of the Article, which preceded the English translation, the word 'abuse' appears as 'abusive exploitation'. This seems to imply that not even exploitation of dominance is prohibited, unless it is abusive (a point made by a number of European commentators, who saw a change of emphasis when the official English version was published in the early 1970s). This apparently tolerant attitude towards monopoly is consistent with the thinking of some of those involved in the founding of the EEC, that one of the aims should be to encourage the development and continuing strength of major European enterprises, able to achieve economies of scale and to finance research and innovation.

Article 86 does not define 'dominant position', a point already discussed at some length in Chapter 2. Neither does it define 'abuse' (or 'abusive exploitation') but it provides some specific examples:

> Such abuse may, in particular, consist in:
> (a) directly or indirectly imposing unfair purchase or selling prices or unfair trading conditions;
> (b) limiting production, markets or technical development to the prejudice of consumers;
> (c) applying dissimilar conditions to equivalent transactions with other trading parties, thereby placing them at a competitive disadvantage;
> (d) making the conclusion of contracts subject to acceptance by the other parties of supplementary obligations which, by their nature or

according to commercial usage, have no connection with the subject of such contracts.

While (b), (c) and (d) are reasonably specific, (a) is something of a catch-all, as the word 'unfair' is subject to wide interpretation.

As in the application of Article 85 dealing with restrictive agreements, the CEC has extensive powers under Regulation 17 to investigate complaints of abuse and to initiate its own inquiries on *prima facie* evidence. Where an abuse is proven, the Commission can require its termination and can impose fines of up to 10 per cent of turnover.

In interpreting Article 86, the Court of Justice has insisted that the existence of a dominant position be proved independently of the abuse. This insistence has been much criticised by both lawyers and economists (see Chapter 2) who have argued that the abusive conduct itself was the best evidence of dominance. One implication of the Court's interpretation of the Article is the dubious principle that certain kinds of business conduct are prohibited only when the firm pursuing them is in a dominant position. The debate surrounding this somewhat peculiar logic is described on page 106–7.

As was pointed out in Chapter 3, in almost all Article 86 cases the Commission has used the same logical approach to the definition of dominance, without ever making this explicit. This approach, also followed by the UK Monopoly and Mergers Commission, seems well grounded in economic principles. The three stages are (i) delimitation of the market, in terms both of product range and geography, and calculation of market shares; (ii) assessment of potential competition; (iii) examination of the degree to which the effects of any dominance defined by (i) and (ii) on overall welfare are mitigated by competition in downstream or wider markets. This analytical framework is consistent with the view that the ultimate concern of competition policy is aggregate welfare — in theoretical terms the sum of consumers' and producers' surpluses.

Certain actions by a firm may have serious adverse effects on one or more other firms dependent on it without necessarily affecting overall welfare. An obvious example would be a decision by a producer to undertake its own distribution and to deny supplies to distributors, who had previously specialised on dealing in its products — a recent (1991) cause of dispute in the motor trade in the UK and certain other European countries. The pronouncements of the Court in a number of cases suggest that such actions may be regarded as abusive conduct under Article 86, although we still await a case where the issue is clear-cut. This controversial aspect of European policy is on page 107–12.

A further interesting problem, highlighted in a recent UK Green Paper (DTI, 1992) is the apparent inapplicability of Article 86 to non-collusive oligopoly. Certain adverse effects of dominance of a market by a small number of firms — price leadership or downward inflexibility of prices, brand proliferation, excessive advertising and promotion expenditures — may fall outside the ambit both of Article 85 and Article 86. This is discussed on page 112–14.

The wide definition of abuse by dominant firms

There appear to be two basic principles embodied in Article 86 of the EEC treaty. First, the existence of a dominant position is not prohibited, only the abuse of such a position. Secondly, from the examples of abuse given, one may infer that conduct will be prohibited and penalised under this Article only if it is the result of dominance. The second principle, that the Article attacks conduct which would not be possible if the firm(s) concerned were not dominant, is reflected in the view expressed by Waelbroek (1977) (our translation) that: 'In a great number of cases, the proof of the dominant position results from the freedom of conduct enjoyed by the firm.' This has been summarised more recently by Gyselen who asserted that evidence of abuse was the best indicator of dominance.

This second principle is not, however, reflected in the practical application of EEC policy. It is true that the CJEC has always insisted that a dominant position be proven independently of the conduct. In Chapter 3 we saw that the Court has imposed a particular approach to definition of dominance, requiring delineation of the relevant market, and that the Commission has added to this consideration of potential competition and of competition in downstream or wider markets. However, both institutions have departed from what appears to have been the original (second) principle by applying the prohibition of Article 86 to conduct which is not dependent on a dominant position. In other words, firms with evident market power have been penalised for conduct which they could have pursued with impunity if they had not enjoyed this dominant position.

Before discussing specific examples of this, we shall consider why this departure from principle is remarkable. In its judgement on the *Hoffman-Laroche* case (1979), the Court included as one dimension of abuse 'recourse to methods differing from those which condition normal competition'. This is consistent with the principle that 'abusive exploitation of a dominant position' (to revert to the original non-English wording) comprises conduct which would not be possible in a competitive environment, illustrated by the specific examples listed in the Article.

It is quite puzzling that the Court's implied support for this principle should come six years after its conclusion, in the *Continental Can* case (1973) that a (friendly) takeover of a competitor by a firm already in a dominant position could constitute abuse of that dominance. In fact, in this earlier case, the Court decided that the Continental Can company did not enjoy a dominant position in foodstuffs packaging and that the Commission had defined the market too narrowly, so there was no abuse. This judgement gives even greater emphasis to the peculiar logic — the 'conduct' (a merger) took place even though in the Court's view Continental Can did not enjoy a dominant position. If, for example, the US parent had also controlled subsidiaries producing glass and plastic containers then the Court might have agreed that it had market power and prohibited the takeover. This is clearly inconsistent with the notion of 'abusive exploitation of dominance'. The coming into force of the Merger Control Regulation in 1990 probably means that there will be no future merger cases under Article 86 and the *Continental Can* case may seem to be of only academic interest. The implied negation of the principle that the Article can prohibit only conduct which would be impossible without a dominant position is of great practical significance.

Another case where the principle was again refuted is *Michelin Nederland* (Commission Decision 1981, upheld by the Court 1983). Michelin held around 65 per cent of the replacement market for heavy vehicle tyres in the Netherlands and also supplied a very wide range of tyres intensively marketed among final users, so that dealers had a strong incentive to stock some Michelin tyres. The abuse for which Michelin was fined by the Commission was a retroactive discount scheme, whereby annual bonuses to dealers were based on the increment of sales of Michelin tyres over a 'target' based on the previous year's sales. Obviously, this led to differential pricing, according to the performance of each dealer. Another conclusion of the Commission seems almost equally obvious, namely that the scheme restricted dealers' freedom of choice and was 'aimed at tying the dealers to Michelin and thus making it difficult for other producers to gain a foothold in the market'.

However, it is hard to disagree with Hay that, unless the discount meant that Michelin was selling below cost (unlikely because the replacement market is the main source of profit for tyre producers), there is no obvious reason why the practice should have been condemned. The logic of the Commission, upheld by the Court, is that action by a dominant firm to maintain or increase its market share is by nature anti-competitive. This places an emphasis on the desirability of a fragmented market structure which was not évident in the EEC treaty and is not consistent with much current economic thinking. (Note that Vickers and Hay put the same interpretation on the findings in this case but, because they favour a structuralist approach, are much less critical.)

There are two conclusions to be drawn from the *Continental Can* and *Michelin Nederland* cases. First, the conduct of a dominant firm which increases its market share is condemned, even though the same conduct by a smaller competitor would be tolerated. Two small firms may merge to enable them to compete more effectively; small firms may implement loyalty discounts with impunity. It is difficult to see how identical conduct by a dominant firm can be defined as abusive exploitation of its market power. Secondly (and moreover!), *any* conduct by a dominant firm which strengthens its position can be condemned. In the *Continental Can* judgement the Court went so far as to make this explicit: 'the strengthening of the position held by the enterprise can be abuse and is prohibited under Article 86 of the Treaty regardless of the method or means used to attain it'. George and Jacquemin pointed out that, at least in theory, this 'dictum raises the possibility that Article 86 could be used to prevent dominant firms from extending their dominance even through internal growth unaccompanied by any anticompetitive behaviour.' Fortunately, the Commission has not attempted to interpret it in this way.

We shall see that this is one respect in which UK competition policy is more logically acceptable than that of the EEC. The terms of reference of the Monopolies and Mergers Commission in monopoly cases are to determine whether a statutory monopoly exists and, if so, what the monopolist is doing to exploit or to maintain it — the two are separated. The MMC is then asked to report on whether any of its findings conflict with public interest. This avoids the anomaly in some EEC cases where action by a dominant firm to retain its dominance (ie to compete) can be regarded as an abuse of its dominance.

Protection of competition or of competitors?

As long ago as 1961, M A Adelman (p 236), commented (on an extension of US control over mergers) that 'Legislators have never shown much interest in consumer welfare. Their chief concern has always been to protect some business firms against others, chiefly larger ones …' A number of authors (quoted in Chapter 1) have urged priority to the maintenance of fragmented market structure and consequent diffusion of economic power as an aim in itself, even at the cost of efficiency. Many antitrust/competition policy cases arise from complaints by small and medium-sized companies that they have been unfairly treated by a dominant trading partner, on whom they were dependent.

Michael Glais, a leading French economist in this field with whom Cranfield has collaborated for some years, has emphasised the importance of the notion of *partenaire obligatoire,* a company without whose supply or custom another company cannot trade, and of the implied *état de dépendance* (state of dependence) — see Glais and Laurent (1983) or Glais (1989). The prohibition of abuse of an *état de dépendance* was introduced as a separate element in French competition law in 1986, alongside that of abuse of a dominant position.

Although the terms 'dominance' and 'market power' (monopoly, monopsony) are used synonymously, which is normal practice (as in this book), there is an important distinction between a dominant position and a state of dependence. The key question is dominance over whom? A firm enjoying market power (or dominance) is generally defined in economics as one which can exploit that power in such a way that aggregate welfare — consumers' plus producers' surplus is diminished. The dominance is over society as a whole.

The CEC has, on the evidence of cases examined in Cranfield research over the years, consistently adopted a definition of dominance which reflects this latter emphasis. The key element in the analysis is the examination of the degree to which a dominant position in the relevant market, secure from potential competition, is constrained by competition in a downstream or wider market. If so, then exploitation of dependence of trading partners within the dominated market would result in redistribution of producers' surplus with little or no effect on consumer welfare.

The Commission has consistently adhered to these basic economic concepts in the definition of dominance. However, a number of its Decisions, upheld (at least in this respect) by the Court, have implied that abuse of dominance over trading partners, with no material effect on final consumers, may contravene Article 86.

An early case demonstrating this questionable interpretation was *Commercial Solvents Corporation (CSC) v Zoja* (Commission decision 1972, upheld by the Court on appeal in 1974). The US company (CSC), which had a worldwide monopoly of nitropropane decided, after a protracted commercial dispute, to cease supply of a derivative product, aminobutanol, to an Italian pharmaceutical company, Zoja. CSC had itself recently acquired an Italian subsidiary and had extended its activities forward to produce the antitubercular drug ethambutol, for which aminobutanol was an essential component. By refusing to supply aminobutanol to Zoja, it was eliminating a competitive producer of ethambutol. Zoja claimed that this was an abuse of dominance by CSC.

The patents relating to the methods used by CSC to produce nitropropane had expired and, although production and marketing on a small scale would have been uneconomic, one could argue that the company's market power had now become limited by the possibility of entry by one or more major chemicals producers. We shall, however, leave aside this aspect (discussed more fully in Fishwick, 1986, p 112) and concentrate on another part of the defence put forward by CSC. The company claimed that, even if it did have a monopoly in the supply of derivatives of nitropropane, including aminobutanol, this latter product was not relevant to antitrust policy, because of competition in the final market for antitubercular drugs. According to this argument, if CSC were to abuse the stronger position in the supply of ethambutol, which it had gained by eliminating competition from Zoja, users of this product would turn to other antitubercular treatments.

The CEC investigated this argument and concluded that it was false: that ethambutol was one of a number of antitubercular drugs used complementarily, in rotation, rather than as substitutes. This meant that any abuse of dominance in an intermediate product market would not be constrained by competition in the market for the final product.

Although the Commission's analysis demonstrated that CSC did have a dominant position which could be exploited to the detriment of aggregate welfare, it is questionable whether vertical integration by CSC and the subsequent elimination of Zoja from the market constituted such an abuse. If, as a result of the change, there had been an increase in the price of ethambutol, or some other adverse effect on the final consumer, the argument would have been different. The judgement of the Court demonstrates its view that a redistribution of profits between firms, with no aggregate effect, constitutes an abuse of dominance:

> An undertaking being in a dominant position as regards the production of raw material and therefore able to control the supply to manufacturers of derivatives, cannot, just because it decides to start manufacturing these derivatives (in competition with its former customers), act in such a way as to eliminate their competition.

Fox (p 401) shared the author's own critical opinion of this decision, stating:

> *Commercial Solvents* is a case of internal vertical integration. The decision

to vertically integrate did not, as the Court said, eliminate a competitor; it substituted one competitor for another.

The *Commercial Solvents v Zoja* case was not a one off. Another very similar case was *Hugin v Lipton* (CEC December 1977, Court Judgement on appeal 1979). Hugin was a manufacturer of cash registers, wholly owned by the Swedish consumers' cooperative organisation. Under an agreement in 1969 it appointed Lipton, a London dealer in cash registers from a wide range of manufacturers, as its main (but not exclusive) agent in the UK, with rights to service and repair. Hugin warned that this arrangement, timed to coincide with the introduction of decimal currency in the UK and a consequent boom in demand, might be of only short duration. It was: in 1972, when demand was much less buoyant, Lipton's agency was terminated. Later in the year Hugin refused to supply either machines or spare parts to Lipton (or to any other UK company) at wholesale prices, reserving this business to a new wholly-owned subsidiary. Hugin stated that this was part of a policy of guaranteeing quality and providing comprehensive repair and maintenance in less favourable trading conditions. Lipton claimed that the refusal to supply spare parts undermined the repair and maintenance service which it had set up as main agent for Lipton and threatened its own survival.

The 'abuse' in this case was made possible by Hugin's control over the supply of spare parts for its own machines. The CEC has been criticised by many observers for defining these spare parts as the relevant product. Logically, it had no alternative — it was Hugin's 100 per cent control of supply of spare parts (it closed alternative channels by other vertical links) that enabled it to deny them to Lipton. However, was this a dominant position which could be exploited to the detriment of aggregate welfare?

In seeking to answer this last question, the Commission acknowledged that Hugin was ranked fourth in the UK market for cash registers, with 13 per cent, contrasting with the 40 per cent held by the market leader, National Cash Registers. It was therefore hardly dominant in the final market. Hugin argued that its monopoly of spare parts and consequently of the repair, maintenance and reconditioning of its own machines could not be abused to the detriment of final customers, because the quality and cost of maintenance was one of the criteria used in the selection of cash registers. Exploitation of the monopoly of spare parts, repair and maintenance would ultimately induce customers to buy other machines.

The Commission countered this argument with the observations that sales of spare parts accounted for only 3 per cent of Hugin's UK turnover and that the average annual maintenance charge for cash registers was only around 5 per cent of their purchase price. In other words, Hugin could have increased final prices of spare parts and of repair services without encountering much customer resistance. It held a dominant position which it could abuse to the detriment of aggregate welfare.

The Commission's factual evidence was disputable (see Fishwick, 1986, p 120) but one cannot fault its approach in trying to prove the existence of a dominant position by showing that this could be exploited to the detriment of final customers, in the form of monopoly profits. Perhaps one might argue that this potential adverse effect on consumers could hardly be of major significance. It could occur only because it was too slight to influence their choice of cash register. However, the main objection to the Commission's action in *Hugin v Lipton* case is that the alleged abuse did not itself affect the final customer. It may well have increased Hugin's profits at the expense of those of Lipton but its effect was purely redistributive. The view of the CJEC on this case is not known, because Hugin's appeal was upheld on grounds of geographical market definition — the Court decided that the relevant market was the UK and that the alleged abuse had no inter-state effects within the European Community. The Advocate-General supported the Commission on all other aspects of the case and it is probable that the Court would have upheld its logic, if it had not decided that the relevant market was purely national (mistakenly in the author's view — see Fishwick, 1986, p 118).

In neither the *Commercial Solvents v Zoja* nor *Hugin v Lipton* case was the alleged abuse directed at the final consumer. Nor was the Commission able to show that it was directed at eliminating competition in order to secure a position from which abusive conduct would be possible. From a number of cases, it has been established beyond doubt that abuse of dominance in one market segment to secure it in another contravenes Article 86, even though abuse to the detriment of the final consumer may not yet have occurred. For example, in 1985, the Commission decided that AKZO Chemie had abused a dominant position in the European market for organic peroxides by selective and below-cost price cutting aimed at damaging specifically a comparatively small UK firm, Engineering and Chemical Supplies Ltd, which had begun to extend its activities to a wider product market in Germany. This would have brought it into direct competition with AKZO. The CJEC upheld the Commission's Decision in 1990.

Another example is the *Eurofix and Bauco v Hilti* case (1987), in which the CEC decided that Hilti, the major European manufacturer of nail guns, had contravened Article 86 by preventing independent firms from selling nails for use in Hilti guns. One of the methods used was the supply of nails free of charge with cartridges, for which Hilti enjoyed patent or copyright protection. The Commission rejected Hilti's argument that its wish to exclude competitive supplies of nails was motivated purely by safety and also considered that competition in the wider market for building fasteners (comprising also power drill systems) was too remote to prevent exploitation of the monopoly of nail-gun cartridges. This case is less clear than AKZO: the Commission's argument would have been strengthened if it had been able to show that where Hilti did not face competition from other nail producers it exploited this monopoly position. An appeal against this decision is still (in July 1993) under consideration by the Court of First Instance of the CJEC.

The concern raised by *Commercial Solvents v Zoya, Hugin v Lipton* and, less definitely, by the *Eurofix and Bauco v Hilti* cases is that the Commission and the Court appear to be interpreting Article 86 as protection for competitors or other individual traders. Some economists and other specialists believe that this approach is an effective way of ensuring competition and diffusion of economic power which may, in the long term, be best for aggregate welfare (see Chapter 1). This view is highly disputable. Most economists would today favour a principle that the definition of abusive conduct should be confined to actions which either directly reduce aggregate welfare (rather than merely redistributing it) or which have as their motive or effect the establishment of a position which poses a threat to aggregate welfare.

In all the cases examined here, the Commission established that the undertaking accused of abuse did hold a dominant position which could be abused to the detriment of aggregate welfare, even though the particular 'abuses' may have had only redistributive effects. It would be interesting to observe its reaction, and that of the Court, to a case of alleged abuse of this kind, essentially of a 'state of dependence', in a situation where exploitation of dominance were irrefutably constrained by competition in a downstream or wider market. Such a case has occurred in the application of UK policy (*Ford Motor Company Ltd* summarised in Chapter 5) and the MMC's decision appears to regard such downstream/wider competition as sufficient to justify the non-intervention of competition policy. It is by no means certain that the CEC and, more particularly, the CJEC would take the same view as the MMC.

Oligopoly and collective dominance

A possible gap in the coverage of EEC competition policy appears to be implied by the CJEC's interpretation of dominance in conditions of oligopoly (see Chapter 2). The parallel conduct resulting from interdependence among a small number of firms dominating a market is normally considered a matter of concern for antitrust/competition authorities, as also are the large expenditures on possibly 'wasteful' non-price competition which may occur. Unless there is evidence of collusion between the firms concerned, parallel conduct cannot be prohibited and penalised under Article 85, which refers specifically and exclusively to agreements. There is, of course, no way of interpreting Article 85 so as to prohibit non-price competition.

The difficulty in applying Article 85 to parallel pricing was evident in the 1991 CJEC hearing of the *Woodpulp* case. Suppliers of a homogeneous raw material to technically sophisticated users must obviously charge uniform prices (irrespective of market structure). The CEC's case against suppliers of bleached woodpulp to the EEC market, all of them located outside the EEC in Scandinavia and North America, was that prices were not reduced at times of excess supply and rose in parallel in periods of excess demand. There was some evidence that suppliers encouraged transparency in the market and that certain individual suppliers may have communicated price information to competitors, but this was fragmentary. The case rested substantially on the observed price behaviour. However, as was pointed out by numerous specialist antitrust economists called as witnesses by the suppliers, this price behaviour was consistent with non-collusive oligopoly (see Cockram and Fishwick, 1991).

There are two reasons for suspecting that parallel pricing of the kind observed in the *Woodpulp* case would not be viewed by the CJEC as an abuse of (joint) dominance under Article 86. In the recent (1992) case of *Italian Flat Glass*, the Court of First Instance was reluctant to accept that this Article could be applied to an oligopoly of three independent producers (see Horspool and Korah, 1992, pp 343–4). This was the first case brought before the Court referring explicitly to oligopolistic abuse of dominance. Secondly, in the definition of a dominant position, the Court has tended to emphasise the gap between the market share of the leading firm and that of its nearest rival. George and Jacquemin (p 231) comment:

> This would seem to imply that the Court is of the view that dominant firm market structures pose a greater threat to competition than tightly-knit oligopolistic ones where, say, two or three well-matched firms account for the bulk of sales. Although Article 86 covers oligopolistic as well as monopolistic abuses of dominance no case against an oligopoly has yet been heard under EC law.

Our own research has found a similar emphasis on the inequality of market shares — single firm dominance — in the CEC's implementation of the Merger Control Regulation, a point discussed on page p 131.

The UK Department of Trade and Industry regards the difficulty in application of Article 86 to joint dominance as a 'shortcoming' (DTI, 1992, para 3.13–3.15). It lists a number of anti-competitive practices which result from non-collusive oligopoly (particularly duopoly) but would be hard to prohibit as abuse of dominance, given the CJEC's reluctance to apply this concept to structurally independent companies. This perceived difficulty is one of the reasons why the UK government decided in April 1993 not to modify UK policy on abuse of market power to bring this closer to the conformity with Article 86.

Some concluding remarks about Article 86

The DTI 'Green Paper' (1992) listed two other 'shortcomings' of Article 86 as the sole basis for control of abuse of market power.

First, it pointed out that there have been very few cases under this Article relating to 'the exploitation of market power at the expense of customers or suppliers'. As an example of such exploitation it gives excessive prices. In the context of the discussion above, it appears that the DTI is referring to exploitation at the expense of aggregate welfare. This criticism is supported by Horspool and Korah who observe that most of the cases started by the Commission have related to exclusionary conduct. Such conduct is aimed at maintaining or reinforcing a dominant position rather than exploiting it in the ways specifically listed in the Article.

A second shortcoming, also noted in the 1992 Green Paper, is the inability of the CEC or the CJEC to remedy a situation which has led to abusive conduct. When a firm charges excessive or discriminatory prices, reduces product quality or otherwise abuses a dominant position the authorities may bring a case against it and impose substantial fines. However, there are no powers in EEC law whereby the dominant position may be removed or diminished, by divestment or fragmentation. Nor is there any provision for regulation of prices or other market conduct.

The absence of laws to eliminate or diminish market power in the EEC reflects the favourable attitude of the Community's founders towards big business. In the evolution of competition policy, Article 86 has been increasingly interpreted as a means of protecting small companies from 'abuse' by bigger trading partners on whom they depend and also as a means of protecting a competitive market structure. These do not appear to have been its original purposes.

MERGERS AND ACQUISITIONS

The Merger Control Regulation and the historical background

The drift of policy towards the maintenance of a competitive structure is emphasised by growing pressure for control over the process of concentration, a control conspicuously absent from the 1957 Treaty of Rome. The founders of the EEC were inclined to favour greater concentration: sub-optimal size of European firms was one of the economic arguments for the Common Market. With the consequent economies of scale, European companies would become more competitive in world terms. As early as 1965 the Commission proposed the introduction of a control over mergers and the first draft regulation was awaiting approval by 1973. Meanwhile the *Continental Can* case was an application of Article 86 to prohibit a further acquisition by a firm already in a dominant position. The CJEC overruled the Commission's Decision on this case but only on the grounds that the relevant market had been misdefined and potential competition understated. The Court upheld the principle that expansion by acquisition on the part of a firm already dominant would constitute abuse of that dominance (however perverse it may appear when summarised like this!). This ruling left a serious anomaly in EEC law: a merger involving at least one firm in a dominant position might be prohibited under Article 86; a merger between a small number of equal-size firms would contravene no law even if it created a 100 per cent impregnable monopoly.

In 1987 the Court ruled in the *Philip Morris* case that agreed share transactions between companies could constitute a restrictive agreement under Article 85, thus giving the Commission power to intervene in 'friendly' mergers and acquisitions which might affect interstate trade. This Judgement encouraged a number of firms affected by mergers to complain to the Commission and there were a few notable interventions backed by the threat of action under Article 85. For example, the CEC forced British Airways to reduce slots at Gatwick Airport by 10,000 per annum and to surrender a number of intra-EC routes as a condition for approval of the merger with British Caledonian (following a complaint to it by Air Europe). The anomaly in the application of Article 85 to mergers was the restriction to friendly (ie *agreed*) changes. A merger or acquisition which did not involve a firm already dominant and which was not the subject of a positive agreement (as opposed even to passive acquiescence) could not be subject to Community intervention, even if it would result in a considerable market power.

There were several reasons for the growing support during the later 1980s for direct control over mergers and acquisitions:

1. The Commission had acquired powers to intervene in certain conditions under either Article 85 or Article 86, but the applicability of these powers to any particular case depended on irrelevant criteria — was the merger positively agreed or was one of the firms already dominant in any market?

2. Given the powers of the Commission and the probability of overlap with national policies, where these existed, there was a strong case for a 'one-step' clearance procedure to avoid unnecessary delay and expensive investigation and litigation, particularly for mergers with no adverse competitive effects.

3. Again given the Commission's powers, there was a case for defining procedures more rigorously, to ensure maximum speed and efficiency.

4. A growing proportion of mergers was between companies in different EC countries or between EC companies and enterprises outside the Community. Note however that in the more recent recession this international merger activity has declined. (See Table 4.1 below.)

Table 4.1 Mergers and acquisitions affecting EC companies[*]

12 months to May	Purely national	Intra-EC transnational	International	Total
1984	101	29	25	155
1985	146	44	18	208
1986	145	52	30	227
1987	211	75	17	303
1988	214	111	58	383
1989	352	225	89	666
1990	353	315	165	833
1991	280	198	118	596
1992	288	159	60	507

*Mergers or acquisitions of majority holdings
Source: CEC — Annual Reports on Competition Policy

5. With the programme towards implementation of the Single Market by end-1992 (a process begun in 1985), there was recognition of the need to prevent the reduction of competition in the wider market through increased concentration across intra-EC boundaries.

It seems reasonable to suggest that the appointment in January 1989 of Sir Leon Brittan as Commissioner with responsibility for competition was a major factor in the rapid achievement of compromises, reflected in adoption of a final regulation in December 1989 — Council Regulation (EEC) No 4064/89 on the control of concentrations between undertakings, normally called in English the Merger Control Regulation (MCR).

The British government had been one of those least willing to accept 'interference by Brussels' in the affairs of private business in Member States; it therefore wished to raise turnover thresholds to limit the number of cases falling within the ambit of the regulation. The British government also considered that effects on competition should be the only criterion for assessment under the EEC regulation. This seems rather remarkable because UK law allows consideration of increased efficiency as a defence of a merger and this principle is strongly supported by the 'free market' Chicago School in the USA, highly regarded by leading UK politicians at that time. Commenting on this apparent anomaly, George (1990) attributed the British view to suspicion that any efficiency defence in the EEC regulation would be used to complement broad industrial and social strategy. In other words, the insertion of criteria other than competition might imply a reversion to the concept of European champions, cherished by the federalist founders of the EEC in the mid-1950s. Finally, the British had some sympathy for the German view that national governments should not be forced to relinquish control over mergers when these might have anti-competitive effects in their own national markets.

Comparison of the final version of the regulation with the published draft still extant in May 1989 (see *European Economy* No 40 of that month) shows a remarkable movement towards the British view.

1. *Thresholds and the ambit of the MCR*

   Table 4.2 (overleaf) shows the changes in thresholds for inclusion within the scope of the regulation.

   Perhaps to pacify those who thought that the Commission would have very few cases to consider and that its newly constituted Merger Task Force would have no work, Article 1(3) of the final version states that the thresholds will be reviewed before the end of four years from its adoption and that any changes proposed by the Commission can be approved by a qualified majority of the Council of Ministers. Since the Commission had strongly proposed a turnover threshold of 2000 million ecu rather than the 5000 million specified in the adopted

Table 4.2 Merger Control Regulation — thresholds for application

	Published draft May 1989	Final adopted version
Aggregate worldwide turnover of undertakings concerned (million ecu)	1000	5000
Community-wide turnover of each of at least two of undertakings concerned (million ecu)	100	250
Regulation not to apply if each of undertakings concerned achieved more than following ratio of Community turnover in some Member State	3/4	2/3

regulation, it appeared probable at the time of adoption that the scope of the MCR would be widened by the end of 1993.

The regulation came into force on 21 September 1990, at a time of peak activity in concentration. Between this date and the end of 1991, 75 proposed mergers and acquisitions were notified to the Commission (CEC: XXth and XXIst Reports on Competition Policy). Perhaps there was relief that lower thresholds had not been fixed.

With the adoption of the MCR, the Commission declared that it would relinquish any powers under Articles 85 or 86 to investigate mergers falling below the thresholds. Such mergers would remain subject to any national competition laws. The principle of 'one-stop' clearance was implemented, subject to very rare exceptions described under 3 below: mergers and acquisitions meeting the three threshold criteria set out above (and in Article 1 of the MCR) would be assessed exclusively by the CEC; others would be subject only to national control.

It should be noted that the MCR applies to any mergers which fulfil the criteria, even between undertakings located outside the Community. The application of EC law to mergers between US or Japanese companies because the EC turnover of each of them exceeds 250 million ecu raises obvious difficulties, particularly if this represents a relatively small proportion of their world-wide turnover. There have been discussions between the CEC and the US antitrust authorities to ensure mutual recognition of parallel laws in this area and the

Commission has already considered mergers between firms based outside the EC — Northern Telecom/Matra Telecommunications, Delta Air Lines/Pan American Corporation and Dresser/Ingersoll are three examples. Fortunately, in view of the legal wrangles which might have followed, there have been no serious doubts about their compatibility with the Common Market.

2. *Criteria for assessment*

Given the history of the European Communities (the EEC and the ECSC) and the growing acceptance of the 'efficiency' defence for mergers in US antitrust policy, it seems quite extraordinary that the Merger Control Regulation finally adopted requires that assessment be based exclusively on the effects on competition. Article 2 (paragraph 2) states quite unequivocally that 'A concentration which does not create or strengthen a dominant position as a result of which effective competition would be significantly impeded in the common market or in a substantial part of it shall be declared compatible with the common market.'

Likewise Article 2(3): 'A concentration which creates or strengthens a dominant position as a result of which effective competition would be significantly impeded in the common market or in a substantial part of it shall be declared incompatible with the common market.' Note the use of the word *shall*, which is not a linguistic error — Overbury (1992, p 79) emphasises its obligatory implications; Gyselen (para 67) states (our translation): 'Concentrations which create or reinforce a dominant position *will always* be declared incompatible with the common market. They cannot be justified for reasons which do not arise from competition policy' (our emphasis).

This quite extreme position contrasts with that implied by the penultimate draft still under consideration in May 1989. In this draft there was a qualifying clause to Article 2(3) quoted above. This read:

> ... unless authorised on the ground that their contribution to improving production and distribution, to promoting technical or economic progress or to improving the competitive structure within the common market outweighs the damage to competition. In this respect, the competitiveness of the sectors concerned with regard to international competition and the interests of consumers shall be taken into account.

This conditional escape clause was deleted from the final version. It would have made it possible for mergers which created or reinforced market power to have been approved by the Commission on vaguely defined grounds of efficiency, progress or competitiveness.

The deletion of the escape clause and insistence that the creation or strengthening of a dominant position be the only criterion in assessment mainly reflects British government opposition to industrial policy. Sir Leon Brittan, an ex-member of that government, played a major role, as Commissioner for Competition from January 1989, in getting the regulation adopted. At a seminar for the Royal Institute of International Affairs in September 1990 he emphasised his own determination that mergers policy would be based exclusively on competition considerations:

> It will be my task to ensure that the consideration of particular mergers will be based on an approach fundamentally rooted in competition and that we will not seek to use the Merger Regulation as a means of imposing some kind of industrial policy, whereby the Commission picks winners across the Community. We, I happen to believe, are in no way qualified to do that, any more than national governments (in my view) are, but if we were qualified to do that, this would most certainly not be the appropriate vehicle for doing so. This is a competition regulation and not something else.
>
> (From a recording made with the speaker's consent)

Strong words, which explain why Article 2(3) was cut short. However, the unambiguous terms of Articles 2(2) and 2(2) are preceded by a rather vague preamble in Article 2(1), which has been described (by Hölzler, 1990) as a 'veritable pot pourri of possible factors which may be taken into account'. Among these is 'the development of technical and economic progress, provided it is to consumers' advantage and does not form an obstacle to competition'. Why do these words remain? The two subsequent paragraphs state that mergers which do not create or strengthen a dominant position shall be approved, those which do shall be prohibited. The explanation lies in the history of negotiations on earlier drafts — the list of other factors is a residue of reference to public interest wider than competition, almost but not quite eliminated from the final version. (See Hölzer for full discussion).

There can be little doubt that the late modifications of the draft of the Regulation went too far — it is now too rigid. Neven et al (1993) describe a number of decisions, notably *AT&T/NCR* and *Drager/IBM/HMP* in which potential cost savings brought about by synergies between the merging firms were seen as negative factors, because they might strengthen a dominant position. It cannot seriously be argued that greater efficiency is undesirable because it may lead to competitive advantages for the firms concerned.

The final form of the MCR and the Commission's interpretation of it both strongly reflect the personal views of Sir Leon Brittan who played a key role in getting it adopted in 1989. His replacement as Competition Commissioner in January 1993 by a Belgian Socialist raises the question of possible changes in interpretation, to give greater weight to 'efficiency' considerations. Because of unambiguous wording of the Regulation, it is difficult to see how such considerations could easily be introduced.

3. *Reference to national authorities — the 'German clause'*
One concern about the 'one-stop' procedure was that mergers with 'a Community dimension' might be cleared by the CEC even though they would not have been permitted under national policies. This would occur where these national policies were more stringent than those applied at Community level. The country with the most stringent policies in Western Europe for many years has been Germany (BRD) and the German government resisted the adoption of the draft regulation on the grounds that this would usurp its authority over mergers.

This objection to loss of national control over the process of concentration was overcome by an apparent compromise in the form of an additional article added to the draft regulation in the latest stages — Article 9, which was not present in the version extant in May 1989. Within three weeks of the notification of a merger (or other 'concentration') a Member State may inform the Commission of its concern that this threatens to create or strengthen a dominant position in a distinct market within that Member State (universally interpreted to mean either the entire territory or part of it). It is then the prerogative of the Commission to decide whether (i) such a distinct market exists, and (ii) whether the proposed concentration would indeed create or strengthen a dominant position. It may then decide either to deal with the case itself, 'in order to maintain or restore effective competition' or to refer it to the Member State in order that national law may be applied.

Even a preliminary reading of Article 9 makes it clear that this concedes no authority to the Member State. The latter can express its concern but, if the merger proposal falls within the scope of the MCR, the Commission is the sole arbiter on whether concern is justified. Conflict between a Member State and the Commission may well arise where the criteria applied by national competition authorities to assess dominance are different from those used by the Commission.

Such conflict has already arisen, with regard to the problem of oligopoly. We have already noted that Article 86 (abuse of dominance) has not been applied successfully to non-collusive parallel conduct attributable to interdependence among a small number of big firms. German competition law (GWB = *Gesetz gegen Wettbewerbsbesch-rankungen*, or 'law against restrictions on competition') is essentially concerned with market structure. Section 22(3) of the GWB contains the presumption that competition is threatened by joint dominance if the three largest firms have a combined market share of at least 50 per cent, or if the top five have a combined share of two-thirds. The merger between *Alcatel and AG Kabel* produced the first result in Germany and was the subject of German representations, but the Commission cleared the merger as compatible with the common market, on the grounds that the power transmission cable market would become Community-wide over the next few years.

As we shall see in the discussion of the definition of a dominant position under the MCR, the Commission has tended to emphasise single-firm dominance. Indeed, it has encouraged the development of oligopoly, in preference to the continued existence of inequality between firms in the market. This may produce further disputes with competition authorities of Germany and, to a lesser degree, the UK where there is also concern about the form (or absence) of competition in markets dominated by a small number of independent firms.

A detailed analysis of the operation of the MCR by Neven et al shows that the Commission has received requests for referral from Member States with respect to five cases. Four of these, all from Germany, were rejected; the remaining case, *Tarmac/Steetley*, which might have led to regional monopoly of certain building materials within the UK was partly referred to the UK, for consideration by the MMC.

From this analysis, it may be concluded that Article 9 is relatively insignificant as a compromise of the principle that the Commission has sole jurisdiction over mergers which clear the thresholds for 'community dimension'. There remains an opportunity for Member States to retrieve control in circumstances specified in Article 21(3), relating to mergers which affect 'legitimate interests other than those taken into consideration by this Regulation'. Such interests include 'public security' (presumably defence industries), 'plurality of media ownership' and 'prudential rules' (on what, we do not know). Hölzler expressed some concern about the vagueness and, therefore, potentially wide application of this provision for national government intervention. In the 30 months since the MCR came into force, there seems to have been no recourse to Article 21(3). Perhaps some escape clause of this kind was politically inevitable; its use may prove politically difficult to justify.

The detailed provisions of the Merger Control Regulation and its practical implementation

The MCR lays great emphasis on rapidity of decision by the Commission. This feature would undoubtedly astonish any specialist economist or lawyer who were to read it immediately after recovering from (say) ten years, lack of consciousness. The tight time limits set down in the regulation contrast markedly with the slow processes experienced with cases under Articles 85 and 86. The reduction of the length of time allowed for the Commission to consider cases was one of the major issues in the later stages of negotiations on the draft regulation.

Insistence on rigorous time limits can be understood in the context of widespread support within most Member States for a policy of giving maximum freedom to restructuring of business. British and French policies, for example, were explicitly in favour of minimal restraint on mergers except where these raised objections on grounds of competition. The key point here is that when a proposed merger or acquisition is referred for thorough investigation, this can dramatically affect the outcome. This is obviously true of a hostile take-over, especially if it is being effected insidiously: reference to an investigation by public authority provides a delay for defensive action or for intervention by another party. It is also true of takeovers aimed at securing the survival of firms as going concerns (the 'failing firm' defence of a merger is one which is hard to rebut). Since only a small minority of merger proposals are ultimately found to have anticompetitive effects in national jurisprudence, it is undesirable to delay, and thereby perhaps prevent, a significant proportion of the rest.

Related to this all-pervading emphasis on rapid decisions is the institution of a two-stage clearance process. This is very similar to corresponding arrangements introduced in France at the end of 1986 and in the UK early in 1988.

Article 40 of the French Competition *Ordonnance* of December 1986 provides for voluntary notification by any affected enterprise of 'concentrations', either proposed or completed in the last three months. Two months of silence on the part of the Economics Ministry implies tacit acquiescence on the government's part; there may be a delay of six months if the merger or takeover is referred to the *Conseil de la Concurrence* (the Council for competition, quite similar in both terms of reference and composition to the UK Monopolies and Mergers Commission).

In 1988 the UK government introduced a voluntary notification system. Provided that a proposed merger is notified to the Office of Fair Trading and publicly announced to give affected parties an opportunity to air any objections, four weeks of silence may be interpreted as automatic clearance. Conditional clearance may be given within this period. Only if there are substantial doubts may the merger be referred to the MMC for full investigation, which may take a few months (see Chapter 5 for fuller discussion).

Notification is not obligatory under either French or UK policy. However, in both countries, the parties to non-notified mergers run the risk that these will be referred to the *Conseil de la Concurrence*/Monopolies and Mergers Commission at a much later date.

These recent changes in France and the UK preceded the final design of the EEC regulation. It is not surprising that this also includes a two-stage process. The Commission has a maximum of one month from notification to decide one of the following (Article 6.1):

(a) the concentration does not fall within the scope of the Regulation;
(b) it falls within the scope of the Regulation but 'does not raise serious doubts as to its compatibility with the common market';
(c) it falls within the scope of the Regulation and does raise serious doubts.

Where the decision is (a) or (b) the concentration is effectively approved. In situation (c), the Commission has a further period of four months in which to decide under Article 8 of the Regulation that the concentration (i) is compatible with the common market, possibly subject to conditions or modifications agreed with the parties, or (ii) that it is not compatible, must not proceed and, if already implemented, must be reversed (the undertakings re-separated). The four-month time limit may be extended exceptionally if firms delay provision of information or, by not cooperating fully, require the Commission to conduct a formal investigation.

The only other variations to the time limits described would occur when the Commission received representations from national authorities under Article 9 (see the previous section). When this occurs, the time-limit for a preliminary decision under Article 6 is extended to six weeks and the Commission has then another three months in which to decide whether to refer the case to these national competition authorities. (If it

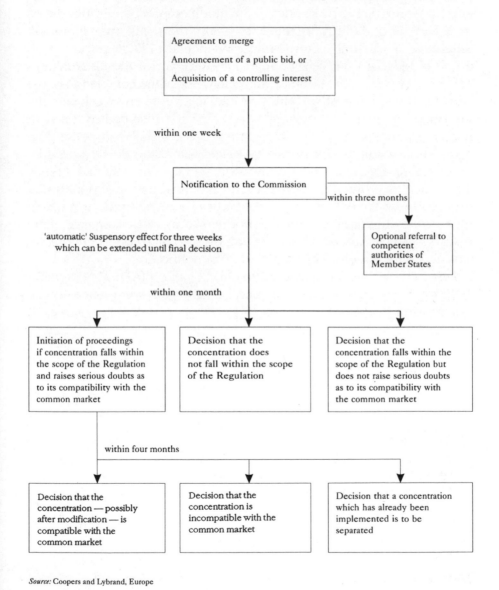

Source: Coopers and Lybrand, Europe

Figure 4.1 The Merger Control Regulation — how it works

decides not to do so, its own final decision is still required within four months of the preliminary decision under Article 6.)

The decision process under the MCR is summarised in Figure 4.1, which is based (with permission) on a similar diagram prepared by Cooper and Lybrand, Europe.

Although the procedures for decision making under the EEC Regulation have remarkable similarities to the modified procedures introduced in France and the UK in the late 1980s, there are two important differences. First, notification is obligatory under the EEC Regulation, with a fine of up to 10 per cent of aggregate turnover of the undertakings concerned for failure to notify within one week of the completion of the concentration (at the latest). This possible delay until one week after the merger or takeover has been achieved was not included in the draft regulation until a very late stage, during 1989. It makes it possible to complete a secret and/or hostile takeover before the delay caused by reference to the Commission. Secondly, unlike the UK and French authorities, the Commission cannot acquiesce in silence: decisions under Article 6.1 are notified in writing to the parties concerned and are available for access by the public. (They are produced only in the language of the case, but in most cases this has been English.) Notified concentrations are suspended for three weeks after the date of notification.

Research by Neven et al shows that in the period from 21 September 1990 to 25 March 1993, 141 decisions on mergers were made by the Commission. These were as follows:

Article 6.1	(a) MCR not applicable	17
	(b) MCR applicable but no serious doubts on compatibility	113
	(c) Serious doubts — full investigation	11
Article 8 of which		
	Cleared without conditions	2
	Cleared with conditions	6
	Declared incompatible	1
	Decision still pending	2

Source: Neven et al, p 252

The one prohibition so far is *Aerospatiale-Alenia/De Haviland.* The CEC's decision that this would create a dominant position in the world-wide market for turbo-prop commuter aircraft caused a storm from those favouring a European challenge to US hegemony in the civil aircraft industry.

It may be argued that these results show that the pressure for merger control in the EEC was much ado about nothing, that if only one of 141 mergers between very big firms had serious anti-competitive effects the process is superfluous. The conclusion would be reasonable, if every decision taken by the Commission that no dominant position would be created or strengthened was correct. This last assumption is challenged in the next sub-section.

Interpretation of the 'creation or strengthening of a dominant position'

We have seen that the decision of the Commission on any merger or acquisition with a Community dimension must, at least in principle, depend exclusively upon whether it creates or strengthens a dominant position. The term 'dominant position' is not defined. Article 2(1) states that in appraising concentrations 'the Commission shall take into account:

(a) the need to preserve and develop effective competition within the common market in view of, among other things, the structure of all the markets concerned and the actual or potential competition from undertakings located either within or without the Community;

(b) the market position of the undertakings concerned and their economic and financial power, the opportunities available to suppliers and users, their access to suppliers or markets, any legal or other barriers to entry, supply and demand trends for the relevant goods and services, the interests of the intermediate and ultimate customers, and the development of technical and economic progress provided that it is to consumers' advantage and does not form an obstacle to competition.'

Criticism of (b) has already been noted. With regard to definition of dominance, there is nothing in this second paragraph which cannot be subsumed in the first — for example, elements such as barriers to entry and supply and demand trends are relevant because of their implications for potential competition. Some of the things listed towards the end of (b) are merely the residue of those elements in early drafts which were listed as considerations in a trade-off with restrictions on competition. In the final version such trade-offs are ruled out as we have seen on page 119 above.

Paragraph (a) of Article 2.1 suggests that the definition of a dominant position under the MCR may be based on the same principles as that adopted for Article 86 — (i) existing market shares, (ii) potential competition and (iii) actual or potential competition in downstream or wider markets. The third principle is not made explicit but, as the CEC has applied it in a number of Article 86 cases where it was particularly relevant — *Commercial Solvents v Zoja, Hugin v Lipton* and *Eurofix and Banco v Hilti,* it seems reasonable to assume that it will apply to the analysis of market structures. There are, however, some basic differences in the logical approach.

The procedures for identifying and punishing abuse of dominance are concerned with proof that a firm *was* in a dominant position at the time of the abuse. Moreover, although the CJEC has always insisted that the existence of dominance cannot be proved solely by evidence of exploitation, such evidence does provide a starting point for analysis. The Commission can begin its examination of market boundaries and of potential competition by asking the question: why was the firm able to indulge in the particular anti-competitive or monopolistic conduct? With mergers and takeovers there is no past evidence to go on: the question is about the future — *will* the concentration mean the creation or reinforcement of a dominant position?

To answer this question it is necessary to look into the future and predict what competitive conditions would exist with and without the merger. This means much more emphasis on potential competition, on the possibilities of longer term demand-substitution or of supply-side substitution, than would be applied in an Article 86 case, where these would be relevant only to the degree that they restrained business conduct at the time of the alleged abuse. Because the progressive implementation of a Single European Market is expected to break down the barriers between national markets, potential competition is expected to increase substantially in many markets over the next few years. It is envisaged that many existing monopolies will be eroded and that dominant positions which may be created or reinforced in the short term will also be considerably weakened within a few years.

One methodological question to be considered is whether, in view of the decisive importance of potential competition, the Commission should continue to consider this separately from actual competition in a market defined by current trading patterns. It may be argued that the difficult process of market definition can be avoided by consideration of a direct question about the freedom of manoeuvre of the combined undertakings. Gyselen (p 96) (our translation) puts it thus:

> Given that its assessment takes place before any abusive behaviour — the best indication of dominance — can arise, the Commission examines

whether the concentration gives to the merged enterprises the power to behave *in a lasting manner* independently of the other operators in the market.

(original author's emphasis)

In principle it would be possible to approach this hypothetical question without introducing the notion of a 'market'. Ability to behave independently depends upon freedom from actual or potential competition from substitutes. Economic analysis does not require the grouping of substitutes into those within a market and the rest.

However, the preamble to the MCR contains the presumption that a concentration is unlikely to impede effective competition where 'the *market share* of the undertakings concerned does not exceed 25 per cent either in the common market or in a substantial part of it' (our emphasis). At first sight, this may appear to require the definition of the relevant market, in terms both of product and geographical boundaries, in every case. In practice this is a helpful rather than onerous presumption for the CEC. In many instances, the Commission has been able to avoid precise market delimitation by examining whether, under any combination of the narrowest reasonable definitions of product and geographical markets, the 25 per cent threshold would be reached. This approach facilitates rapid clearance of concentration proposals not creating combined shares of this level, to the advantage both of the parties concerned and of the Commission itself in lower administrative costs. An analysis (by Cranfield researchers) of all the cases cleared under the four-week procedure as raising no serious doubts on compatibility with the common market, up to July 1992, revealed 65 with horizontal effects (product range combined with geographical overlap). In 21 of these 65 cases, the Commission was able to leave aside the definition of the market because even with the narrowest definition the 25 per cent threshold would not be attained.

Having established that within one or more markets defined by current business patterns, the merger or acquisition would lead to a market share in excess of the threshold, the Commission must examine potential competition, but over what period? US Merger Guidelines (described in Chapter 2) to some extent bring supply substitution into market definition — the denominator for computation of market shares is the (hypothetical) quantity which would be supplied to the market within one year of a 5 per cent long-term price increase. They also require separate consideration of likely entry within two years of such a price increase. The CEC has no such guidelines. Fishwick and Denison recommended, on the basis of results from research financed by the Commission, that the latter should consider a minimum period of two years in assessing to what degree a newly created or reinforced dominant position would be undermined by longer term demand-switching or an increase in supply.

Colin Overbury, Director of the Commission's Merger Task Force, has discussed (Overbury) how the Commission should regard a concentration that will result in a dominant position, limited in time because of the integration of the Single Market. He concluded that acceptance should depend upon

(i)   the certainty that, as a result of the integration process, competitors not presently contesting the merging undertakings' market will do so within a defined short period of time,

and on the judgement that

(ii) the degree of dominance resulting from the operation is not excessive in the light of this time scale.

The use of two years as 'a defined short period of time' is suggested as a compromise, to allow for lagged response to any exploitation of increased market power while recognising the welfare consequences of such exploitation before the response can be effective.

We have already seen that the Commission has cleared the large majority of proposed concentrations falling within the ambit of the MCR within four weeks of notification, because they do 'not raise serious doubts as to compatibility with the common market'. There are two groups of mergers accepted by the Commission which, according to some observers, may have significant anti-competitive effects. These raise issues for continuing debate.

The first group comprises mergers of firms with large shares of different national markets, currently distinct but likely to become integrated during the next few years with the implementation of the Single Market. So far in each case the Commission concluded that the merger would not strengthen a dominant position because it would not increase shares of these separate markets — there was no overlap. However, to the degree that such a merger might diminish the prospect of future competition in the future integrated market, it could be seen as maintaining existing dominance. Dominant positions in the different markets would be stronger in the future if the merger went ahead than if it were prevented. In this sense, it could be seen as *strengthening* the dominant positions.

One example of this situation was the decision on the partial merger between Renault and Volvo, which unified decision making on trucks and buses. The Commission decided that, because of past procurement policies, the markets for buses remained national in 1991. In 1989 Volvo (having acquired Leyland Bus) supplied 64 per cent of buses sold in the UK, while Renault supplied 70 per cent of those registered in France. Both Volvo's share of the French market and that of Renault in the UK were negligible. However, it could surely be argued that with the ending of national preference in public procurement (combined with privatisation of most bus services in the UK), Renault and Volvo would, as independents, have become major competitors in the European bus market. The merger eliminated a potential competitor from each of the two national markets. In fairness to the Commission, it did consider this possibility but decided that there would remain sufficient potential competition. This decision may not convince all sceptics — at what stage will the Commission raise the drawbridge on further mergers? Is this fair on those firms which are a little slower in combining with competitors?

Another case was the *Fiat/Ford New Holland* acquisition, which raised Fiat's share of the Italian tractor market from 41.4 to 44.1 per cent. This was hardly a major rise but Ford NH held nearly 8 per cent of the EC market, being active mainly in the UK, Denmark and Ireland. Certain factors which had sustained Fiat's share of the Italian market were in decline and, in the context of the Single Market, one might have expected Ford NH to attack the Italian segment more aggressively. Once again, the Commission did consider this aspect but concluded that, because of the presence of other multinational suppliers and excess capacity throughout Europe, sufficient potential competition would remain to prevent market dominance. The same comments apply as to the *Renault/Volvo* Decision.

In the insurance industry, five mergers or joint ventures had been cleared by mid-1992. In each case, the Commission argued that life insurance, in particular, remained parcelled in national markets because of delay in implementation of Single Market directives. If mergers continue at this rate, how much potential competition will remain by the time the directives are implemented?

The second category of mergers approved by the Commission but viewed with some apprehension by many observers are those which have led to more concentrated oligopoly. The Commission's apparent readiness to tolerate the sharing of markets by two or three firms, as long as no single firm is dominant, contrasts with US policy, with national policies in Germany and, to a lesser degree, in the UK and with some of its own earlier policy documents. In Chapter 3 the US use of the Herfindahl-Hirschman index (the sum of the squares of market shares) was explained. Under US Guidelines a market structure in which one firm held 50 per cent and no other held more than 1 per cent of the market (HH < 0.255 or 2550) would be preferred to one with three firms holding 40, 35 and 25 per cent (HH = 0.345 or 3450). Piesch and Schmidt (1983), in a monograph financed and published by the CEC, recommended the use of this same index in EEC policy, though admitting that there would be problems in distinguishing between tight oligopoly and single-firm dominance.

In a number of decisions about merger proposals notified under the MCR, the Commission has demonstrated quite clearly that it is more concerned about inequality between the largest and the next largest firm than about collective dominance by an oligopoly. On page 113 above we noted the observation by George and Jacquemin that this inequality was perceived as the greater threat to competition by the CJEC, as revealed by its judgements on Article 86 cases.

In two cases, *Varta/Bosch* and *Nestlé/Perrier,* the Commission demonstrated its priorities quite clearly by making the bolstering of the second largest player in the relevant market a condition of approval.

In the *Varta/Bosch* case a proposed joint subsidiary of the two German companies was to take over their business in starter batteries. This would give it a 44.3 per cent share of the replacement market for starter batteries in Germany and 44.5 per cent of that in Spain. (The definition of national markets for a product susceptible to arbitrage by middlemen in the integrated market has been widely criticised, but that is not our current focus.) In Spain a second firm, Tudor SA, already had a similar share; the Commission noted that this duopoly 'could lead for several reasons to the alignment of the behaviour of both competitors'. Its main concern, however, was with the German market, where the next largest competitors appear to have had less than 10 per cent shares. (The precise figures are not disclosed.) The case was therefore subjected to a full four-month investigation.

During this four-month period two changes were implemented which enabled the Commission to give its approval. First, Varta undertook to cease cooperation and overlapping board membership with another German producer, Deta/Mareg, making the latter a more independent player with about 10 per cent of the German market. The Commission's reaction to the second change is particularly revealing. The Italian firm Fiat acquired the French battery producer CEAc and also the German firm Sonnenschein. These acquisitions increased Fiat's share of the German market to well above 10 per cent. Moreover, the Commission observed that 'Due to the merger of Fiat/CEAc/Sonnenschein, a strong competitor will emerge whose competitive potential will be significantly greater than the sum of the separate potential of each of the companies before the merger'. While this line of reasoning is consistent with much recent thinking about the nature of competition, it has never been made formally explicit that oligopoly is preferable to more fragmented structures in European competition policies! The Fiat acquisitions substantially increased the level of concentration in the German market as measured by the HH index. The argument that the new Varta/Bosch subsidiary Starterbatterie would now face stronger competitors must be set against the argument that it would have fewer competitors to deal with in securing acceptance of its market leadership. By overtly acquiescing in the creation of a duopoly in Spain, the Commission further emphasised that its prime concern was single-firm dominance.

The Commission's 1992 Decision on the *Nestlé/Perrier* merger, also the result of a full investigation, shows its recognition of the joint dominance issue, in an explicit discussion of the application of the MCR to oligopolies. In 1991, Nestlé, Perrier and BSN accounted for 78 per cent of the volume of bottled water sold in France and 82 per cent of the value. Of waters officially recognised as 'mineral water', this three-firm concentration ratio was 93 per cent. (Mainly because of the low value-to-weight ratio and the requirement that waters be bottled at source, actual and potential competition from imports was negligible.) Perhaps to avoid refusal of the merger on grounds of single-firm dominance (Nestlé and Perrier had a combined market share of 60 per cent in 1991), Nestlé proposed to sell one subsidiary, Volvic, to BSN. The Commission objected to the Nestlé/Perrier merger explicitly on the grounds that this would create 'duopolistic dominance'. Paragraph 112 of the Decision begins: 'The Commission considers that the distinction between single firm dominance and oligopolistic dominance cannot be decisive for the application of the Merger Regulation because both situations may significantly impede effective competition under certain market structure conditions.' Paragraph 120 adds further emphasis to the enhanced likelihood of parallel conduct: 'The reduction from three to two suppliers (duopoly) is not a mere cosmetic change in the market structure ..... (It) would make anticompetitive parallel behaviour leading to collective abuses much easier.' This Decision, unlike that in the *Varta/Bosch* case, deals specifically with the problem of duopoly and the dangers of (not necessarily collusive) joint exploitation of dominance. The solution negotiated between the CEC and Nestlé does, however, indicate again the Commission's emphasis on inequality between firms. Nestlé agreed to sell brand names and source capacity of 3000 million litres per annum, about 20 per cent of the combined capacity of Nestlé, Perrier and BSN, *to a single entity*, to be approved by the Commission. Meanwhile Perrier was to remain a legal and commercially distinct company. The Commission emphasised that

> the establishment of an effective competitor vis à vis Nestlé and BSN depends on the strength of the purchaser to develop the sources and brands which will be sold to it. The purchaser must in particular have:
>
> > sufficient financial resources to develop a nationwide distribution organization and to adequately promote the acquired brands;
>
> and
>
> > sufficient expertise in the field of branded beverage or food products.
> >
> > (Decision, para 137 — part)

Many industrial economists will applaud the Commission's logic — a third major player with resources to take over 20 per cent of the market (there is excess capacity) may well provide greater deterrence to exploitation of joint dominance by Nestlé and BSN. The use of this logic does, however, raise two questions: first, why has there been no general statement that the Commission is, in principle, more concerned about inequality of competitors than about absolute concentration and secondly, is this principle also held by national competition authorities throughout the Community? After all, in terms of the HH index, which would be applied in the US, the divestment of substantial capacity by Nestlé to a single new enterprise is a less satisfactory solution than a similar sale to a number of independent smaller competitors.

The most likely inconsistency with any national policy would be with that of Germany. Under German competition law (GWB) there is a legal presumption of 'dominant oligopoly' if five firms hold a market share of over two-thirds or if three firms have a share exceeding 50 per cent. We have already seen on page 122 that the Commission cleared the *Alcatel/Kabel AG* merger because the merged firm would have a market share of less than 25 per cent, even though it increased the three-firm concentration ratio in Germany to 58 per cent and would have been presumed undesirable under the German law. The German request under Article 9 of the MCR for authority to decide upon this merger confirms this different emphasis.

This case is interesting in two respects. First, it shows that the Merger Control Regulation cannot be used, without reversal of the assumption regarding market share, to prevent a merger or takeover which does not create a market share of more than 25 per cent, even if it significantly increases oligopolistic dominance. The Commission has shown in the *Nestlé/Perrier* case that it will use the Regulation to prevent mergers which substantially increase oligopolistic concentration (in that case creating a duopoly). However, the *Alcatel/Kabel AG* Decision seems to place a limit on this application.

Secondly, the case is of considerable political significance. The Merger Control Regulation reflects a compromise of philosophies which is much less focused on market structure than the underlying philosophy of German competition policy. Under the one-stop principle, only partly modified by Article 9 of the MCR, mergers with a Community dimension become the concern of the Commission, exclusively. If, on any of the three criteria, this merger had not fallen within the scope of the MCR, it might have been prohibited by the German competition authority (*Bundeskartellamt*). Because it involved large firms with transnational interests it fell within the jurisdiction of the CEC and was permitted.

This last feature is rather anomalous. Within the Single Market there is much to be said for international consistency in competition policies; otherwise, firms may claim an 'unlevel playing field'. In the next chapter, we examine how UK policy differs from that of the EEC and the steps under consideration to achieve greater consistency.

5

UK Competition Policy in Relation to that of the EEC

INTRODUCTION

The main focus of Cranfield's research has been the implementation of EEC competition policy and that remains the focus of this book. UK policies on restrictive practices, monopolies, mergers and anti-competitive practices remain substantially unchanged from those set down in consolidating legislation enacted over the period 1973–1980. In 1993, the details of these policies are of diminished interest to UK companies. Because of the growing internationalisation of business combined with the widening of EEC powers (in particular the Merger Control Regulation), a growing proportion of cases is likely to fall within EEC rather than national jurisdiction. Moreover, with regard to restrictive agreements the UK Government has put forward proposals which would make UK policies more consistent with Community law. Rather surprisingly, it has decided not to adapt other elements of UK competition policy to reflect principles inherent in that of the EEC.

With regard to restrictive trade practices, proposals for realignment of UK policy with Article 85 of the EEC treaty were presented in a White Paper (Government legislative proposal) in July 1989 (DTI). Lack of progress in implementing these proposals is officially attributed to congestion in the legislative timetable (see DTI, 1992, p 1) but, as on many aspects of European integration, there may also be potential political hazards. Alternative options for changes to controls on monopolies, to align these with Article 86 on abuse of dominance, were presented in a Green Paper (consultative document prepared by Government) in November 1992 but in April 1993 it was announced that the different approach embodied in UK policy would be maintained. The practical implementation of the legal control over mergers, but not the substance of the law itself, was modified in 1989. While there are many similarities between the UK arrangements for merger control and those in the Community's new Merger Control Regulation, there are also some significant and controversial differences.

So, it is still necessary for business managers, lawyers and other specialists to be aware of the principal elements of UK competition policy. Perhaps regrettably, they will have to remain reconciled to the anomaly of two parallel competition policies with different procedures and, in some respects, different criteria for decision making.

Over many centuries the exploitation of market power by single-firm monopolies or by cartels was restrained in England both by common law and by statutory legislation. However, by the early twentieth century these legal restraints had tended to lapse and during the economic crises of the 1920s and 1930s government policies tended to favour concentration and collusion in business — the antithesis of competition policy.

The conception of present-day policies occurred in 1944 in the White Paper on Employment Policy. This emphasised the adverse effects of restriction of output by monopolies on employment and the consequences of lack of competition for efficiency, competitiveness and long-term employment prospects. Because it originated from concern about employment and also was enacted by the (overtly Socialist) Labour government in 1948, modern UK policy on monopolies and restrictive practices was based on a range of social and economic criteria — not just competition. In the early years of this policy the emphasis was on investigation with no presumption that monopoly or restrictive practices were against the public interest. This ambivalence was reflected in the absence of any control over mergers until 1965. A rebuttable presumption that restrictive agreements are against the public interest was introduced in the Restrictive Trade Practices Act 1956. With regard to monopolies, the neutral stance formally survives; if anything, the policy on mergers is still biased in their favour. This historical background, important for an understanding of current policies, is analysed on page 138–44.

The law on restrictive agreements provides for their registration and judicial appraisal. Unless agreements are approved as consistent with public interest under criteria set out in the legislation, the restrictive practices concerned become invalid. Operation of a restrictive practice before judicial consideration is not penalised retrospectively, nor is failure to register an agreement, formal or *de facto*. This absence of prohibition contrasts with EEC policy and is one of the reasons why UK policy may be realigned with the latter. The economic issues relating to UK law on restrictive agreements are examined on page 145–50.

The absence of retrospective penalties is also a key difference between UK and EEC laws on monopoly power and its consequences. In certain respects, the economic principles underlying UK and Community policies are similar. In particular, the practical definition of monopoly power by the UK Monopolies and Mergers Commission (MMC) is quite close to that used by the Commission of the European Communities (CEC) to define a dominant position. Also, under neither UK nor EEC policy is monopoly or dominance condemned *per se*. Perhaps because approval by Member States necessitates greater formality in the application of EEC policy, that in the UK tends to be more flexible. In particular UK policy provides for control of adverse effects on oligopoly and of anti-competitive conduct by individual firms, without the requirement in the latter case to prove either dominance or collusion. Lack of such a control seems to be a gap in EEC policy. The desirability of preserving these particular powers was one of the reasons given by the UK government for choosing not to align its policy on monopoly power and its abuse with that of the EEC. Pages 150–63 examine these aspects.

Government powers to investigate mergers and to prohibit those which are shown to be against the public interest were enacted in the UK in 1965. UK law on mergers appears in the view of many observers still to imply a presumption that these are economically beneficial unless proven otherwise. This key difference between UK and EEC policy on mergers is remarkable in political terms, because the criteria for appraisal by the MMC remain much broader than anti-competitive effects alone. These criteria encompass the factors which enthusiasts for 'industrial policy' objectives wanted to see in the EEC's Merger Control Regulation. These were the very factors removed from the early 1989 draft of the MCR largely through British influence. In practice this contrast between the two policies is less significant than it may seem. In recent years, the UK government, in deciding whether to delay a recent or proposed merger for investigation, has been influenced explicitly and almost exclusively by potential effects on competition. Meanwhile, the CEC, formally obliged to prohibit a concentration which would create or strengthen a dominant position, has in some cases been more permissive than some economists might have expected (see Chapter 4). Policies on mergers are contrasted on pages 163–74.

HISTORICAL AND POLITICAL BACKGROUND

Competition policy in the UK began in its present form in 1948, but historically there were many antecedents. From Saxon times until the economic liberalisation of the early nineteenth century both common law and statute laws were used to regulate the prices of basic commodities, at central or local levels. The granting of royal monopolies, the origins of the patent system, dates back to the thirteenth century and during the seventeenth century there were battles between the Crown and Parliament regarding the extension of this right. The issue was largely resolved by the Statute of Monopolies 1623, which confined the award of private monopoly rights to 21-year patents. After 1750 other aspects of the law on monopolies fell into disuse. (See Merkin and Williams, 1984, p 7.)

Legal textbooks (eg *ibid;* Frazer, 1992) devote some space to the historical application of English common law, reinforced by occasional statutes, to agreements interfering with trade. The prosecution of restrictive agreements as criminal offences dated from early medieval times but had lapsed by the mid-eighteenth century. The common law doctrine of restraint of trade survived. This doctrine makes unenforceable any contract which restricts trade unless this is shown to be reasonable with regard to the interests of all parties and to the public interest. Merkin and Williams (1984) assert that with the rise of economic liberalism in the eighteenth century came the general principle that a contract reasonable for all parties would also be in the public interest. There have been occasional cases in more recent times: for example in 1968, there was a common law case concerning an exclusive purchase agreement between Esso and a filling station to which the oil company had given financial assistance. Frazer admits that the common law on restraint of trade has partly been eclipsed by the post–1945 competition legislation but argues that it 'remains an important aspect of competition law'.

The main reason why the legislation introduced in 1948 was such a watershed is that during the economic crises of the 1920s and 1930s government policies were directed more towards restriction of competition and encouragement of concentration. Immediately after the 1914–18 War, during which the government had gained insight into the extent and effects of cartels, a Select Committee of Parliament (the Committee on Trusts) expressed concern about their adverse effects. Consequently, the Profiteering Act 1919 provided for the investigation of prices and costs of cartel-affected goods and for prosecution of firms charging excessive prices. According to Merkin and Williams (1984), 1800 investigative committees were set up and 202 convictions obtained, but the Act was allowed to lapse by 1921. After this, with the ending of the post-war boom, most politicians of both main parties were more sympathetic towards cartels. Staple industries, such as coal, iron and steel, cotton textiles and basic chemicals, were all burdened with excess capacity. In 1929 the Balfour Committee on Industry and Trade commented that the elimination of this excess capacity 'can often be performed more speedily and rationally and with less suffering through the mechanism of consolidation or agreement than by the unaided play of competition'.

(Report p 179, cited by George, p 105) It is quite remarkable, in the light of later legislation, that the governments of the inter-war years should have given legal support to cartels in basic industries by making adhesion to the price- and quota-fixing arrangements obligatory. This happened in coal, iron and steel, textiles and certain agricultural sectors. At the same time, the government gave tacit support to the establishment of large firms by merger ('combination' was the term then used), among them Imperial Chemicals Industries (ICI), Distillers and in the beleaguered textiles industry the Calico Printers Association.

This policy of 'rationalisation' through limitation of competition was accompanied in most cases by measures of protection against imports. Political support for this approach to the problem of structural unemployment is partly explained by the rise of the Labour Party, replacing the Liberals who had most strongly embraced the principles of free trade and internal competition. At that time both the Conservative and Labour parties were concerned primarily with the interests of producers: employers and employees respectively.

Like the 1914–18 War before it, the Second World War gave the government detailed information about the commercial operations of UK industry. Senior civil servants and politicians formed the view that monopoly power or restrictive practices could limit employment opportunities both in the short term, through output restriction, and in the longer term through reduced efficiency, innovation and competitiveness. The emphasis on employment prospects, which from the standpoint of shareholders and managers corresponded to business opportunities, explains why the first outline of proposals to deal with monopolies and restrictive practices appeared in the White Paper on Employment in 1944. There was no presumption that monopoly or restrictive agreements were necessarily harmful. The proposals provided for investigation by an independent body, which would report whether monopoly power or restrictive practices existed and if so whether their existence or their effects were against the public interest.

Following further official inquiries, these principles were finally embodied in the Monopolies and Restrictive Practices (Inquiry and Control) Act 1948. This empowered the government (the President of the Board of Trade) to refer the supply of any good (services were added later) to a Monopolies and Restrictive Practices Commission, which then examined whether one-third of the supply of that good was controlled by a single supplier or by a cartel or whether competition was otherwise restricted, with or without a formal agreement. The Commission had no executive powers. It simply reported whether the specified conditions existed, on the 'things done' to maintain these conditions or because of them and finally whether the conditions and/or the 'things done' were contrary to the public interest. Public interest was widely defined. It included such criteria as efficiency in production and distribution, export performance, employment and 'profiteering'. George points out that there was no implication that competition was the best way of achieving the public interest. The word 'competition' did not appear in the definition.

The Monopolies and Restrictive Practices Commission was (and remains) composed largely of part-time members, providing teams with a full-time chairman and a permanent professional staff to deal with individual inquiries. The members included people from business, the professions, academic institutions and trade unions.

Most of the early references to the Commission related to cartels and in every case it found these to have effects against the public interest. In 1955 the government asked the Commission to produce a general report on Collective Discrimination, which covered a wide range of agreements which had anti-competitive objectives or effects. The Commission's report is highly relevant to the proposed revision of UK policy on restrictive trade practices. It was unanimous in recommending legislation but was split with regard to the form such legislation would take. The majority favoured a system of prohibition with specific provision for exemption, in principle very similar to that subsequently established for EEC policy by Article 85 of the Treaty of Rome. This majority view was not implemented. Instead, the Restrictive Trade Practices Act 1956 (based on the views of the minority of the Commission) set up an arrangement for compulsory registration of all restrictive agreements relating to the supply of goods and for case-by-case judicial evaluation by a specially constituted Restrictive Practices Court. The main departure from the 1948 Act, in terms of economic principles, was the presumption before the Court that restrictive agreements were against the public interest unless shown to be otherwise according to criteria specified in the new Act.

The only element of prohibition in the 1956 Act was that of collective resale price maintenance, which became illegal *per se* subject to exemption by the Restrictive Practices Court. The Court subsequently granted exemptions for books and branded pharmaceuticals but these have been the only exceptions. The Resale Prices Act of 1964 prohibited the enforcement of minimum retail prices even by individual firms; the exemptions granted for books and pharmaceuticals were allowed to continue. It is hard to understand why resale price maintenance was singled out for prohibition, particularly as there is continuing debate by economists as to whether its net effect (especially when it is applied by individual producers) may be pro- rather than anti-competitive.

Responsibility for registration of agreements and for submitting them to the Restrictive Practices Court, together with cases on resale price maintenance, was given to a newly established Registrar of Restrictive Practices. In practice, the Court struck down the overwhelming majority of agreements submitted to it, including some like the Yarn Spinners Agreement which had originally been established with government encouragement. Because of the costs involved in defence before the Court and the evidently low probability of success, many agreements were abandoned (or became covert?) rather than defended. In 1968 the legislation was extended to information agreements; agreements on services were not covered until 1976.

With the establishment of separate organisations for control of restrictive practices, the former Monopolies and Restrictive Practices Commission was scaled down and renamed the Monopolies Commission and its work confined to evaluation of single-firm monopoly and its abuse. In 1965 its work was expanded to include possible reference of services (as well as goods) and also of mergers, where these involved firms with combined net assets of £5 million or more or combined 'market share' of at least one-third.

The introduction of control of mergers by the 1965 Monopolies and Mergers Act illustrates the ambivalent attitude towards business concentration. Monopolies Commission investigations in the early 1960s had shown mergers and takeovers to be an effective way of establishing or reinforcing monopoly power and increasing numbers of firms had resorted to mergers because of the controls on restrictive agreements. The Conservative government included proposals for control over mergers in a White Paper in 1964 and these were adopted by the incoming Labour government in the 1965 Act. Mergers, like suspected monopolies, could be referred by the Board of Trade to the Monopolies Commission which would report within six months on whether they would operate against the public interest. Only if the Commission's decision was adverse to the merger could the President of the Board of Trade require divestment.

Fairburn (1989) describes in some detail the conflict of thinking in government circles in the late 1960s, with a predominantly favourable attitude towards mergers tempered by concern about competition and efficiency in certain cases. In 1966 the government set up the Industrial Reorganisation Corporation (IRC) with the specific objective of encouraging 'concentration and rationalisation to promote greater efficiency and international competitiveness in British industry' (Pickering, 1974). Under the Minister of Technology (surrounded by phrases like 'a British lead in the white heat of technology') the IRC encouraged mergers and takeovers in a wide range of manufacturing industries, especially in electronics and electrical engineering but also including motor vehicles, mechanical engineering and paper. It even helped finance hostile takeovers and intervened financially in competitive bids.

In the first eight years after the 1965 Act, only 18 mergers were referred to the Monopolies Commission, seven of which it condemned as against the public interest (seven were cleared, four abandoned). In the following eight years, 39 cases were referred (10 condemned, 15 cleared, 14 abandoned). This contrast reflects a change which occurred in the early 1970s. In both political parties there was a move away from the corporatist inventionist philosophy which had reached its peak in the 1960s, with the creation of the National Economic Development Council and the Economic Development Committees (big and little 'Neddies'), a National Plan, the Ministry of Technology and Department of Economic Affairs. Although most of this French-style 'indicative planning' is associated with the Labour governments of 1964–70, the Neddy organisations and their administrative support originated from the Conservative government of 1959–64. By 1973 there was less enthusiasm for this approach, even in the Labour Party. Although the National Enterprise Board set up by the Labour government in 1975 had formal resemblance to the earlier IRC, its role in practice was to sustain ailing industries, which brought it into conflict with EEC competition policy (Article 92 — state aids). Within the UK, since about 1973, competition policy has been more consistent philosophically with other government objectives.

The basic outlines of present-day competition policy in the UK are those established by the legislation up to 1965. In the 1970s there were three Acts of Parliament which consolidated previous legislation: the Fair Trading Act 1973, dealing mainly with monopolies and mergers, the Restrictive Trade Practices Act 1976 and the Resale Prices Act 1976. Of these only the 1973 Act introduced substantial changes.

First, it created the post of Director General of Fair Trading (DGFT) with administrative support from an Office of Fair Trading (OFT). The DGFT took over the responsibilities of the former Registrar of Restrictive Practices and directed the administration of policy on monopolies and mergers; the operation of competition policy therefore became integrated for the first time. Secondly, the 1973 Act modified the thresholds for investigation of monopolies and mergers by the (renamed) Monopolies and Mergers Commission: the criterion 'market share' (share of UK sales of the reference product) for definition of a monopoly was reduced from one-third to 25 per cent. The same change was also applied to reference of mergers to the MMC; the alternative assets threshold was increased later. Thirdly, the 1973 Act introduced the concept of a 'complex monopoly', comprising a group of firms with a combined share of the reference product at least 25 per cent linked together through some common anti-competitive practice (not a formal registrable agreement).

The last of these innovations was aimed specifically at parallel conduct under oligopoly (DTI, 1992, para 2.3) but its practical effectiveness has been limited, first by the difficulties for the OFT in identifying markets to be referred and secondly by problems for the MMC in obtaining data from firms not identified *a priori* as statutory monopolists (Merkin and Williams, p 133).

Since 1973, apart from the consolidating legislation of 1976, one major change has been the extension of the legislation on restrictive agreements to services in 1976, early in that year, before the introduction of the Restrictive Trade Practices Bill. Considering that the services sector accounts for well over 50 per cent of GDP, this extension seems incredibly late. A second development was the Competition Act of 1980 which empowered the DGFT to investigate and subsequently refer to the MMC an allegation that a single firm, not necessarily possessing a 25 per cent share of any market, is carrying out a specific anti-competitive practice. This set up a much simpler procedure (six months) for the investigation of conduct by one company than the full monopoly investigation, which requires the MMC to assess the structure of demand and supply throughout the market for the reference product. Finally, there have been some changes in the procedure for dealing with mergers, including a facility for rapid clearance, introduced in 1989.

The formal structure of UK competition policy has evolved over the last 45 years, the protectionist years of the 1920s and 1930s having provided a break from the remnant of much earlier controls on monopoly and restraint of competition. Over the 45 years, there have been wide variations in prevailing economic and political philosophy. In one country, where the electoral system gives comparatively unlimited legislative and executive power to the elected government, it is much easier to effect changes than in a Community of member states like the EEC. As a result, UK competition policy is rather like a patchwork quilt, with fragments reflecting prevalent thinking at the time of their introduction. Alignment with the principles of EEC policy would provide an opportunity to give UK policy greater consistency, transparency and clarity of purpose. Only limited alignment is currently proposed and we do not yet know when that will take place.

POLICY ON RESTRICTIVE AGREEMENTS

More detailed examination of current policy

Although UK legal and official parlance refers to restrictive agreements as 'restrictive trade practices', use of this term will be avoided here, because in ordinary English it would embrace a much wider range of anti-competitive activity. The Restrictive Trade Practices Act 1976, which consolidated legislation since 1956, is concerned exclusively with agreements to restrict competition.

The first stage of the procedure set out in the Act is the registration of any agreement which formally fulfils three criteria:

(a) There must be an 'agreement', but this need not be contractual or even written — this is made explicit in the Act and creates problems for lawyers, but the flexibility is welcomed by some (see for example Frazer who provides a detailed and illuminating commentary on this legislation);

(b) At least two of the parties must carry on business in the UK;

(c) At least two of the parties must accept restrictions relating to any of the following:

> sale or purchase prices;
> recommended prices for resale;
> terms and conditions of supply or purchase;
> quantities or descriptions of goods to be supplied or acquired;
> process of manufacture;
> persons with whom they will trade.

Agreements to exchange information are also registrable and, apart from this extension to information agreements (why the exclusion?), agreements relating to services are affected similarly to those relating to goods. (Frazer, points to some anomalies which result from the separation of goods and services.)

Failure to register an agreement is not a criminal offence. Although the Act declares the implementation of an unregistered but registrable agreement to be 'unlawful', this merely means that any firm adversely affected by it can bring a civil action for its cessation and possibly for damages. According to Frazer there has been only one publicised successful claim of this kind, by the Post Office against cable suppliers in 1979.

The 1988 Green Paper (DTI) listed 47 categories of exemption from the need to register agreements, 18 of them included in the Act itself. These include agreements in certain sectors of the economy (coal, steel, agriculture and fisheries) and in most professional services, agreements to comply with approved standards, those relating to conditions of employment and also (effectively) most vertical agreements other than those relating to resale prices.

Despite these exemptions, which may well leave significant restrictions untouched by the legislation, the formal nature of the registration criteria has led to a veritable flood of registrations — a cumulative total of over 10,000 at the end of 1992. This imposes a very heavy workload on the Office of Fair Trading, which must examine each agreement and decide whether it is likely to have harmful effects. If so, it may then negotiate modifications with the parties concerned in order to remove this danger. Agreements deemed to be innocuous, with or without modification, are referred by the DGFT to the Secretary of State for Trade and Industry for clearance. About 40 per cent of registered agreements are dealt with in this way. The procedure can take a long time. The DTI 1988 Green Paper reports a survey in 1985 which showed average time for negotiations of 33 months, with over 10 per cent of cases taking longer than eight years to resolve.

Agreements which cannot be exempted through negotiation are then submitted for judicial review by the Restrictive Practices Court, first established in 1956. This Court meets as required, now rarely. In practice it normally consists of a non-specialist judge (president) and two from a panel of six lay members, mainly academic and business economists. There have been only 36 contested cases since the RPC was established in 1956 and only one since 1972 — the *Association of British Travel Agents* case in 1984. This very light volume of work occurs because parties to an agreement not acceptable to the DGFT, even after long negotiations, normally decide not to defend it. They may abandon it completely or may decide to continue its operation clandestinely.

The appraisal by the Restrictive Practices Court of an agreement defended by the parties must be based on one or more of eight 'gateways' to exemption set out in the Act, seven dating from 1956, the eighth added in 1968. These are as follows:

1. protection of the public against injury;
2. other specific and substantial benefits to the public;
3. need to counteract anti-competitive behaviour by other businesses;
4. need for the parties to be able to negotiate fair terms with dominant suppliers or customers;
5. avoidance of adverse effects on employment;
6. avoidance of adverse effects on exports;

7. need to support other restrictions which the Court has approved;
8. no material discouragement of competition.

Note: truncated wording based on OFT publicity material.

The Court is also required by a 'tailpiece' to the list of gateways to balance the gateway arguments with any detrimental effects on parties outside the agreement and on the public.

In most of the 36 cases when agreements have been defended before the RPC the parties have, not surprisingly in view of its vagueness, attempted to use gateway 2. This gateway — the yielding of specific and substantial benefits to the public — has also formed the basis for nine of the 11 decisions of the Court to uphold the defence of the agreement and therefore to allow it to stand. Proceedings in such cases tended to be very lengthy, with an average lapse of nearly three years from the time when an agreement was referred by the DGFT (before 1973 the Registrar of Restrictive Practices).

The UK control over restrictive agreements is therefore a highly formal and legalistic one in principle, normally effected in practice by informal negotiations between the parties (often a trade association representing them) and the OFT.

Assessment of current arrangements and proposals for reform

As long ago as March 1979 the government of the day issued a consultative document (Green Paper) reporting the results of an inquiry into policy on restrictive agreements. This concluded that the policy had been 'very effective' in controlling the formal price-fixing and market-sharing agreements endemic in Britain up to the late 1950s, with good effects on competition, prices and efficiency. However, the inquiry had also revealed 'growing evidence of evasion by failure to register' and the scope for avoidance of registration by changing the form of the agreement.

The 1979 review document put forward for consideration three major proposals for change: (i) facilitation of agreements with desirable economic effects, which tended to be deterred by the existing formal system (research and development agreements were given as an example); (ii) modifications to simplify and accelerate procedures and to make them more comprehensible; (iii) stronger enforcement.

The combination of the slow, cumbersome and expensive procedures and the absence of a general prohibition with retrospective penalties means that firms can exploit unregistered agreements with impunity.

When such agreements are detected, proved to exist and refused exemption to continue then they must cease — but this may take some years. Registered agreements may continue to operate during negotiations on their future with the OFT or (now no longer occurring in practice) proceedings in the Restrictive Practices Court.

The proposals presented in the 1988 Green Paper and refined in the prospective legislation set out in the 1989 White Paper (DTI, 1988 and 1989) go much further than those put forward in 1979. They are modelled closely on Article 85 of the Treaty of Rome, the basis of EEC policy in this area. There will be a general prohibition with penalties on the parties concerned for operating an agreement or concerted practice before this has been specifically exempted, unless it falls within a category for block exemption. The criteria for exemption and the categories for block exemption will be essentially those set out in Article 85 (3) and in the block exemption regulations (see Jacobs and Stewart-Clark, Chapter 5).

As under the EEC legislation (see page 98 of Chapter 4 above) the White Paper proposes exemption for agreements affecting mainly small businesses, unless these relate to price-fixing. These *'de minimis'* proposals are based on turnover (initially £5 million, for horizontal agreements, but subject to variation without legislation) rather than market share — as with the CEC Notice on Agreements of Minor Importance, this absolute turnover threshold has little economic justification. However, the White Paper states that the Government expects that, in the light of experience, the DGFT will later issue a market share criterion.

Like Article 85, the new legislation will cover vertical as well as horizontal agreements, a departure from existing policy which does not require registration of agreements relating to the chain of supply of the same goods. The White Paper states that 'The Government therefore believe that it cannot be wholly for suppliers and dealers themselves to decide where and how far intra-brand competition should be suppressed and that vertical agreements must be brought under the control of the new legislation' (para 2.21). Nevertheless, recognising that vertical agreements may have a greater effect in stimulating competition between goods ('inter-brand') than in reducing competition between distributors of the same good ('intra-brand'), the Government proposes a £30 million turnover threshold for vertical agreements. Many such agreements may also fall within the categories for block exemption, such as exclusive distribution.

For reasons which must perplex many economists, agreements to maintain resale prices will not qualify for *de minimus* exemption, even if the resale price maintenance (rpm) agreement is purely vertical. The exemption granted by the Restrictive Practices Court in 1962 for collectively enforced rpm on books will cease to have effect.

This last case leads us to the transitional arrangements proposed in the White Paper. Such agreements upheld by the RPC will be allowed to continue for one year extendable to two by the DGFT, during which period the OFT will investigate anti-competitive effects. If a registered agreement was modified through negotiation with the DGFT and not submitted to the RPC (declared 'not significant' under Section 21(2) of the 1976 Act), the transitional period will be five years. This seems rather arbitrary — parties who conceded to the DGFT and compromised are given better treatment than those who defended their case before the Court and won.

The logic behind this apparently unjust anomaly is that the criteria to be applied under the new legislation will give less scope for exemption on non-economic grounds. Modified agreements were cleared by the DGFT because any anti-competitive effects had been made insignificant. Those upheld by the Court were justified because anti-competitive effects were outweighed by benefits to the public interest defined by one or more of the eight 'gateways', which are no longer relevant.

The procedures for operation of the new arrangements will be substantially different from those operating at present (and since 1956). · The Office of Fair Trading (like DGIV of the CEC) may be notified of an agreement by the parties concerned, who may seek negative clearance or exemption, or alternatively it may be made aware of an alleged agreement or concerted practice by a third party. After investigation, the DGFT will issue a conclusion that the agreement be cleared or prohibited. In the case of a notified agreement not yet put into effect, the parties may be able to negotiate changes to enable the DGFT to give 'negative clearance', a statement that he does not regard the agreement as falling within the criteria for prohibition. Like the corresponding EEC system, such negative clearance will not guarantee immunity from prosecution, by private action or by the DGFT, if the agreement is subsequently shown to have significant anti-competitive effects.

If the DGFT decides that a notified agreement does fall within the prohibition and cannot be exempted then it cannot be put into effect. If it has already operated, the parties concerned may be subjected to fines — notification will not guarantee interim immunity (a difference from the EEC system). If the DGFT finds that firms have carried out concerted practices, or have operated a non-notified agreement with significant anti-competitive effects, they can also be fined. Initially the maximum level of fine will be £1 million, subject to increase up to 10 per cent of turnover on application by the DGFT to the High Court.

When the DGFT's decision is unfavourable, the parties to the agreement will be able to appeal to a new Restrictive Practices Tribunal, replacing the Restrictive Practices Court. This will consist of people drawn from the MMC, plus about ten new (but similar) appointees. For each individual case there will be a panel of three, including one lawyer; other members will be drawn from 'business, economics and the professions'. The RPT will draw on MMC staff for support. Hearings will be private and will be less judicial in form than earlier RPC hearings. If the RPT decides against an agreement, the parties to it will be able to appeal to the High Court. If its decision overturns that of DGFT, third parties will be able to appeal to the High Court against the decision of the Tribunal.

Although the proposals will make the process of assessment much easier and less arbitrary, with reliance on economic criteria, the procedures themselves appear more complex, if anything. In particular, the two-stage appeals procedure could provide substantial earnings opportunities for lawyers and consultants in antitrust economics. With the threat of fines up to 10 per cent of turnover in major cases, companies may well consider it worthwhile to pursue the appeals procedure to the limit.

The delay in bringing forward this legislation may be attributable partly to political factors. Some junior ministers at the Department of Trade and Industry with inclinations to the rightist free-market philosophy are believed to have been unhappy at the prospect of greater surveillance of business practices, retrospective fines and bureaucratic investigation. There may also be mixed feelings about the imposition on the UK of what is essentially an EEC policy. However, the new arrangements will be much closer than those now existing to the recommendations of the Monopolies and Restrictive Practices Commission in 1955 and, at least in underlying philosophy, to the systems of control in the USA, Canada and most other European countries.

MARKET POWER AND ITS ABUSE

More detailed examination of current policy

The current system of control remains one of investigation, recommendation and, if appropriate, action to prevent or limit further effects harmful to public interest. There is no general prohibition of abuse of market power and no retrospective punishment of such abuse.

The responsibility for initiating action under the 1973 Fair Trading Act lies with the Director General of Fair Trading who may refer the supply of a specified good or service (perhaps within a limited geographical area) to the Monopolies and Mergers Commission. This power to refer is subject to veto by the Secretary of State for Trade and Industry, who may make references on his/her own initiative, but neither the veto nor the direct reference power has been used. In deciding what products to refer to the MMC, the DGFT has a statutory duty to collect information about market structure and business conduct and is also the formal recipient of complaints to government by any organisations or individuals consider-ing themselves adversely affected by abuse of market power.

The Fair Trading Act 1973 defines both (i) single-firm or 'scale monopoly' and (ii) 'complex monopoly'. The actual wording is rather abstruse but it amounts to the following: (i) at least 25 per cent of UK supply of the reference product is by or to one organisation or group of interconnected organisations, possibly in a specific geographical market or (ii) at least 25 per cent is supplied by or to members of a group of firms who 'whether voluntarily or not, and whether by agreement or not, so conduct their respective affairs as in any way to prevent, restrict or distort competition'. This second, complex monopoly definition is designed to catch parallel conduct under conditions of oligopoly, where one or more players may individually account for less than 25 per cent of sales or purchases of the reference product. Note that the term 'monopoly' (single seller) is extended to subsume monopsony (single buyer). Likewise, references in UK competition policy documentation to 'oligopoly' normally subsume oligopsony, an increasingly common situation (as with many fast moving consumer goods) where a few major buyers (supermar-ket chains) dominate purchases. The first question considered by the MMC in a monopoly reference is whether a 'monopoly' exists, that is whether one firm or a group of firms with common anti-competitive policies controls 25 per cent or more of the UK market (or specific part thereof) for the referred product. If so, the firms are identified. If not, the investigation will end at this stage. Indeed it is possible for a reference to be limited to this question (section 48 of the 1973 Act) but no such 'facts only' reference has ever been made.

If a statutorily defined 'monopoly' is found to exist, the MMC will then proceed to investigate what practices or actions are adopted either to maintain the monopoly or to exploit it. Finally, it is required to report on whether the 'monopoly' situation or the practices, actions or other consequences attributable to it currently operate or may operate against the public interest.

Each reference contains a time limit within which the MMC will report.

In recent years this has been reduced from a norm of 18–24 months to less than 12 months (Frazer). In order to accelerate proceedings and reduce the burden of work for the MMC and for firms involved in the proceedings, the DGFT may restrict the reference to confirmation of the statutory monopoly and certain specified effects, such as pricing policy (eg *Contraceptive Sheaths*, 1982 and *Tampons*, 1986) or exclusive dealing (eg *Car Parts*, 1982).

The 1980 Competition Act was introduced as a measure to deal with 'anti-competitive practices' operated by individual firms without the need to prove an agreement with other firms or the existence of a 'monopoly' position. This obviates the need for a full monopoly inquiry and also accelerates the control procedure. An anti-competitive practice is any conduct which has the objective or effect of restricting, distorting or preventing competition in the supply or acquisition of goods or services in the UK or any part of it.

The first stage of enforcement of the 1980 Act is an investigation by the Director General of Fair Trading, normally in response to a complaint from a party alleging injury from anti-competitive conduct. This must first verify that the complaint does not concern a firm with UK turnover of less than £5 million and with less than 25 per cent of any definable market. (Although the 1980 Act was designed to obviate the need to define monopoly positions, a very small firm with no dominance even in local or niche markets could not indulge in anti-competitive conduct and survive.) The DGFT usually reports within a year. If anti-competitive practices are found, the firm concerned may undertake to discontinue them; such undertakings are published and subsequently monitored.

If the firm concerned disputes the DGFT's conclusions, the latter can take no action without first referring the case to the MMC as a 'competition reference', for a second-stage investigation. The MMC is asked to report within six months (exceptionally extendable to nine) on

1. whether conduct specified in the DGFT's report has been pursued by the named firm(s) within the preceding twelve months;
2. whether this constitutes an anti-competitive practice;
3. whether such practice operates or may be expected to operate against the public interest.

Frazer, apparently the only source of detailed analysis of this legislation, reports that up to March 1991 there were 30 reports by the DGFT on anti-competitive practices and eight of these cases were referred to and subsequently reported on by the MMC; in only one case (*UniChem*, 1989) did the Commission not confirm the DGFT's findings.

With respect both to monopoly and competition references, the MMC has no executive power, except in an indirect negative sense. Its reports are published and may be expected to influence public opinion. If it believes that certain effects of monopoly or anti-competitive practices operate against the public interest, its report may include recommendations for government action. Responsibility for enforcement rests with the Secretary of State for Trade and Industry. In practice, the firm(s) involved normally negotiate with the DGFT and try to agree upon legally enforceable undertakings aimed at preventing or greatly reducing adverse effects on public interest identified by the MMC. Only when such solutions cannot be negotiated, as in the mid-1970s case involving the Swiss group Hoffman-Laroche (*Chlordiazepoxide and Diazepam*), does the Secretary of State make a statutory order to implement all or some of the Commission's recommendations.

From the standpoint of the business economist, there are two aspects of the process of investigation of monopolies and anti-competitive practices by the MMC which merit further examination. The first of these is the fairly consistent use of the concept of dominance or market power described in Chapter 3. This has little connection with the 25 per cent market share thresholds specified in either the 1973 or 1980 Acts. There is no reference to dominance or market power in the legislation, but the concept is normally implicit in the MMC's analysis. This is discussed on the next four pages. The second element which we need to study further is the assessment of public interest. The criteria for this latter evaluation are laid down in the 1973 Act; they reflect the long history of disputes among economists and politicians about the pros and cons of monopoly. This aspect is studied on pages 157–8.

In the final part of this section, we compare the UK system of control over market power and its abuse with that in force under EEC legislation, and proceed to study the different options proposed by the DTI to make UK policy more compatible with that of the Community, together with the reasons given for deciding on only a minor change (see pp 159–63).

Analysis of market power by the MMC

It is unfortunate that in public discussion of monopoly cases the term 'market share' is sometimes used to describe a share of UK sales of the reference product. The reference product and the threshold share of sales (25 per cent) only provide a starting point for analysis. If this threshold is not reached (either for a single firm or a group demonstrating parallel anti-competitive conduct), then the monopoly investigation must cease.

If the threshold is exceeded, the MMC will normally then investigate whether monopoly power exists in an economic sense.

Unlike the procedure under Article 86 of the EEC treaty for dealing with abuse of dominance, the terms of reference of the MMC do not require it to prove the existence of market power or dominance before it may condemn the consequences. With monopoly references it needs only to establish that a statutory 'monopoly' exists (a term which includes monopsony, oligopoly and oligopsony). It is not formally required to study whether the reference product constitutes a relevant product market in the economic sense, that is whether it has no close substitutes accepted as such by consumers. It is not formally required to consider whether the UK is the appropriate geographical definition of the market, whether international trade (either existing or potential) implies a wider definition, or whether more local boundaries would be more valid. It is not formally required to consider potential competition or the influence of competition in downstream or wider product markets.

In the case of competition references under the 1980 Competition Act the MMC is not required to consider 'market shares' at all except in a case concerning a firm with annual turnover of £5 million or less, which can proceed only if it can be shown that there is a distinct market (for example at local level) where the firm concerned has a share of at least 25 per cent. Some examples of local dominance by small firms have been identified in competition references concerning local newspapers. This need to define local or niche market share in the case of small firms accused of anti-competitive practices is the only formal requirement to prove market power imposed by the legislation on either the MMC or the DGFT.

If this absence of formal obligation were reflected in the practical implementation of policy, that policy would be very suspect on economic grounds. In earlier chapters we saw that in the presence of competition from existing or potential substitutes, or in wider or downstream markets, firms cannot continue conduct which adversely affects consumers (or, in the case of alleged monopsony, suppliers). With regard to 'anti-competitive' practices, it is necessary to recognise that the same practice may be viewed as 'pro-competitive' when it is used by a smaller competitor to improve its market position. A loyalty rebate, for example, would be condemned by economists only when its objective and effect were to keep competitors out of a market, so that an existing firm could continue to hold (and exploit) a dominant position. Market dominance, or absence of competition is a necessary precondition of continuing adverse effects on aggregate welfare.

Several commentators have criticised UK policy-makers for failing to set out a consistent logical framework for analysis of market power. For example, Merkin and Williams (p 149), call for a more transparent and predictable methodology for MMC investigations, possibly including rules for definition of the relevant market in the true economic sense. Similar views have been expressed by Fairburn and George. In a research paper recently published by the OFT, Ridyard et al (p 18), report on an analysis of market definition in MMC cases. They comment quite critically:

> We found that many reports do not deal explicitly with definition of the relevant product market and reports frequently take a relaxed approach to terminology when talking about "markets", "market sectors", "market segments", "sub-markets" and so on. In carrying out the case studies, we did not find a consistent thread to the approach taken on market definition, nor any indication that this was in principle regarded as an activity on which a rigorous approach needed to be taken.

> ... In many cases we felt that insufficient attention had been taken in defining the market when to do so might have improved the direction of the enquiry itself.

Our research at Cranfield has also involved analysis of MMC cases, mainly for comparison with similar EEC investigations. While one must agree about the regrettable lack of formal definition of market power or dominance (this goes much further than market share), there does seem to have been a fairly high degree of consistency in the analytical methods applied by the MMC in practice. The framework used is essentially that set out in Chapter 3.

Stage One is consideration of substitute products, taking into account both functional (will the product serve the same purpose?) and reactive (do purchases recognise the functional interchangeability?) factors, as well as medium-term barriers to substitution. Substitutability, including consideration of correlated price changes, has played a major part in several MMC investigations among them *Cat and Dog Foods* (1977) and *Ford Motor Company* (1985). Admittedly with regard to a merger reference, for which market definition is more critical, the MMC has gone so far as to use consumer survey data to assess cross-price elasticity (*British Rail-Hoverlloyd,* 1981). Stage Two is assessment of potential competition. One might argue that, by refraining from setting out precise guidelines for market definition, the UK authorities have avoided the thorny and probably irresoluble dispute about whether supply substitution should be included in market definition (see Chapter 3). In practice, it tends to be treated separately, except in the case of interchangeable capacity owned by the same firm (eg Ford's output of body panels for different cars). Potential competition can, however, be a decisive factor. For example, in the *Cat and Dog Foods* (1977) case, the MMC decided that although Mars and Spillers together held 80 per cent of a relevant market surrounded by a substitution gap, this market was potentially contestable by other food producers. The latter held distribution facilities, established reputations with retailers and (perhaps a questionable notion) with pet owners who bought their other products for their own consumption. Stage Three is consideration, when relevant, of competition in wider or downstream markets. The case of replacement panels for Ford cars (*Ford Motor Company*, 1985) provides an excellent illustration of the care taken by the MMC to establish that a firm is in a dominant position in the supply of a product before condemning anti-competitive practices.

This case arose from a complaint that Ford was pursuing an anti-competitive practice, as defined by the Competition Act 1980, in refusing to license independent companies to produce replacement body panels for Ford cars, for which it held a design copyright. Ford had also instituted legal proceedings against independent companies for producing such panels illegally. The case demonstrates how the 1980 Act can be brought to bear on practices which would otherwise be perfectly legal, if they can be shown to restrict or distort competition significantly.

The motor manufacturer suggested that competition in the market for motor cars limited power derived from monopoly supply of body panels. The cost of replacement of crash-damaged panels was reflected in car insurance, and fleet owners financing their own crash repairs were very cost-conscious. Apart from crash repairs, as cars aged and panels corroded the cost of replacement panels became increasingly significant to the car owner; if Ford panels were too expensive, this would depress the prices of Ford cars in the used-car market. The combination of high crash-repair costs (reflected in insurance) and low trade-in values would depress sales of new Ford cars. So, insistence on copyright was not motivated by a desire to charge high prices for body panels, because such high prices would have adverse repercussions for Ford.

The MMC used data from the 1984 Family Expenditure Survey showing that insurance represented 18 per cent of the average cost of vehicle ownership, a significant part of which would be the statistically expected value of crash repairs. It also conducted surveys of fleet owners to see to what extent they were influenced by the prices of replacement panels, either directly or via insurance, in their choice of vehicles. These surveys confirmed the conclusion that the cost of body panels was a significant part of the cost of car ownership and because competition in the car market was intense, this would act as a brake on Ford's ability to exploit its near-monopoly in the supply of panels.

On the other hand, another survey undertaken for the MMC showed that buyers of used cars were not aware of body-panel prices and many of them took out only third-party insurance. The arguments about a feedback between the prices of body panels and used car prices were therefore rejected.

The MMC concluded that Ford's enforcement of copyright did not constitute an anti-competitive practice with adverse effects on public interest, so long as it applied to new cars. However, once a model ceased to be in current production, restriction of competition in the supply of replacement panels could lead to excessive pricing. The recommendation was that enforcement of Ford's design copyright be limited to five years.

This case has been described in some detail, first because it demonstrates the attention paid by the MMC to the existence of market power as a prerequisite for intervention to terminate an anti-competitive practice, but secondly because it shows that UK policy is concerned with aggregate welfare (public interest). Enforcement of copyright by Ford, even for five years, adversely affected other firms who would have liked to supply panels for Ford cars, but their loss was Ford's gain — merely a transfer of producer surplus. The ultimate question was whether the consumer lost. This was answered by detailed and objective analysis.

It is possibly fair to criticise the MMC (and also the OFT) for failing to make its analytical approach to assessment of dominance more transparent. It would probably help if it were set out formally, though the need for flexibility in the treatment of supply-side substitution must be recognised. On the basis of those MMC decisions which we have examined, admittedly a smaller and less recent sample than that of Ridyard et al, the author would conclude that it has consistently used an approach strongly based on established economic principles — that set out in Chapter 3 above.

Market power and public interest

Under UK law neither monopoly power nor even its abuse is prohibited. Moreover, before recommending action to reduce monopoly power or to prevent or limit further abuse, the MMC is required to consider the net effects on public interest.

Some criteria for assessment of public interest are set out in the 1973 Fair Trading Act (Section 84). The word 'some' has been used deliberately because the Act is permissive rather than definitive: the members of the

MMC are required by the Act to take into account 'all matters which appear to them in the particular circumstances to be relevant'. The Act does specify five elements to which they must have regard, which are summarised in OFT publicity material as follows:

(a) maintaining and promoting effective competition;
(b) promoting the interests of consumers, purchasers and other users of goods and services with regard to the prices, quality and variety of the goods and services supplied;
(c) promoting through competition the reduction of costs and the development and use of new techniques and new products; and facilitating the entry of new competitors into existing markets;
(d) maintaining and promoting the balanced distribution of industry and employment;
(e) maintaining and promoting competitive activity in overseas markets.

Although effective competition is at the top of the list, the MMC has itself made it clear (in its report on *Tampons*, 1986) that this does not imply greater priority to this criterion. In that particular case the MMC recommended price reductions, even though this would make the market less attractive to new entrants and hence diminish competition in the longer term.

Criteria (d) and (e) are residues from earlier criteria. They could be used to justify consideration by the MMC of objectives of industrial policy. For example, (d) could be used to justify a benign attitude towards restricted competition with adverse effects on consumers, if the restriction led to protection of jobs in an area of high unemployment. Criterion (e) could be used to support exploitation of domestic monopoly via high prices which facilitated exporting at marginal cost. To some extent, these criteria seem to belong to an earlier period of economic policy, reflecting philosophies of the 1960s rather than the more liberal economics predominant in the 1980s and 1990s.

The MMC seldom refers to the criteria and to some degree they may be regarded as having lapsed. However, since they have not been formally replaced, this means that the definition of public interest becomes even more vague. Partly to reduce the danger of inconsistency and unpredictability, the government has attempted in recent years to introduce the notion of precedent into MMC proceedings (a point made in a public speech in 1991 by the then Secretary of State for Trade and Industry, Mr Peter Lilley). While this may diminish the problem, there remains a risk that the vague terms of reference for investigation of monopolies will lead to an arbitrary element in MMC decisions, also making them vulnerable to pressures of political expediency.

Modification of UK law to consistency with Article 86

Under Article 86 of the EEC Treaty, abuse of a dominant position (insofar as it affects trade between member states) is an offence punishable by fines of up to 10 per cent of turnover. This system also supports compensation for injured parties. The threat of legal action under Article 86, so far initiated exclusively by the Commission of the European Communities but this need not necessarily be the case, may be expected to act as a deterrent to abusive conduct.

In contrast, UK law to deal with abuse of market power is very weak. No conduct is unlawful until after it has been proscribed by an order of the Secretary of State for Trade and Industry or after the firm concerned has given a legally binding undertaking to the DGFT that it will refrain from it. This means that there is no penalty for conduct subsequently found by the OFT or the MMC to be anti-competitive or an exploitation of monopoly power. As the 1992 DTI Green Paper points out, this means that there can be relatively little deterrent effect. Parties injured by abuse of market power have no right to obtain damages for past injury, nor is there any provision for protecting them during OFT and MMC investigations. Monopoly references normally take 9–12 months and, because of the two-stage (OFT and MMC) investigation process, it can take 12 months to condemn an anti-competitive practice. When time is added for consideration and implementation of remedial action, it is understandable that firms may meanwhile be put out of business.

Another problem with the UK legislation is that it accords very limited powers to the OFT to monitor business conduct and to investigate complaints to establish *prima facie* whether there may be abuse of monopoly or an anti-competitive practice. Only after formal proceedings have begun are the investigative powers of the OFT (anti-competitive practices) and the MMC (both anti-competitive practices and monopoly references) considered adequate by the authors of the DTI Green Paper para 2.15.

The simple adoption of Article 86, to be applied by the DGFT to cases not involving inter-state trade, would overcome these disadvantages. Abuse of market power would become a punishable offence and could be subject to penalties of up to 10 per cent of turnover — this would act as a deterrent. Additionally because the abusive conduct would be illegal, there would be scope for injured parties to sue the offending companies for damages; temporary injunctions prohibiting particular conduct could be obtained during proceedings. The DGFT would have powers of investigation similar to those of the CEC in EEC-level cases — these might include power to enter and search business premises, subject to magistrate's warrant. This prohibition system was presented as Option 2 in the DTI's 1992 Green Paper.

There are, however, some advantages in the present UK system which would be lost if there were simply a switch to a prohibition arrangement based on Article 86. These are as follows:

1. The UK law provides greater scope for control over oligopoly. This results partly from the low threshold for definition of a statutory single-firm 'monopoly' (25 per cent of UK sales of the reference product). In some markets, for example in the *Credit Cards* case, there may be two or three scale 'monopolists' perhaps pursuing non-collusive parallel conduct to the detriment of consumers. The definition of dominance used by EEC institutions, which places much emphasis on the size of the largest firm in relation to that of its nearest competitor, would not cover such a case. Definitions based on 'freedom of manoeuvre' (*comportements indépendants*) or 'dependency' (*état de dépéndance*) also miss the oligopoly situation unless these terms are applied to the oligopolists collectively, which has never yet been done. The complex monopoly provisions, whereby the law is extended to firms pursuing parallel anti-competitive conduct provided their combined share of sales of the reference product exceeds 25 per cent, add even further flexibility for investigation of oligopoly.

   In the 1992 Green Paper para 2.10, the DTI points out that fewer than half of the MMC's monopoly and competition references in 1980–91 were concerned solely with the exercise of market power by a single company.

   The flexibility created by the Competition Act 1980, which provides for investigation of anti-competitive practices by single firms without the need to establish the existence of a statutory 'monopoly', is probably not relevant to this argument. As explained above, the MMC has recognised and condemned anti-competitive practices only when these have been carried out by firms with market power — an approach consistent with economic logic. This is the approach adopted by the CEC and insisted upon by the Court of Justice in Community-level cases under Article 86. A switch to an Article 86 type system might require more formal exposition of the proof of market dominance (for which most UK observers and affected businesses would be grateful); in cases about the conduct of individual firms its practical effect would be relatively minor.

2. The monopoly provisions of the 1973 Fair Trading Act provide for

remedies other than the prohibition (in the future) of practices resulting from monopoly power. These may include divestment by monopoly companies (as in *Domestic Gas Appliances*, 1980 and *Beer*, 1989), particularly appropriate when market power is so strong that further abuse (perhaps in another form) is considered probable. Another remedy may be government regulation, eg price controls imposed in *Contraceptive Sheaths* (1982), *White Salt* (1986), *Opium Derivatives* (1989) and *Matches* (1992). EEC legislation provides neither for divestment/fragmentation nor for regulation. It is directed at punishment of abuse of market power; only the size of the penalties ensures that abuse is not repeated.

Given these advantages of the present UK system, an alternative to harmonisation with Article 86 would be to strengthen that system. The only elements which could be strengthened without changing the entire principles are *a)* the granting of greater powers of investigation to the OFT; *b)* additional scope for the DGFT to obtain binding undertakings in order to shorten investigations; *c)* provision for back-dating of damages and perhaps civil penalty to the time when a reference to the MMC is made. These changes would still leave a fairly weak deterrent effect (a view expressed in paragraph 4.5 and Annex C of the DTI Green Paper). This strengthening of the present system is Option 1 put forward in the 1992 Green Paper.

A third option (Option 3) was application of the prohibition system based on Article 86 to UK national cases, combined with retention of those parts of existing legislation which provide advantages over the EEC system. These advantages, the flexibility in dealing with oligopoly and the availability of 'structural' and 'regulatory' remedies (breaking up of monopolies or controls over their behaviour) follow from the monopoly provisions of the 1973 Act. If these were retained alongside the prohibition system the result would be wide and flexible powers to limit the adverse effects both of monopoly and oligopoly.

The main problem with this option would be the existence of parallel systems which would to some degree overlap. Businesses would not know by which route proceedings would be taken against them. The deterrent effects on anti-competitive conduct would be very strong, but the complexity caused by two parallel sets of controls might prove too heavy a burden on management.

On 14 April 1993 (answer to Parliamentary Question by Mr Neil Hamilton, a Minister of State in the DTI) the government announced that it would adopt Option 1, a strengthening of the present UK system rather than either of the other two options. The proposed changes are:

- greater investigative powers for the DGFT in advance of a full investigation;
- power to the DGFT to accept enforceable undertakings before a formal investigation under the Competition Act (anti-competitive practices) or in lieu of a monopoly reference to the MMC;
- power to the Secretary of State for Trade and Industry to make interim orders to prohibit alleged anti-competitive practices during the period of MMC investigation;
- extension of the legislation to deal with anti-competitive abuse of certain specific property rights.

The first of these changes will make it easier for the OFT to identify cases where intervention is required; the second will accelerate the termination of anti-competitive conduct and, in cases where the company concerned is unwilling to give an appropriate undertaking, the third will ensure protection of allegedly injured parties during the second stage of investigation of alleged anti-competitive conduct, by the MMC.

The explanation of the government's decision in Mr Hamilton's statement emphasises the 'burden of bureaucracy' and uncertainty which would be borne by companies if a prohibition system were adopted. These problems would be even greater with the dual system which had been considered as Option 3. Another factor was the flexibility of the present system: Mr Hamilton concluded his statement as follows: 'The conclusion is that a prohibition would bite on fewer market situations than our present legislation. This is particularly true in markets where there is more than one major player.' This decision is a little difficult to reconcile with the analysis in the DTI's own Green Paper. The lack of retrospective penalties contrasts with legislation not only in the EEC but also in the other four countries examined in that document (DTI, 1992, Annex G). It means that nothing which is done to maintain or to exploit monopoly power can be illegal, until the particular firm has agreed or been ordered not to do it. It is true that the British system has been more effective in dealing with oligopoly, but this is more a reflection of the interpretation by the CEC and the CJEC of 'joint dominance'. German competition law, which provides for prohibition, also deals with joint dominance. Similarly with regard to remedies: the EEC law provides only for fines, with provision neither for divestment nor regulation, but powers to apply the alternative remedies could be added to a prohibition system. French competition law applies penalties for abuse of dominance but also contains provision for divestment.

It is hard to believe that business managers will welcome the existence of two different systems for dealing with alleged abuse of market power.

One of these provides for retrospective punishment with no exemptions; it will apply where any alleged abuse affects inter-state trade within the EEC. The other (UK) system is an investigative process with exemptions based on vaguely defined public interest, which does not punish past conduct but might end up in fairly draconian restrictions on future action.

As with many other aspects of economic policy, the UK looks like ending up the odd one out among Member States in the principles applied in curbing abuse of market power. The conclusions that this distinct difference should continue is not easy to reconcile with some of the analysis in the November 1992 Green Paper (DTI). The response to that Green Paper may have swayed government opinion towards the chosen option. However, even if in an objective sense the UK system is more cost-effective than that applied in the rest of Europe (and in North America), there is much to be said for adopting the latter. It would make life much simpler for both the business community and consumers to have a common system. Rather than adopt its own approach to the dwindling number of cases which will fall under its jurisdiction, might not the UK government try to secure improvements in EEC policy, such as the control of oligopoly and powers to require divestment? Broader political factors may be involved here.

POLICY ON MERGERS

The term 'merger' applies to any action which results in two or more 'enterprises ceasing to be distinct' (Fair Trading Act 1973). It therefore covers any form of amalgamation, including mergers in the more specific sense (pooling of shareholdings and management), takeovers whether friendly or hostile and joint ventures.

In the outline history of UK competition policy (pages 145–50 above), we saw that, at least in the twentieth century, British politicians have generally been in favour of mergers. Powers to intervene in mergers were not introduced to competition legislation until 1965 and this measure was very much one of extending to mergers the system of investigation applied to cases of alleged existing monopoly power. This late development of merger control policy has had two important consequences. First, it means that much of the procedure and many of the criteria for assessment of mergers are derived from and similar (in certain respects identical) to those applied to existing monopolies. Secondly, the generally favourable attitude towards mergers was reflected in the legislation and, in the opinion of some well-known and experienced specialists, continues to be reflected in the way the legislation is applied.

The next few pages outline the mechanisms for control of mergers in the UK and describe, with comment, certain major changes introduced since 1988. The point must be made at the outset, though it will be reinforced at various stages of the exposition, that the legislation on mergers is permissive. Merging firms are not required to notify the authorities (the OFT or the DTI) of their proposed or recently accomplished amalgamation. Only the Secretary of State for Trade and Industry is allowed to refer a proposed or recent merger to the MMC; he is not required to do so (except in the special case of newspapers with large circulation). This means that influence of the power to control mergers depends primarily on how much and in what ways the power is used.

Pages 170–4 compare the UK system with that of the EEC based on the Merger Control Regulation of 1989. This comparison is used as a framework for discussion of some of the current issues surrounding UK and EEC policy in this area.

Outline of UK system for control over mergers

A merger will qualify for investigation under the Fair Trading Act 1973 if four criteria are met. These are as follows:

1. Two or more enterprises must 'cease to be distinct'. This may occur either because they are brought under common ownership or control or because there is an arrangement between them that they will withdraw from overlapping activities (for example by joint ventures). 'Control' includes not only majority control but also shareholdings sufficient to lead to '*de facto*' control or even material influence over policy. OFT guidance material (OFT) states that a shareholding of more than 25 per cent is likely to be regarded as conferring material influence over policy and any acquisition which takes a holding above 15 per cent is liable to attract the scrutiny of the OFT. In exceptional circumstances even lower holdings may attract attention.

2. At least one of the enterprises must be operating in the United Kingdom or be controlled by a UK-based company. A merger between two foreign companies may qualify for investigation if either controls an enterprising operating or incorporated in the UK. Where the merger falls within the ambit of the EEC Merger Control Regulation, it becomes the responsibility of the Commission of the European Communities and, unless it is referred back under Article 9 of the MCR, the UK authorities have no jurisdiction.

3. The merger must either not have taken place or have taken place within the six months before the reference is made. An exception to

this time limit applies to a merger which has not been publicly announced or about which neither the OFT nor the DTI has been privately informed. In such cases the six months time limit begins from the time that the information does become known. The issue of notification is quite important and has been affected by recent policy changes outlined below.

4. *Either*, the merger must result in a rise to at least 25 per cent in the merged company's share of sales (or purchases) 'of goods or services of a similar kind' in the UK or substantial part of it ('market share test') *or* the gross value of the world-wide assets acquired must exceed £30 million. (From 1973 to April 1980 this figure was £5 million and from April 1980 to July 1984 it was £15 million — this criterion is known as the 'asset test'.)

The first stage of merger control policy is consideration by the DGFT with a view to recommending whether it be referred to the MMC. A Mergers Panel, comprising civil servants from different departments, participates in this decision whether or not to refer; very little about procedures or recommendations is made public. This preliminary assessment normally takes about one month and, according to the OFT guidance document, focuses mainly on competition, particularly on market definition, market shares, international competition, market contestability and vertical links insofar as these have horizontal effects.

The Secretary of State for Trade and Industry is not required to act on the DGFT's recommendation — he or she may decide not to refer a merger to the MMC even though such reference has been recommended and equally may make a reference against the DGFT's advice. The MMC has six months to report on any merger referred to it, extendable to a legal maximum of 12 months. The publication of the final report of the MMC is mandatory, subject only to the omission of confidential data.

The first stage in the MMC's investigation is to ensure that the four criteria for intervention are met. If not, the investigation ends immediately. It then proceeds to evaluate the implications of the merger for public interest, using the same permissive and wide-ranging criteria that are applied in monopoly references (see page 158 above). There is a formal presumption that mergers are beneficial and unless the MMC reports a proven case that a merger is against the public interest it must be allowed to proceed. The Secretary of State has no power to prohibit or regulate a merger unless the MMC has reported adversely, though he or she may allow a merger to proceed despite a negative recommendation from the Commission — such cases have been very rare.

It is probably already clear from this summary that merger control policy remains limited in effect. There is no obligatory notification. Relatively few mergers are referred to the MMC (between 2 and 3 per cent of qualifying cases in the late 1980s; in 1990 the proportion rose to 10 per cent for special reasons explained below). In the assessment by the MMC there is a presumption that mergers are beneficial unless proved otherwise: even though cases are referred to it only when there are *prima facie* grounds for concern, the MMC recommended against the merger in only 21 of 47 decisions made in the years 1985 to 1991. Finally, even when the MMC does recommend against a merger, the Secretary of State can still allow it to proceed.

For completeness, it must be pointed out that the explicit bias in favour of mergers in UK legislation is substantially reversed in cases involving concentration of the press. The Secretary of State's written consent is required for mergers which concentrate a circulation of 500,000 paid-for copies into the ownership (defined as 25 per cent control) of one person (or company). Such consent cannot be given without a report from the MMC that the merger is not against the public interest. Mandatory reference to the MMC also applies to mergers of water or sewerage undertakings above a threshold size.

The permissive nature of UK policy is, of course combined with wide discretion in its application. One of the problems produced for business managers by a potentially severe control which is applied sparingly is unpredictability. Although very few mergers are referred to the MMC, the process whereby the DGFT decides whether to recommend a reference remains shrouded in secrecy. Since the final decision on reference rests with the Secretary of State for Trade and Industry, a senior politician, there might still be scope for non-economic considerations to influence the outcome. Once a merger has been referred to the MMC, this puts it into six months or more of suspension. In the case of bids for public companies, the rules of the (London) City Code on Takeovers and Mergers require that an offer is conditional on non-reference to the MMC and will lapse if the merger is referred. Even though the chances of clearance may remain high, the vague nature of the MMC's formal decision criteria aggravates the uncertainty. Where a takeover is being resisted, its suspension may effectively lead to its abandonment. Where there is a rival bid, perhaps without a horizontal market overlap and therefore not qualifying for reference, the merger proposal referred to the MMC is unlikely to survive. Frazer found that nearly 25 per cent of mergers referred to the MMC are abandoned soon after reference.

In order to reduce some of these difficulties for business, the UK government has introduced some changes in recent years which truncate procedures and make them more transparent — but, in both respects, only slightly. These measures to truncate and accelerate merger control procedures were introduced in 1989. They include a voluntary pre-notification procedure and the acceptance of legally binding undertakings which remove threats to competition considered by the DGFT to be posed by the merger.

Firms may now choose to notify the OFT of a proposed merger, at the same time submitting information on a standard questionnaire about the business concerned. Provided that the proposal is also publicly announced, so that third parties may voice any objections, 20 working days of silence from the OFT may be interpreted as automatic clearance. If the OFT does raise doubts during this period, it can extend the time for consideration by two further periods of 10 and 15 days respectively. At the end of the 20-day period (extendable to 45), three outcomes are possible — clearance, recommended reference to the MMC or legally binding undertakings to deal with objections on competition grounds.

The main form of undertakings given by firms eager to avoid reference to the MMC has been agreement to divest themselves of part of the activities in which they would hold market power. If these undertakings are not subsequently honoured, the Secretary of State can enforce them by law without reference to the MMC.

The main advantage of using the pre-notification procedure is removal of the threat of future intervention. When a merger is not notified or made public, reference to the MMC can take place within six months of the date when full details about it are available to the OFT or the DTI. Another advantage is the rapidity of clearance. The main drawback from the standpoint of the merging or acquiring firm(s) is the danger of giving undertakings which remove some of their gains from the proposed concentration when this would have been allowed without modification under the full procedure. Since only a very small minority of cases are referred to the MMC and the latter condemns fewer than half of these as against the public interest, it may make more sense to take a chance. About 20 per cent of mergers qualifying for investigation are voluntarily pre-notified and some 60 per cent of these receive clearance within 20 days (OFT, cited by Frazer).

The formal pre-notification procedure has another disadvantage in making a proposed merger or takeover known to all interested parties. This loss of confidentiality may be particularly important in the case of a 'hostile' takeover, providing the management of the target company with an early warning. An alternative procedure in such cases is for the company considering the acquisition to seek confidential guidance from the DGFT (who formally advises the Secretary of State) as to whether the proposal would be likely to be referred to the MMC. This guidance is either 'favourable' (reference unlikely) or 'unfavourable'. Although this procedure is believed to be widely used, 'favourable' guidance provides no guarantee, because once the proposed merger is made public the DGFT may reconsider it in the light of comments made by other interested parties.

The second major change in merger policy in recent years has been a modest move towards greater consistency and transparency. In 1984, the then Secretary of State for Trade and Industry (now Lord Tebbitt) announced that references to the MMC would be made primarily on grounds of competition. This 'Tebbitt doctrine' was confirmed in the DTI's formal statement on mergers policy in 1988 (para 2.12). This referred to a divergence between private and public interest:

> ... where a merger confers excessive market power on the new enterprise, so that it offers the prospect of profits to the owners but threatens to damage the public interest, for example, by leading to distortion of the market, reduction of efficiency, and exploitation of the customer. In these circumstances there is a strong case for the public authorities to intervene. This is the rationale for the Government's current policy under which the potential effect on competition is the main consideration in deciding whether to refer a merger to the MMC.

The DTI paper went on to outline the relevant factors to be considered by the DGFT in assessing 'whether the merger is likely to confer market power'. These are the market share of the merged enterprise in relation to those of domestic and overseas competitors, ease of entry, any competitive advantages, scope for collusion in the market, availability of substitute products (it is not clear how this fits in with market share) and finally any countervailing buying or (in the case of monopsony) selling power (*ibid*, para 2.18).

While this document may appear to set out some useful guidelines for merger appraisal, making the operation of policy more transparent, there remain two problems to muddy the waters.

First, the Government, both in the Tebbitt announcement of 1984 and in the 1988 policy statement, did not renounce the power to refer mergers to the MMC on other grounds but preferred 'to retain the open-ended public interest criterion in the legislation, and with it the option of making references to the MMC on grounds other than the threat to competition' (*op cit*, para 2.27). No examples of such other grounds were given.

In July 1990, the Secretary of State for Trade and Industry, Mr Peter Lilley, announced that in future reference might be made when the acquiring company was wholly or partly owned by a foreign state (a response to the acquisition of minority holdings in some privatised UK companies by French state-owned enterprises). Five such references were then made, four of them against the advice of the DGFT, and the DTI urged the MMC to recognise that 'nationalisation by the backdoor' was not in the public interest. However, the effect of this 'Lilley doctrine' was mitigated by the MMC, which did not find such state control to be against the public interest, provided the conduct of the acquired enterprise was sufficiently constrained by competition.

The MMC's ability to modify the implementation of the 'Lilley doctrine' demonstrates its autonomy and executive power, which only legislation could weaken. This autonomy brings us to the second problem for business managers in predicting the outcome of a merger proposal. While the Secretary of State for Trade and Industry, acting almost invariably on the advice of the DGFT, may refer merger proposals to the MMC mainly on grounds of competition effects, there is no reason why the MMC should confine its assessment of public interest to this one criterion. The criteria to be used remain the vague terms of Section 84 of the 1973 Fair Trading Act and reflect the broad economic and social assessment considered necessary in the more interventionist days of the 1960s. In practice, the MMC also focuses on competition and if it did decide to recommend against a merger on other grounds the Secretary of State would be free to ignore this adverse recommendation — but, given media pressure on politicians and even on bodies like the MMC, anything might happen. For example, a merger which would not create market power but which might lead to the closure of a major source of employment in an economically and socially deprived area could in principle be declared against the public interest, on grounds of 'maintaining and promoting the balanced distribution of industry and employment' (one of the Section 84 criteria). If there were a marginal seat in the area, would the Secretary of State overrule such a decision?

Most of the specialists who have examined UK mergers policy in recent years have recommended changes to make this policy less arbitrary and permissive. Those writers include both lawyers such as Merkin and Williams and Frazer or economists such as George — himself a part-time member of the MMC. Most of the proposed changes would make UK policy more like that embodied in the EEC's Merger Control Regulation.

Comparison between UK and EEC policies

The *first* difference in procedure relates to notification: in cases falling within UK jurisdiction notification is voluntary; in cases meeting the criteria for application of the Community's MCR notification is obligatory and failure to notify is punishable by fine imposed by the CEC. Notification to the CEC requires completion of a Form (Form CO) much more complex than that used for notifying the OFT in UK cases. However, in practice, companies are invited to discuss notification at branch offices of the CEC and under certain circumstances completion of the full form is not necessary. A mandatory system has a number of advantages. First, it ensures that the relevant competition authorities are fully informed about cases which may require their intervention. The author feels a vague disquiet in reading in the DTI's formal statement on mergers policy (DTI, 1988) that 'the OFT finds out about many cases from the financial press and follows them up on its own initiative'. Do we want public resources to be spent in amateur detection? Secondly, it avoids the possibility of post-merger divestment or even 'unscrambling'; this did arise with the reference of some completed mergers in the mid–1980s.

The DTI rejected the principle of obligatory notification mainly because 'it creates an additional burden both for the authorities and for business'. This is disputable, first because it would greatly ease the workload of monitoring which the OFT must do if its surveillance of concentration is to be effective and secondly because it would remove much uncertainty faced by business. While it may be argued that voluntary notification achieves the latter objective, the present arrangements make that option potentially less attractive than taking a chance on the merger being cleared without modification.

The *second*, in the author's opinion very important, difference between UK and EEC policy implementation is that the preliminary investigation by the CEC's Merger Task Force is surrounded by much less secrecy than the corresponding evaluation by the OFT. Of the 141 decisions taken by the CEC from the inception of the MCR to 25 March 1993, only 11 were to refer the merger for full investigation. This is somewhat higher than the proportion of qualifying mergers in the UK referred to the MMC, but it is reasonable to assume that similar analysis is used. The more important difference is that the CEC has made a report available to the parties concerned, with a modified public version, on how each of the 141 decisions was reached. While it may be argued that certain decisions have been influenced by political factors and that the economic logic is flawed, at least we have a chance to study and criticise it! This can be contrasted with the secret and poorly understood procedures which precede the decision whether or not to refer a merger to the MMC in the UK.

The *third* major difference between the EEC process of merger control and that in the UK is greater clarity and more formal use of standard criteria. This is partly a reflection of the narrower basis on which the CEC is permitted by the MCR to permit or prohibit a merger — exclusively on whether it will create or strengthen a dominant position. The analysis by which the CEC reaches conclusions on this single essential criterion has been criticised, for example by Neven et al (pp 100–101). At least, the methods of analysis are exposed to such criticism and can be refined in response to it. Business managers can acquire some indications of how their own plans for merger or acquisition may be analysed by referring to earlier cases of a similar nature.

These first three distinctive features of EEC policy and practice compared with those in the UK — mandatory notification, published explanations of interim decisions, explicit use of formal criteria — would all be regarded as desirable by most specialists in competition policy, both lawyers and economists. The other two main differences are the subject of more dispute. One relates to division of responsibility for investigation on the one hand and executive decisions on the other. In the UK, responsibility for investigation lies with the OFT, headed by the DGFT, and independently with the MMC; the decisions to refer a merger to the MMC and to prohibit it or place conditions on it if the MMC recommends this both rest with the Secretary of State for Trade and Industry. Under EEC practice, the Commission of the European Communities (CEC) does everything. The other main difference is, of course, the much wider basis for evaluation of mergers in the UK.

Hölzer discusses the case for a separate authority to vet mergers in the Community, a case supported at different times and for different reasons by the UK and Germany and also by a January 1990 resolution of the European Parliament. The proposal discussed is based on a German model whereby an independent competition authority (equivalent to the *Bundeskartellamt* in Germany) would assess all mergers presented to it purely on grounds of competition. Any prohibition imposed by this body could then be challenged before the Commission, which could consider wider criteria of public interest. This proposal, which Hölzler himself rejects as not politically feasible, goes further than the separation of powers demanded in some quarters. It would change the basis for decision.

Perhaps a model closer to the UK system would have the advantage of removing from the CEC the combined role of police and jury. The four-week procedure leading to Article 6 decisions would remain the sole responsibility of the Commission, in practice carried out by a specific division like the present Merger Task Force. The minority of cases (only

11 out of 141 so far) where this body had 'serious doubts as to compatibility with the common market' (the wording of the MCR), could then be referred for more detailed consideration to an independent tribunal equivalent to the MMC. Only if the latter recommended prohibition or the imposition of restrictions, would the CEC be allowed to stop the merger. This model would appear to overcome most of the objections to the vesting of power exclusively with the CEC. Practically, it may be difficult to establish and it might slow down the process of merger control. Some such proposal may however soon appear on the European Community agenda.

The final major difference between UK and EEC policies on merger control is by far the most perplexing. Any specialist who were to study the two policies immediately after waking from some years of unconsciousness would be nonplussed by the contrast in criteria applied and by the reasons for it. The UK has a system whereby a merger can be prohibited only if it has been proved to be against the public interest by the MMC, which can define its own interpretation of public interest or can call on a string of vague economic and social criteria set down in the legislation. On the other hand, the EEC law does not allow consideration of factors other than competition in the assessment of mergers. And why is the EEC law based on such a narrow assessment? Partly because the British insisted upon it.

The explanation for this apparently illogical outcome is partly historical. Four years after the first legislative control over mergers was introduced in the UK, the then President of the Board of Trade (a title recently re-adopted by the present Secretary of State for Trade and Industry) stated that 'In general, mergers are desirable if they lead to better management or genuine economies of scale without eliminating workable competition. In my view more often than not in Britain mergers will fulfil this condition' (cited by George p 130). This view clearly continues to prevail. The DTI 1988 policy document emphasised the benefits from a liberal policy towards prospective mergers, including 'the discipline of the market over incumbent company managements'. It explicitly rejected any proposal to reverse the burden of proof, currently upon those who oppose a merger.

In the late 1960s and early 1970s there was a consensus among most UK politicians in favour of a pro-active industrial policy. Government was not opposed to mergers but was actively in favour of them. Since 1979 the UK government has consistently adhered to a policy based on supremacy of market forces and the only perceived justification for intervention 'normally' is now the need to preserve competition. The original wording of the legislation still stands but, as all the publicity material of the OFT and the DTI makes clear, the government's use of the legislation will be based on competition alone.

Some of the other Member States of the European Communities, particularly France and Italy, had by 1989 moved less than the UK towards policies based on freedom for market forces. For some of the keener enthusiasts for industrial policy, scope still remained for the creation of European champions to take on the giants of the rest of the world. In Chapter 4, the resolution of this conflict of ideas was described in some detail. The view of the UK government appears to have been that if control over mergers in the EEC were as permissive in form as that in the UK, the Commission could not be trusted to resist 'industrial policies' of this kind — industrial policies which were in place in Britain at the time when the UK legislation was originally conceived.

Whatever the political explanation, the present situation is widely regarded as unsatisfactory. It is hard to disagree with George that what is required in the UK is a reversal of the presumption before the MMC: a merger which will have adverse effects on competition should be declared against the public interest unless it can be shown to be justified on efficiency grounds. The 'efficiency defence' may be hard to prove in many cases — empirical research (admittedly dating from the late 1970s and early 1980s) showed little support for the hypothesis that mergers led to improved performance. However, it is clearly invalid to exclude such arguments. Perhaps inadvertently, the authors of the DTI (1988) , policy document (para 2.19 – at the tail end of a paragraph on criteria for reference to the MMC) stated that after reference of a merger with a significant threat to competition in the UK market: 'It is then for the MMC to conduct a full examination, to assess both the likely damage to competition and any likely benefits to efficiency, and to reach a balanced overall verdict.' This is not far from the logic proposed by George.

Neven et al discuss the case for a similar efficiency defence in EEC policy. They point out that in at least one case, *AT&T/NCR*, greater efficiency brought by synergy between complementary product ranges was seen as a negative factor, because it would help to strengthen a dominant position. In terms of economic principles, such logic is clearly unsatisfactory!

To summarise, there would be much support among specialists for a similar policy on mergers at both national and Community level. This would include:

- mandatory notification;
- publication of analysis leading to the decision to refer (or not) to an

independent advisory body, this decision to be based on competition criteria;

- explicit use of guidelines to define competition criteria;
- consideration by the independent advisory body, based purely on economic criteria but including an efficiency defence;
- a final decision by the responsible executive, which could not be negative unless this were recommended by the advisory body.

This model would combine the best of both systems.

6

Some Major Issues and General Conclusions

INTRODUCTION

Economic policies cannot be divorced from political and social philosophies — nor should they be. The welfare of society cannot be measured without some value judgements. As an economist, the author does not complain about the distortion of economic principles by non-economic considerations in the application of competition policy. However most economists do object to a failure to make such considerations explicit, to make the objectives and processes of competition policy transparent and consistent. When inconsistencies occur, either over time or in the treatment of different problems confronted by competition policy, there is always a doubt: do they reflect hidden policy considerations or do they arise from some confused thinking somewhere in the application process?

This last chapter concentrates on a number of issues within competition policy that have not yet been satisfactorily resolved. On each of these issues, economic theory can point the way not so much to a unique solution (perish the thought!) as to a number of objective factors which will determine the net welfare benefit of each outcome.

After examining how this argument applies to each of the five cases, we end with three general propositions:

1. that competition policies should be directed exclusively towards aggregate welfare unless other objectives are made explicit;
2. that there should be clear guidelines to ensure that these objectives are pursued in every case;
3. for the benefit of business, the objectives, policies and guidelines should be more similar, at least within the European Community.

All five issues have been raised in earlier chapters; they have all been the focus of different parts of EEC and UK policies and they all relate to the broad philosophical positions described in Chapter 1. This chapter is essentially a summary of earlier material presented in a different perspective.

FIVE SPECIFIC ISSUES

Resale price maintenance in relation to other vertical agreements

This is the most specific of the five issues. In choosing to devote a few paragraphs to it, the author has been influenced by the fact that this book appears in the Cranfield Research Series and that resale price maintenance, specifically its continued application to books, has been the subject of extensive research at Cranfield. At the time of writing it is a subject of debate in a number of EC countries and within the CEC itself, where there appears to be some dispute between directorates. Competition legislation in most parts of the world generally prohibits resale price maintenance (subject to specific exemptions in certain countries), while applying a much more tolerant attitude towards other forms of vertical agreement. Economic principles provide no justification for this distinction.

In Chapter 2 it was explained that the net welfare consequences of vertical agreements to limit competition depend on the relative importance of the intra- and inter-brand effects. By limiting competition between distributors in the sale of its product X (intra-brand), a producer may be able to ensure the provision of services and/or to create and maintain other conditions which stimulate sales of X. In theoretical terms, the beneficial effects of the vertical restriction would be to push the demand curve for X to the right. This would lead to an increase in both producers' and consumers' surpluses. It may also lead to a rise in price but this would not be the case if, as seems quite likely, the demand stimulated by the additional services is more price-sensitive than the demand which would have occurred in the absence of the vertical restraint. (For full exposition see Fishwick, 1986b, Appendix 1) An increase in producers' and consumers' surpluses without an increase in price is an undeniable welfare gain.

This theoretical analysis is not new and, as we have seen in Chapters 4 and 5, it is reflected in competition policies in both the EEC and the UK, which generally permit vertical agreements with no horizontal effects. This general principle is found also in the US where the 'rule of reason' is applied to vertical restraints — each is considered on its merits. The only exception, under both American and European laws, is the fixing of resale prices.

Numerous economists, on both sides of the Atlantic, have pointed out that there is no difference in terms of possible economic welfare effects between vertical price-fixing agreements and other vertical restraints: the same comparison of intra- and inter-brand effects is relevant. Vickers and Hay comment, with regard to UK law:

The Resale Prices Act has therefore made vertical restraints involving price almost *per se* illegal. Non-price vertical restraints are, however, treated quite differently ... It is odd that non-price restraints should be treated so differently from those involving price, since their economic effects can be rather similar.

In the US, the arguments for a 'rule of reason' approach to resale price maintenance, providing for evaluation of its net contribution to efficiency, have been presented by Calvani and Langenfeld (1985), Comanor and Kirkwood (1985) and Marvel and McCafferty (1985; 1986), among several others.

The legal position on the fixing of minimum retail prices of books in different parts of the European Community demonstrates the confused state of competition policy on this issue. In the UK, the Netherlands, Germany and Denmark, resale price maintenance is generally prohibited but exemptions are permissible and exemption has specifically been granted to books. In the UK, certain branded pharmaceuticals have also been exempted. In France (since 1981) every publisher or principal importer is legally obliged to fix a retail price for every book and no retailer is permitted to give a discount of over 5 per cent; for all other products (except again branded pharmaceuticals) resale price fixing is prohibited. In Spain, Portugal and Italy there has been until now informal adherence to fixed retail prices of books but, in order to safeguard this against prospective legislation against restrictive agreements, there are proposals that an obligatory system like that in France be imposed. In the Republic of Ireland, following the enactment of new legislation on restrictive agreements (based on Article 85), book trade associations have requested formal exemption for vertical price-fixing. In Greece and Belgium, resale price maintenance is prohibited and books have not been exempted. A non-government bill before the Belgian Parliament proposes the introduction of a French-style obligatory system.

In trying to analyse the logic behind the various exemptions and legally imposed systems, the author has concluded that only in the UK (and in the request for exemption in Ireland) has the case been based on considerations of economic efficiency. The Net Book Agreement provides for collective enforcement of retail prices for books whenever individual publishers choose to impose them. This was defended before the Restrictive Practices Court in 1962 and was granted exemption from the 1956 Restrictive Trade Practices Act, with further exemption in 1968 from the Resale Prices Act 1964. The arguments presented by both sides were exclusively concerned with aggregate economic welfare — they are summarised below. The same emphasis on objective economic criteria characterised the evidence placed before the Office of Fair Trading in 1989, both by those eager to see an end to the exemption and by those wishing it to continue. (The OFT decided not to refer the issue to the Restrictive Practices Court again, partly because the Net Book Agreement will need to be reconsidered when the proposed new legislation on restrictive practices has been enacted.)

In contrast, discussion of this issue in the rest of the Community appears to be based much more on value judgements, which it must be added also appear in informal debate in the UK. Protagonists of fixed prices for books seem to reject the notion that these should be subject to the normal pressures of the market economy: there is an almost sentimental desire to protect the small to medium-sized bookseller. He or she is perceived not as a profit-seeking entrepreneur but as someone devoted to books, who is motivated primarily by a wish to encourage literary culture. By guaranteeing this non-aggressive altruist protected margins on best-selling titles, resale price maintenance will provide cross-subsidisation of less profitable books. Economic logic would deny first the likelihood of such behaviour (which requires the majority of booksellers to reject profit-maximisation) and secondly its desirability, if it were to occur. Its welfare-redistributive effects would almost certainly be adverse — buyers of mass-market paperbacks would be subsidising those purchasing more specialist and erudite works; the latter customers are probably better off. (For further discussion, see Fishwick, 1989b, p 13–14, where evidence is presented to show that the 'cultural' argument may in reality work in reverse.)

In contrast, those who oppose resale price maintenance tend to base their opposition on a sweeping generalisation that it is a restrictive practice and therefore, like all such practices is bad. This presumption seems to have become established in parts of the Commission of the European Communities which has resolutely resisted any concessions which would allow vertical price-fixing to extend across national frontiers within the EEC. In 1985 it prohibited the imposition of fixed resale prices on books traded between the Netherlands and Belgium; in 1988 it prohibited the application of the Net Book Agreement to books exported from the UK to the Republic of Ireland. The Netherlands-Belgium decision (*VBVB/VBBB*) has been upheld by the Court of Justice, that on UK-Ireland (*UK Publishers Association*) has been upheld by the Court of First Instance but is still, at the time of writing, the subject of an appeal to the full Court.

In both decisions the CEC emphasised that its concern was about the collective enforcement provision, with use of standard conditions. This emphasis contrasted with the conclusions of the UK Restrictive Practices Court (accepted by the Registrar of Restrictive Trade Practices, the precursor of the DGFT), that the fragmented structure of publishing and bookselling meant that if resale price maintenance were to be permitted it must be collectively enforced. It also avoided discussion of the economic assessment of resale price maintenance. However, the Press Notice issued after the 1988 Decision makes clear the Commission's view:

> The other forms of competition — stocking, specialisation, service offered and ordering facilities — must be regarded as secondary to price competition ... Among booksellers, competition is eliminated in respect of a substantial part of the products in question. This conclusion is in no way affected by the fact that a degree of price competition exists among publishers.

In other words, the Commission's Press Office urged us not to consider the trade-off between intra- and inter-brand competition, fundamental to the analysis of vertical agreements!

The 1985 and 1988 decisions were based on analysis by DGIV — the Directorate-General for Competition. A similarly negative view is reflected in a decree introduced in January 1990 to modify the French law requiring a fixed price. This decree, which emanated originally from DGIII of the CEC — the Directorate-General for Industry — makes an exception to the fixed price rule for lower prices resulting from 'an advantage obtained by the importer in the country of publication' (where that country is another Member State). The CEC has therefore established a policy which firmly resists the application of vertical price-fixing across national boundaries. Meanwhile another directorate (DGX — the Directorate for Cultural Affairs), with encouragement from the European Parliament, has been considering (for some years!) an obligatory system of minimum resale prices to be applied Community-wide, the European 'floor price'.

The present legal position within the European Community on resale price maintenance for books is obviously unsatisfactory, with conditions varying from obligatory price-fixing in some countries (enforced by the police) to prohibition of the practice in others. The European Commission, on the one hand has done all it can to undermine the practice, its Press Office justifying the decisions with statements that appear inconsistent with established economic principles; on the other hand, it has seriously considered an obligatory system. In matters like this, within a

Single Market, business is entitled to demand a uniform and transparent approach.

Politically, it may not be an appropriate time to advocate a pan-European policy on a subject as specific as resale price maintenance on books. It may be argued, anyway, that different conditions in each Member State may require differences in the detail of policy. What is reasonable to demand is consistency of approach, preferably based on the application of transparent guidelines derived from economic analysis.

Resale price maintenance, like any vertical restriction, restricts and distorts competition at one horizontal level of the supply chain. It replaces price competition with competition in services, which may be a waste of resources; it impedes the restructuring of retailing and may perpetuate inefficiency by safeguarding a quiet life for less enterprising retailers. There can be little dispute among economists that resale price maintenance imposed by effective cartels of distributors would have negative welfare effects — though given the contestable nature of bookselling such cartels seem unlikely to be effective. Similarly, economists would, for the most part, be very concerned about the consequences for efficiency of externally imposed fixed resale prices (see Ecalle, 1988, for a critique of the French system for books).

However, what about vertical price-fixing imposed by producers? *A priori*, one would expect them to want efficient distribution of their product and so to welcome price competition among retailers. Their motives may not necessarily be pro-competitive. For example, resale price maintenance may form part of collusion on prices between the producers themselves (Allan and Curwen, 1991). There may also be a desire to prevent the restructuring of retailing, because this would lead to the emergence of powerful customers (oligopsony) able to demand a larger gross margin and other improvements in terms. Neither of these strategies on the part of producers would justify resale price maintenance as a means of increasing aggregate welfare.

The pro-competitive benefits of resale price maintenance apply when it is necessary to sustain the provision of services and conditions which increase the sales of the individual product. The threat of price-cutting and consequent 'free-riding' on such services was emphasised as a justification for fixed retail prices by Telser (1960), a seminal work on this subject. 'Services' should be extended to include not only pre-sales facilities, such as free trial or professional advice, but also the mere act of stockholding and display. Surveys have shown that nearly 50 per cent of all book purchases are the result of impulse — hence a publisher's desire to encourage display of his or her titles. Note also that this principle applies not only to the degree of service in each outlet, but also to the number of outlets willing and able to stock the product at all.

This is not a book about resale price maintenance. The objective here is to show the factors which would be taken into account by a competition authority seeking to assess the net welfare effects of a particular application of vertical price-fixing. They can be grouped quite clearly into a comparison of the negative effects of suppression of intra-brand competition with the positive effects of stimulation of inter-brand competition.

The obvious conclusion is that each case needs to be considered on its merits. In general, the imposition of resale price maintenance by law or by collective agreement of either distributors or producers may be presumed to have negative economic welfare effects. However, an arrangement which allows individual producers to choose to fix retail prices, even if supported by a system of collective enforcement of those prices which are voluntarily fixed, cannot be condemned in principle on economic grounds. There should be no general prohibition and the criteria for assessment of each case should be consistent between all competition authorities.

Control over oligopoly

In teaching economics in business schools for over 30 years, the author has repeatedly found it necessary to emphasise that oligopoly is not just an intermediate stage between monopoly and competition. It is not possible to measure the effects of oligopoly on some kind of sliding scale where perfect competition would be zero and extreme monopoly (virtually undefinable in practice) 100. The consequences of domination of a market by a small number of major players necessitate a different kind of analysis from that applied to monopoly on the one hand and something approaching atomistic competition on the other.

The model of oligopoly was outlined in Chapter 2. The main feature of this model are interdependence between the major dominant firms and their recognition of this interdependence. This tends to result in periods of 'oligopolistic détente' punctuated by aggressive action (to secure first mover advantages) followed by defensive reaction. With a reasonably homogeneous product distinct from more distant substitutes (eg petrol, toothpaste, cigarettes or plate glass), aggregate demand is generally insensitive to price and to other marketing variables but the market share of each player is highly sensitive. Because price cuts can be followed fairly rapidly (and indeed must be), the aggressive action rarely takes this form.

A price war may be initiated if one player believes that one or more of its competitors cannot survive for long with low prices, but this requires the acquisition of an initial cost or resource advantage. Instead, competition tends to take the forms of heavy advertising, insubstantial changes in product design, multiple branding, free 'gifts' — a whole range of non-price incentives. Often such bouts of competition begin with a 'good marketing ploy', which competitors will need time to emulate.

Oligopoly also tends to encourage collusion. This is comparatively easy to organise between a few major players and also, because of the inelasticity of aggregate demand for the product, is profitable for all concerned. Such collusion may ultimately have little effect on aggregate welfare, for example if it results in a reduction in mutually offsetting advertising expenditures or wasteful and trivial changes in product design. When it applies to prices or to product quality (for example, electric lamp bulbs or vehicle tyres), its implications are more serious.

The conduct associated with oligopoly raises a number of different problems for competition policy:

1. One problem is that the forms of competition normally prevalent — heavy advertising and other promotional expenditure plus multiple branding — create barriers to entry of new firms, that is they sustain the oligopoly. Even though the strategies of individual firms may cancel each other out in the aggregate, so that market shares are relatively stable, they may succeed in differentiating existing brands from those of new entrants. Entry may require even heavier promotional expenditure plus lower prices (see Chapter 2 for fuller discussion, also Fishwick and Denison for extended analysis).

    This anti-competitive effect of non-price competition under oligopoly is difficult to deal with, because the conduct concerned may not be motivated by a desire to create entry barriers. These may be a side effect. In the case of *Household Detergents* in 1966, the UK MMC recommended that the two major companies, Unilever and Proctor and Gamble be ordered to reduce prices by 20 per cent and advertising expenditures by 40 per cent. It argued that advertising costs (about 30 per cent of turnover) were a significant barrier to market entry, but did not suggest that this was the main motive behind them.

    The entry-deterrent effects of heavy marketing expenditures under oligopoly may be exaggerated occasionally. The success of retailers' own-label products in the markets for many fast-moving consumer goods suggests that, except where the product concerned involves an element of risk or status symbolism, brands may be less important than once considered (see Fishwick and Denison with extensive bibliography). However, where these factors are present, this element of concern must remain.

2. The second problem for competition policy arising from conduct under oligopoly is the risk of 'X-inefficiency'. The entry barriers created by marketing expenses can leave the firms within the market in a state of cosy détente. Linda (1972; 1976), at that time a senior official in DGIV of the CEC, saw this as a major cause of concern to competition authorities. He directed attention particularly to the situation where a small number of equal firms pursue the same general strategies. 'The inequality of the firms and the diversity of their motives, their environment and their level of information' ... (*inter alia*) ... 'are the most powerful stimulants of competition' (Linda, 1972, p 328). It is, of course, true that this inertia and lack of competition would bring about the demise of the incumbent oligopolists if the market were contestable. In other words this danger depends partly on the existence of the barriers described under 1. However, particularly in a mature, static market (as many oligopolistic markets are), new entry may be deterred also by the limited rewards in prospect.

3. The third concern for competition authorities is that the forms of non-price competition characteristic of oligopoly are wasteful of resources. Aggregate demand for the product is increased only negligibly, prices are higher than they would be with price competition so that consumers' surplus is reduced but the potential profits of producers are dissipated in marketing expenditures. The only people to gain are those involved in advertising and promotional media. (There are obvious spin-offs in lower newspaper prices, the transmission of television broadcasts and so on, but these are not subject to direct testing by the market mechanism — should Mr Smith who does not watch commercial television pay for it when he buys household cleaning materials?)

Obviously, competition policy cannot become a vehicle to ensure that television is financed either by public levy, itself objectionable on economic efficiency grounds, or by pay-as-you-view reception, the economist's ideal if it were not so expensive to install. However, one might expect it to intervene where the distortion becomes excessive, as in the *Household Detergents* case in the UK in the 1960s and (to a lesser degree) in the *Cat and Dog Foods* case of 1977.

4. The final major consequence of oligopoly of concern to competition authorities is the likelihood of collusion, particularly with respect to prices or product quality. A great difficulty faced by the authorities is that collusive conduct may be indistinguishable in certain circumstances from what would have occurred under tacit détente of oligopoly — at times of excess capacity prices remain unchanged for long periods and rise in parallel when demand grows beyond existing supply.

The *Woodpulp* case, which was under consideration by the CEC and CJEC for nearly nine years, has already been quoted in this respect. Although there were over 30 suppliers of bleached sulphate pulp to EEC paper mills, there was a wide range of complementary types of pulp used in the composition ('furnish') of any single category of paper. For each specific type of pulp, the buyer had access to a relatively small number of suppliers, perhaps three or four. Technically sophisticated customers, within a market characterised by transparency and an informal information network, bought exclusively on price and quality. In this classic case of oligopoly, the behaviour of prices could be explained either by non-collusive oligopoly or by collusion. Without direct evidence of collusion it could not be deduced from the facts on prices alone.

From this list of possible concerns, it is clear that competition authorities may reasonably be expected to devote considerable attention to the consequences of oligopoly, particularly as this is the form of market structure most commonly found in practice.

We have seen in Chapter 4 that EEC policies have not been applied effectively to oligopoly problems and, in Chapter 5, that this is one of the reasons why the UK has decided not to bring its own policies on abuse of market power into line with those of the Community. It is also a cause of some dispute between the CEC and Germany, which has rigorous structural thresholds based on concern about oligopoly built into its own system of control over mergers. The CEC has refused all eight requests from Germany, submitted under Article 9 of the MCR, that its own competition authorities be allowed to consider and decide upon mergers which would create tight oligopolies within Germany.

In EEC law the main problem seems to be in the interpretation of the term 'dominant position' under Article 86. The Court of Justice (CJEC) has shown reluctance to accept the application of this concept to groups of companies not financially or otherwise structurally linked. Moreover, in the definition of a dominant position, the Court has tended to emphasise the gap between the market share of the leading firm and that of its nearest rival. Jenny (1990) describes how, despite an attempt in 1979 by the *Commission de la Concurrence* (roughly equivalent to the MMC in the UK) to apply the definition of a dominant position to a small group of independent firms indulging in parallel conduct, the interpretation of French law has tended towards that of the CJEC.

Because of the problem of distinguishing between the effects of tacit collusion ('concerted practice') and of non-collusive parallel conduct in an oligopolistic stalemate, Article 85 has proved inadequate to deal with price rigidity in a market dominated by a few producers of a homogeneous product. This leaves a gap in EEC competition policy — an inability to deal with what ought to be a subject of major attention.

The discussion of cases arising under the Merger Control Regulation has shown a tendency for the Commission (the CEC) to follow the definition of dominance preferred by the Court in Article 86 cases. In the *Varta/Bosch* and *Nestlé/Perrier* cases in particular, the decisions of the CEC showed a preference for a tight oligopoly of more equal competitors over a structure in which one company (or in the *Nestlé/Perrier* case two companies) would compete with a larger number of smaller competitors. This is inconsistent not only with German interpretation of dominance but also, as mentioned earlier, with the analysis of Linda and of Piesch and Schmidt who did background work on this subject for the Commission on this subject. The latter study recommended the use of the HH index as the main measure of concentration for EEC competition policy, as in the US (while admitting the possibility of dispute in the treatment of oligopoly).

Once again we have an unsatisfactory situation — policy inconsistencies between Member States and between Member States and the Community. The UK and Germany both have policies to deal specifically with problems arising from oligopoly, including both prevention of the development of joint dominance and remedies for its effects. France and the EEC have a different interpretation of 'dominant position' which means a gap in their competition policy. One multinational company might have to deal with two or more of these authorities.

In the author's view, this situation should not be resolved merely by each country deciding to retain its own statutory arrangements. For reasons set out earlier in this section, it seems reasonable to argue that the UK and Germany are correct in recognising the importance of the consequences of oligopoly for competition policy. But their producers and their consumers are also going to be affected by the policies of the EEC and, to a lesser extent, of other Member States. The differences could surely be resolved by reference exclusively to economic analysis of welfare effects and a common system of guidelines for application of individual cases developed. If, for some non-economic reason, national governments wished to bring in their own jurisdiction, these should at least be explicit and available for general reference.

In fact, one must suspect on this issue that the differences have arisen mainly through inadequate consideration of the factors involved. The CJEC in particular may not have been formally made aware of the arguments which suggest that oligopoly leads to many of the problems which ought to concern competition authorities.

The trade-off between market power and efficiency in the control of mergers

We have already considered this topic at some length at several stages of this book, particularly in Chapters 4 and 5 where the policies of the EEC and the UK were contrasted. The UK arrangements for merger control allow the MMC, which has a semi-judicial role in this system, to assess impact on public interest on a wide range of criteria, of which competition is only one. There is an explicit presumption that mergers are beneficial unless proved otherwise. This is very similar to the arrangements in France as modified in 1986. In Germany, the presumption is reversed: a merger which would create or strengthen a market-dominating position must be prohibited unless there are improvements in competitiveness which outweigh the disadvantages of market domination (Kantzenbach, 1990).

The essential point is that in all three Member States with established arrangements for control over mergers there is provision for trade-off between effects on competition on the one hand and other economic effects on the other. As an economist, the author would like to see other considerations confined to economic effects, but perhaps that is a little idealistic given the propensities of politicians and the vagaries of public opinion to which they respond.

The main economic considerations other than competition are *a)* possible economies of scale or scope and *b)* better prospects for research, development and innovation. In theory the net effects of these benefits combined with those of enhanced market power can be assessed by consideration of changes in consumers' and producers' surpluses in the short and long term.

When we turn to merger control policy at EEC level, as set out in the 1989 Regulation, we find that there is no scope for trade-off: if a merger creates or strengthens a dominant position it shall be prohibited, if not it shall be permitted. Quite simple and unequivocal; no 'efficiency defence' like that implicit in French, German and UK policies and in those of the US or Canada. And why not? Because the UK, despite the bias in its own policies towards mergers, pressed for the removal of the clauses providing for an efficiency defence from the draft of the MCR before it was approved in 1989.

As explained in Chapters 4 and 5, the main reason for this pressure (which was partly supported by Germany) was the desire to avoid the risk that the MCR could be used as an adjunct of industrial policy, of supporting European winners. For example, the MCR might have been used to prevent the acquisition of a European company by a US or Japanese firm, in order to assist a takeover of the same target company by another European enterprise. Given the history of the European Community, this fear is understandable but the rigidity of the Regulation is now excessive. Chapter 4 quoted instances where the CEC expressed misgivings about certain mergers which would lead to significant cost savings, on the grounds that these would enhance the competitive advantages of the firms concerned. Such logic is obviously unacceptable.

So what changes are needed? Once again the same company may be affected at different times by both national and EEC jurisdictions. Consistency is needed and common guidelines could be based again on the objective economic criteria of aggregate welfare, which would of necessity include assessment both of market power and of efficiency. The EEC Merger Control Regulation would need amendment to take account specifically of the efficiency criterion — the risk that this might be broadened to encompass wider non-economic objectives could be removed by explicit exclusion of these other considerations. Countries which did wish to add non-economic considerations to their own criteria could do so, but one would hope that these would be explicit and specific. Vague and all-embracing definitions (which allow authorities to include anything they wish) are not helpful to business.

Definition of abuse of market power

Although the categories may be hard to delineate precisely, most of the actions which have been condemned by UK or EEC competition authorities can be placed into one of three groups:

1. exploitation of power over a market to the detriment of customers (in the case of monopsony, suppliers) in that market;

2. exploitation of power over one market to secure a competitive advantage in another market;
3. exploitation of power over a market to ensure that this power is maintained or strengthened.

Of these, category 1 is the one most frequently presented and discussed in economic theory. In any elementary treatment of monopoly attention is focused upon exploitation of this kind. Most of the analytical approaches to definition and measurement of market power (or dominance) start from the ability of the monopoly firm to raise prices above the competitive level. These higher prices may result in higher profits or may be dissipated in higher costs because of lack of competitive pressure. Apart from price, one could list within category 1 such practices as limitation of product life, planned obsolescence or lack of product improvement and innovation.

Adverse effects of oligopoly are difficult to fit into this category because they do not necessarily result from intentional exploitation. It may be argued that disadvantages of oligopoly for consumers, particularly higher prices to finance duplicated and ineffective marketing expenditures, are a consequence of the structure itself and cannot be prevented by prohibition of abuse of dominance. This is another perspective on the topic discussed in the last sub-section.

In practice, relatively few cases of abuse of dominance considered by the CEC under Article 86 have fallen within category 1. The DTI Green Paper on Abuse of Market Power (DTI, 1992) presented this as one of the shortcomings of a prohibition system. (Somewhat remarkably this observation was given little emphasis in its conclusions and was not mentioned explicitly in the announcement of the decision not to move to this approach.) The DTI's explanation of the reason why there have been so few cases under Article 86 concerning excessive prices is supported by the author's own discussions with officials of DGIV of the Commission over the years:

> This partly reflects the difficulty of establishing in any particular case whether a supplier is earning a reasonable or unreasonable return. The problem of assessing whether profits and prices are excessive is not confined to a prohibition system. Nevertheless, it is likely to be more difficult to establish that a pricing practice is abusive, and therefore unlawful, than to find that such a practice is operating against the public interest and should be controlled for the future.
>
> (DTI, 1992, para.3 16)

An example of this problem is provided by industries characterised by high research and development costs. The price of a successful product may be required to cover research and development costs of those products which did not reach market launch or which failed to attract enough demand. How are profits to be assessed? If the competition authority finds that overall profits in the industry are not high but that research and development has been on an excessive scale, perhaps reflecting personal ambitions of senior management, is this a punishable offence under a prohibition system? It may be perfectly legitimate for an organisation like the MMC to recommend some limit on pricing or on length of patents to force the firm to change its policies in the public interest, but could the CEC legitimately impose fines retrospectively?

The only case under Article 86 where the Commission did impose fines for unjust pricing *per se*, and even here among a number of other 'abuses', was *United Brands* (1975). The point that prices may have been excessive was made in a number of other cases (eg *Hoffman-Laroche*, 1979) but this was not the central issue. This is surprising because the imposition of 'unfair purchase or selling prices' is the first particular form of abuse listed in Article 86 itself; the second 'limiting production, markets or technical development to the detriment of *consumers*' (our emphasis) would also fall within category 1. This concern with consumer welfare in Article 86 itself has not been reflected in the nature of cases arising from this Article of the Rome Treaty.

Category 2 in our tentative classification, exploitation of power over one market to secure a competitive advantage in another, covers many more EEC cases. Conduct which would fall within this category includes product-bundling, by which purchases of one product, in which a firm enjoys a degree of monopoly power, are tied to purchases of another complementary product for which it would otherwise face competition. An example is *Eurofix and Bauco v Hilti* (1987), where Hilti AG held a virtual monopoly of the supply of cartridges for its own nail guns, which also dominated sales of that particular appliance. By supplying nails with the cartridges, Hilti significantly reduced the opportunities for other nail producers to compete in selling nails for Hilti guns. Another example of conduct within this category is price discrimination used as a predatory device. A notable example is *AKZO v ECS* (1985), where the major EEC supplier of organic peroxides responded to an attempt by a relatively small UK competitor to extend its activities to Germany by selling at below-cost prices to flour mills in the UK, the main market of ECS. This amounted to exploitation of market power elsewhere to cross-subsidise predatory pricing in the particular UK segment. Another case of predatory pricing was *Tetrapak II* (1991). This producer of cartons for liquid foods had exploited a monopoly of the supply of aseptic cartons (used for UHT-treated 'long-life' liquids) to cross-subsidise entry into the gable-top carton, fresh liquid, segment.

This last case raises a difficult question. The Commission's report accepted that the aseptic carton market was declining as preferences turned towards fresh liquids (milk, fruit juices and so on), facilitated by wider ownership of domestic freezers. Did it not make simple commercial sense for Tetrapak to milk its 'cash cow' of aseptic cartons for as long as it could and to use the proceeds to extend in the expanding segment? There was, of course, a negative aspect to this strategy, in that pushing prices of aseptic cartons too high might accelerate their decline. Obviously, the fact that Tetrapak was able to cross-subsidise its activities in the gable-top segment from profits elsewhere put its competitors in the latter segment at a disadvantage, but was its strategy not legitimate? In this particular case, the Commission showed that the net effect, already obvious, would be dominance by Tetrapak of both segments and, on the grounds that prevention is better than cure, its decision is defensible. However, the issues are not clear-cut and judgement must depend partly on the degree of cross-subsidisation and its net effects.

The economic welfare approach implies that ultimate concern must be with the combined interests of all producers plus that of consumers (producers' plus consumers' surplus). Where exploitation of power in one market enables a company to gain or to maintain a dominant position in another, then this is to the disadvantage of consumers. Regrettably, some decisions under Article 86 and particularly the observations of the Court on these decisions appear to ignore this basic ultimate concern with aggregate welfare.

One example, admittedly from 20 years ago, is the *CSC v Zoja* case of 1972, already described in greater detail in Chapter 4. The world-monopoly producers of nitropropane had attempted in 1970 to acquire Zoja, a producer of an anti-tubercular drug (ethambutol) based on this chemical. Having failed, it established its own (new) manufacturing facility for the anti-tubercular drug and, first through a sharp increase in the price of nitropropane and then a denial of supplies, forced Zoja out of production.

In applying Article 86 to this case, the Commission demonstrated that CSC's monopoly in nitropropane gave it power over the ultimate consumer, the purchaser of the final derived product ethambutol (actually one of many derived products, but that is not significant here). This was because anti-tubercular drugs were used complementarily and ethambutol had no effective close substitute. This was consistent with economic theory. But what were the welfare consequences of the abuse? CSC wanted to integrate forward to the final product, and because Zoja resisted this it put Zoja out of business (as far as this product was concerned). The structure of supply of ethambutol was unaffected. As the US antitrust legal expert Eleanor Fox pointed out: '*Commercial Solvents* is a case of internal vertical integration. The decision to vertically integrate did not, as the Court said, eliminate a competitor, it substituted one competitor for another' (Fox p 401). As Fox stated, the CJEC did indeed uphold the Commission's decision that elimination of a competitor (a former customer) constituted an abuse of dominance, even though the consumer was unaffected, either directly by the abuse or any change in market structure.

The decision on *Hugin v Lipton* (1975), where a Swedish cash register company decided to take over the distribution and servicing of its own machines in the UK, raises similar issues. Again, as explained in Chapter 4, the CEC defined the existence of dominance in complete accordance with the three-stage analytical framework (existing substitutes, potential competition and downstream or wider competition). Criticism of its definition in some of the literature is, in the author's view unjustified. The definition of abuse is less satisfactory. Hugin's decision to distribute and service its own machines could be viewed quite credibly as a marketing strategy in a diminished and very competitive market — it had no appreciable effect on the structure of the servicing of Hugin machines in the UK as far as consumers were concerned. It was harsh on Liptons — but they had been warned by Hugin before becoming dependent on the Swedish supplier.

The *Eurofix and Bauco v Hilti* case is similar to *CSC v Zoja* and *Hugin v Lipton* in that the nature of the abuse was the same: exploitation of dominance in one market to force a competitor out of another. However, the net effect was different (and probably the objective). In neither of the two earlier cases was the ultimate consumer affected, whereas the tying of nails to the sale of cartridges guaranteed Hilti a dominant position in the supply of nails to the ultimate consumer.

We return in the final sub-section to the philosophy reflected in decisions of this kind, which appears to be directed towards the protection of small and medium-sized firms as an objective in itself. Before this, we should note that category 3 of the different kinds of abuse, set out at the beginning of this current discussion, has a built-in bias against larger firms. Use of market power to maintain or strengthen it can include specific actions by larger companies which would raise no objections if carried out by smaller competitors.

This last point is stated explicitly and unambiguously in the UK Office of Fair Trading's publicity material on Anti-Competitive Practices: 'The decision on whether a practice is anti-competitive thus rests on the position of a particular company within its market' (OFT, 1991, p 6). The practice is not condemned because of its nature but because of 'its effect of restricting distorting or preventing competition'. Among Article 86 cases which demonstrate this principle are *Hoffman-La Roche* (1976) and *Michelin Nederland* (1982) both of which related to fidelity rebates offered by dominant firms. This particular competitive weapon would be perfectly acceptable unless its effect were to create a barrier to entry to new entrants. Note that prohibition as an abuse of dominance can cover actions which are perfectly legal in other senses — in *Tetrapak I* the defendant was found guilty of abuse by legally obtaining an exclusive licence for liquid packaging machinery. In the UK, the DGFT referred to the MMC for consideration as an anti-competitive practice Ford's enforcement through the courts of its copyright on car panel designs.

The decision which stretches the interpretation of abuse of dominance to the limits of credibility is that of the CEC with regard to *Continental Can* (1972). Though this was rejected by the CJEC in 1973, the Court's objection related purely to market definition; the definition of abuse was accepted. In this case, the US company was accused of abuse of dominance by acquiring a majority shareholding of another European packaging company, with the approval of the acquired company. The logic of the Commission's argument was very strange. In order to condemn a takeover by the US company of a near-monopoly supplier in Belgium and Holland, it had to prove that the US company's German subsidiary had a dominant position in Germany! The merger was not a consequence of any dominance of Germany; since the Commission (mistakenly in the view of the Court) defined a distinct German market, it did not create or strengthen dominance in any one market. The logic seems to have been that Continental Can had become big enough in Europe and, having got a monopoly in Germany, it should not also be allowed to take over an existing monopoly in the Benelux countries.

With the introduction of the Merger Control Regulation, we are assured that there will be no more cases like *Continental Can* under Article 86. The decision in that case leads to apprehension, expressed by George and Jacquemin that the Court (in particular) would regard as an abuse of dominance any action by a dominant firm which enhanced its competitive advantage — even actions which improved its efficiency. Fortunately the Commission has not interpreted the concept in this way and, it is to be hoped, never will.

Protection of competition or of competitors

In the previous sub-section we have seen that the EEC authorities have in a number of cases regarded as abuse of dominance any action by a large firm with market power which puts a smaller firm out of a particular line of business. This view has extended to cases where the consequences for the ultimate consumer were negligible, because the smaller company had previously been dominant in the specific segment from which it was displaced. In *Hugin v Lipton* and *CSC v Zoja,* forward vertical integration by the larger companies led to the replacement of the 'victim' company with no change in the structure of supply in its specific market segment. We have also described the tendency for the Commission and, to an even greater extent, the Court to define as abuse of dominance any action by a dominant firm which strengthens or maintains its market position. Both of these attitudes reflect a bias noted by several observers of EEC competition policy (Jacquemin and de Jong, Korah, George and Jacquemin) towards its use to protect small firms against big. Unless the damage inflicted by predatory action ultimately affects the welfare of consumers, a transfer of producers' surplus from small firms to large ones has no immediate aggregate welfare effects.

It may be argued that in the longer term the maintenance of a more fragmented structure of business will ensure that market power never becomes concentrated and that society will never become dominated by giant undertakings with fingers in every pie. There is however a counter to this argument about long-term dynamics. A presumption that companies with market power should not be allowed to increase or even defend it runs the risk of removing the incentive to compete in the first place, which is to win against the competition. It is equivalent to insisting that a football team which secures a good lead in a match should not try to score any more goals, or even use the security of its lead to pack its defence to prevent the opposition from scoring. If the rules of the game were like this, would it be worth scoring in the first place?

Some of the more bizarre interpretations of Article 86 could be avoided if there were explicit recognition that the ultimate criterion for the application of competition policy should be aggregate economic welfare. This seems, after all, to have been in the minds of the original authors of Article 86, whose first two categories of 'particular' abuse were both explicitly directed at consumers. The authorities may believe, in a specific case, that aggregate public interest (and not just that of a victim company) would gain from the protection of a small company, even though immediate effects on market structure are insignificant. If so, they should make this explicit.

The *Ford Motor Company* case described in some detail in Chapter 5 showed how abuse of dominance might be assessed in purely economic terms. The MMC verified that Ford could not exploit a dominant position to the significant disadvantage of the ultimate consumer by charging high prices for replacement body panels for cars in current production, because this would be reflected in insurance costs or heavy repair costs to fleet owners. Since these costs were a significant proportion of the total expense of car ownership, high panel prices would reduce sales of Ford cars. Ford's insistence on copyright prevented other metal-stamping companies from competing in this specific market but, because of wider competition, this did not imply any net aggregate welfare loss — Ford's gain offset the opportunities denied to its would-be competitors and the consumer was unaffected.

It is rather strange that the Community institutions should have acquired a bias towards care for small and medium-sized firms; part of the philosophy behind the original common market concept was based on a desire for economies of scale — for European Titans. In objective economic terms a more neutral stance is desirable.

CONCLUSIONS

Those who have read this chapter from the beginning will anticipate the first two conclusions to be drawn from this examination of five major issues and the third follows fairly obviously from them.

The first conclusion is that, unless there are special factors which need to be made explicit, competition policies should be guided exclusively by considerations of aggregate welfare. This principle will ensure consistency and help business by introducing more predictability into the application of the policy.

The second conclusion is that guidelines based on this principle need to be used by all institutions concerned — the OFT, DTI and MMC in the UK and the CEC and CJEC in the European Community. These should be published and decisions should be explained with reference to them. This does not mean that special factors outside the guidelines could not be considered — politicians would never surrender the discretion given to them by the use of the word 'normally'. It simply means that those factors must be identified and their exceptional influence explained.

Finally and perhaps most controversially, inconsistencies between national and Community policies need to be removed. It is bad enough for business managers to be faced with two jurisdictions; it is intolerable that these should apply different principles. Unfortunately, the problem cannot be resolved by agreement on the part of all Member States to apply policies identical to those of the EEC, because (as we have seen in the comparison with UK policies) some of the EEC policies are subject to widespread and considered criticism. The following outcome appears most reasonable on economic grounds and will, in the author's view, ultimately become established throughout the Community:

1. For restrictive agreements, a prohibition system on lines of Article 85 is generally regarded as acceptable. Transparency and consistency in the application of policy might be increased by more explicit reference to the combined market power of the parties to any agreement or concerted practice, because without such power the adverse effects of an agreement cannot be substantial.

2. The prohibition of abuse of dominance, apart from being explicitly defined in terms of aggregate welfare, needs to be supplemented by other policies to deal with the effects of particular market structures. Such measures would provide for regulation of conduct, not just retrospective punishment, and also for imposed fragmentation of monopoly power through divestment. The need for such policies to deal with the effects of oligopoly, not easily defined as 'abuse of dominance', is paramount. German competition law includes most of these provisions; Option 3 of the DTI's alternative proposals for the UK (now abandoned) went along these lines. This means more powers for the Commission of the EC and may be resisted for this reason, but it is hard to dispute the existence of policy gaps at present.

3. The EEC's Merger Control Regulation contrasts with those of Member States in allowing no consideration of trade-off between enhancement of market power and increased efficiency. The exclusive application of the market power criterion is indefensible in terms of economic theory (the aggregate welfare approach) and is inconsistent with the fundamental objectives of the common market. It is the result of a contorted political power game (described in Chapter 4). In the long run common sense must prevail and the criteria for assessment must be modified. Let us hope that this is done explicitly, rather than by finding a way round the existing criteria, which would add further confusion.

The title of this book *Making Sense of Competition Policy* could be interpreted in two ways. The main objective has been to explain the economic arguments underlying competition policies and the ways in which these are reflected in their design and application. A second interpretation is that certain aspects of competition policy do not currently make sense. The proposals summarised here would do much to remedy this deficiency.

APPENDIX

Tables of Cases

EEC CASES UNDER ARTICLES 85 OR 86

Case	Commission decision (Official journal – publication)		Court of Justice judgement (ECR – page)	
AKZO v ECS	1985	L374	–	
Commercial Solvents v Zoja	*1972	L299	*1974	223
Continental Can	*1972	L7	*1973	215
Eurofix and Bauco v Hilti	1988	L65	pending	
Grundig-Consten	*1964	2545	*1969	1
Hoffman-Laroche	1976	L223	1979	461
Hugin v Lipton	1978	L22	1979	1869
Italian Flat Glass	1989	L33	–	
Michelin Nederland	1982	L353	–	
Philip Morris	–		1980	2671
Publishers Association	1989	L22	1992	1059
Tetrapak I	1988	L272	–	
Tetrapak II	1992	L72	–	
VBBB and VBVB	1982	L54	1984	19
Woodpulp	1984	L85	(Report awaited)	

*Not available in English, references are to French version

197

EEC MERGER REPORTS

	Commission case number and official journal publication		
AT & T/NCR	50	1991	L16
Aerospatiale/Alenia/de Havilland	53	1991	L334
Alcatel/AEG Kabel	42	1992	L6
Dräger/IBM/Hmp	101	1991	L236
Delta/Pan Am	130	1991	L289
Dresser/Ingersoll Rand	121	1992	L86
Fiat/Ford New Holland	9	1991	L118
Nestlé/Perrier	190	1992	L356
Northern Telcom/Matra	249	1992	L240
Renault/Volvo	4	1990	L281
Varta/Bosch	12	1991	L320

CASES REPORTED BY UK MMC

Title (as used in text)	Publication		
Beer	1989	Cm	651
British Rail-Hoverlloyd (merger)	1981	HC	374
Car parts	1982	HC	318
Cat and dog foods	1977	HC	447
Chlordiazepoxide and Diazepam	1973	HC	197
Collective discrimination	1955	Cmnd	9504
Contraceptive sheaths	1982	Cmnd	8689
Credit card services	1989	Cm	718
Domestic gas appliances	1980	HC	703
Ford Motor Company	1985	Cmnd	9437
Household detergents	1966	HC	105
Matches	1953	HC	161
Opium derivatives	1989	Cm	630
Tampons	1986	Cmnd	9705
UniChem	1989	Cm	691
White salt	1986	Cmnd	9778

FRANCE

Super-centrales d'achat (Hypermarket pool purchases)	Commission de la Concurrence Rapport Annuel 1985, Annexe 1.

Bibliography

Adams, W and Brock, J W (1991) *Antitrust Economics on Trial*, Princeton University Press

Adelman, M A (1961) 'The Measurement of Industrial Concentration', *Review of Economics and Statistics*

Allan, W and Curwen, P (1991) *Competition and Choice in the Publishing Industry* (Hobart Paper), Institute of Economic Affairs, London

Bain, J S (1956) *Barriers to New Competition*, Harvard University Press, Cambridge, Mass

Baker, J B and Bresnahan, T F (1992) 'Empirical methods of identifying and measuring market power', *Antitrust Law Journal*, Vol 61

Barrie, Sir G (1989) 'Merger Policy Concern', in Fairburn, J A and Kay, J A (eds) *Mergers and Merger Policy*, Oxford University Press, Oxford

Baumol, W J (1982) 'Contestable Markets: An Uprising in the Theory of Industry Structure' *American Economic Review*, Vol 72,

Brennan, T J (1982) 'Mistaken Elasticities and Mistaken Rules', *Harvard Law Review*, Vol 95,

Cairncross, A *et al.* (1974) *Economic Policy for the European Community*, Macmillan, London

Calvani, T and Langenfeld, J (1985) 'An Overview of the Current Debate on Resale Price Maintenance', *Contemporary Policy Issues*, Vol III, Spring

Cockram, R and Fishwick, F (1991) *Parallel pricing in the supply of bleached sulphate woodpulp to the European Community — concertation or competition?* submitted to Court of Justice of the EC, Registry of CJEC, Luxembourg

Comanor, W S and Kirkwood, J B (1985) 'Resale Price Maintenance and Anti-trust Policy', *Contemporary Policy Issues*, Vol III, Spring

Comanor, W S (1990) 'United States Antitrust Policy: Issues and Institutions', in *Competition Policy in Europe and North America: Economic Issues and Institutions*, Harwood Academic Publishers, Chur

Demsetz, H (1982) 'Barriers to Entry', *American Economic Review*, March

Bibliography

DTI (Department of Trade and Industry) (1988) *Review of Restrictive Trade Practices Policy — a consultative document*, Cmd 331, HMSO, London

DTI (Department of Trade and Industry) (1988) *Mergers Policy*, HMSO, London

DTI (Department of Trade and Industry) (1989) *Opening Markets: New Policy on Restrictive Practices*, Cmd 727, HMSO, London

DTI (Department of Trade and Industry) (1992) *Abuse of Market Power*, Cmd 2100, HMSO, London

Ecalle, F (1988) Une évaluation de la loi du 10 août 1981 relative au prix du livre, *Economie et Prévision*, May

Fairburn, J A (1989) 'The Evolution of Merger Policy in Britain' in Fairburn, J A and Kay, J A (eds), *Mergers and Merger Policy*, Oxford University Press, Oxford

Fisher, FM (1987) Horizontal Mergers: Triage and Treatment, *Economic Perspectives*, Vol 1, no 2, Fall

Fishwick, F (1977) *A Study of the Evolution of Concentration in the Manufacture and Supply of Tyres, Sparking Plugs and Motor-Vehicle Accumulators for the United Kingdom*, CEC, Brussels

Fishwick, F (1979) *Research into Industrial Concentration in Europe*, PhD Thesis Cranfield Institute of Technology

Fishwick, F (1982) *Multinational Companies and Economic Concentration in Europe*, Gower Press, Aldershot

Fishwick, F and Preston, D (1982) *Book Publishing and Distribution*, Commission of the European Communities, Brussels

Fishwick, F (1985) *Book Prices in Australia and North America*, CEC, Luxembourg

Fishwick, F (1986) *Definition of the Relevant Market in Community Competition Policy*, CEC, Brussels

Fishwick, F (1988) 'Control of Mergers: a necessary role for the European Commission', *European Management Journal*

Fishwick, F (1989a) 'Definition of monopoly power in the antitrust policies of the United Kingdom and the European Community', *The Antitrust Bulletin*, Fall

Fishwick, F (1989b) *The Implications of the Net Book Agreement*, Booksellers Association and Publishers Association, London

Fishwick, F and Denison, T (1992) *The geographical dimension of competition in the European single market*, Commission of the European Communities, Luxembourg

Fishwick, F (1993) 'Definition of the Relevant Market in the Competition Policy of the European Economic Community', in *Revue d'Economie Industrielle*, No 63(1), Paris

Fox, E M (1983) *Abuse of a Dominant Position under the Treaty of Rome — A Comparison with US Law*, Annual Proceedings of the Fordham Corporate Law Institute

Frazer, T (1992) *Monopoly, competition and the law*, Harvester Wheatsheaf, Hemel Hempstead

Galbraith, J K (1957) *American Capitalism*, Hamish Hamilton, London, (reprinted Penguin Books, Harmondsworth, 1973)

George, K D (1985) 'Monopoly and Merger Policy', *Fiscal Studies*, February

George, K (1990) 'UK Competition Policy: Issues and Institutions', in *Competition Policy in Europe and North America: Economic Issues and Institutions*, Harwood Academic Publishers, Chur

George, K and Jacquemin, A (1990) 'Competition Policy in the European Community', in *Competition Policy in Europe and North America: Economic Issues and Institutions*, Harwood Academic Publishers, Chur

Geroski, P A and Schwalbach, J (1989) *Barriers to entry and intensity of competition in European Markets*, CEC, Luxembourg

Glais, M and Laurent, P (1983) *Traité d'Economie et de Droit de la Concurrence*, PUF, Paris

Glais, M (1989) 'Etat de dépendance économique ...', in *Gazette du Palais*, 14–15 June

Glais, M (1992) 'L'application du règlement communautaire relatif au contrôle de la concentration', *Revue d'Economie Industrielle*, No 60

Gyselen, L (1992) 'Le règlement du Conseil des Communautés Européennes relatif au contrôle des opérations de concentration entre entreprises', *Revue Trimestrielle de Droit Commerciale*, 45 (1), janv–mars

Hay, G (1985) 'Competition Policy', *Oxford Review of Economic Policy*, Autumn

Hayek, F A (1945) *The Use of Knowledge in Society*, American Economic Review, 35

Hoet, P (1989) 'Domination du marché ou théorie du partenaire obligatoire', *Revue du Marché Commun*, mars

Holley, D (1977) 'The Concept of Undertakings(s) in Dominant Position and the Systems of Control in US Law', in *La régulation du monopole en droit communautaire*, College of Europe, Templehof, Bruges

Bibliography

Hölzler, H (1990) Merger Control, in Montagnon, P (ed), *European Competition Policy*, Pinter Publishers, London

Horowitz, I (1987) 'Market Definition in Antitrust Analysis: A Regression Based Approach', *Southern Economic Journal*, July

Horspool, M and Korah, M (1992) Competition, *Antitrust Bulletin*, Summer

Hoyer, W D (1984) 'An Examination of Consumer Decision Making for a Common Repeat Purchase Product', *Journal of Consumer Research*, Vol II, December

Jacobs, D M and Stewart-Clark, J (1991) *Competition Law in the European Community*, Kogan Page, London

Jacquemin, A P and de Jong, H W (1977) *European Industrial Organisation*, Macmillan Press

Jacquemin, A (1991) 'Stratégies d'Enterprise et Politique de la Concurrence dans Le Marché Unique', *Revue d'Economie Industrielle*, No 3

Jenny, F (1990) 'French Competition Policy in Perspective', in *Competition Policy in Europe and North America: Economic Issues and Institutions*, Harwood Academic Publishers, Chur

Kantzenbach, E (1990) 'Competition Policy in West Germany: a Comparison with the Antitrust Policy of the United States', in *Competition Policy in Europe and North America: Economic Issues and Institutions*, Harwood Academic Publishers, Chur

Kaplov, L (1982) 'The accurancy of traditional market power analysis and a direct adjustment alternative', *Harvard Law Review*, Vol 95

Kirzner, I (1973) *Competition and Entrepreneurship*, University of Chicago Press, Chicago

Knickerbocker, F T (1973) *Oligopolistic Reaction and Multinational Enterprise*, Harvard Business School

Korah (1986) 'EEC Competition Policy — Legal Form or Economic Efficiency', Current Legal Problems, Vol 39

Koutsoyiannis, A (1979) *Modern Microeconomics*, Macmillan, London

Landes, W M and Posner, R (1981) 'Market Power in Antitrust Cases', *Harvard Law Review*, Vol 94, March

Leibenstein, H (1966) 'Allocative efficiency versus X-efficiency', *American Economic Review*, No 56

Lerner, A P (1934) *The Concept of Monopoly and the Measurement of Monopoly Power*, Review of Economics and Statistics

Linda, R (1972) 'Concurrence oligopolistique et planification concurrentielle internationale', *Economie Appliquée*

Linda, R (1976) *Methodology of Concentration Analysis Applied to the Study of Industries and Markets*, Commission of the European Communities, Brussels

Marvel, H P and McCafferty, S (1985) The Welfare Effects of Resale Price Maintenance, *Journal of Law and Economics*, Vol 28 (2)

Marvel, H P and McCafferty, S (1986) The Political Economy of Resale Price Maintenance, *Journal of Political Economy*, Vol 94 (5)

McWilliam, G (1992) 'Consumer Involvement in Brands and Product Categories', in Baker, M J (ed), *Perspectives on Marketing Management*, Vol 2

Merkin, R and Williams, K (1984) *Competition Law: Antitrust Policy in the UK and the EEC*, Sweet and Maxwell, London

Miller, J P (1955) 'Measurement of Monopoly Power and Concentration', in *Business Concentration and Price Policy*, National Bureau of Economic Research, Washington DC

Monopolkommission (BRD) (1983) Die Sächliche Abgrenzung des relevanter Marktes, Kapitel VII von *Ökonomische Kriterien für die Rechtsanwendung*, Hauptgutachten 1982–3, Nomos Verlagsg

Needham, D (1969) *Economic Analysis and Industrial Structure*, Holt, Rinehart and Winston, Inc

Neven, D, Nuttall, R and Seabright, P (1993) *Merger in Daylight: the economics and politics of European merger control*, Centre for Economic Policy Research, London

OFT (Office of Fair Trading) (1991) *An Outline of UK Competition Policy*, OFT, London

Ordover, J A and Willing, R D (1983) 'DOJ Merger Guidelines: An Economic Assessment', *California Law Review*

Ordover, J A (1990) 'Economic Foundations of Competition Policy', in *Competition Policy in Europe and North America: Economic Issues and Institutions*, Harwood Academic Publishers, Chur

Overbury, C (1992) 'First experiences of European Merger Control', *Competition Checklist*, June , p 79

Phlips, L (1987) 'Information and Collusion', in Hay, D and Vickers, J (eds), *The Economics of Market Dominance*, Blackwell, Oxford

Pickering, J B (1974) *Industrial Structure and Market Conduct*, Martin Robertson, Oxford

Piesch, W and Schmidt, I (1983) *The suitability of concentration measures for*

Bibliography

EEC competition policies, Commission of the European Communities, Luxembourg

Pitofsky, R (1990) 'New Definitions of Relevant Market and the Assault on Antitrust', *Columbia Law Review*, November

Qualls, D (1972) 'Concentration, Barriers to Entry and Long-Run Economic Profit Margins', *Journal of Industrial Economics*

Ridyard, D, Bishop, S and Klass, M (1992) *Market Definition in UK Competition Policy*, OFT, London

Robinson, J (1969) *Economics of Imperfect Competition*, Macmillan (includes comparisons with 1933 edition and with a 1953 comment)

Rothschild, K (1947) 'Price Theory and Oligopoly', *Economic Journal*

Salop, S C (1986) 'Measuring ease of entry', *The Antitrust Bulletin*, Summer

Scheffman, D T and Spiller, P T (1987) 'Geographic Market Definition under US Department of Justice Merger Guidelines', *Journal of Law and Economics*

Schmalensee, R (1982) 'Another look at market power', *Harvard Law Review*

Schmalensee, R (1987a) Standards for Dominant Firm Conduct: What can Economics Contribute? in Hay, D and Vickers, J (eds), *The Economics of Market Dominance*, Blackwell, Oxford

Schmalensee, R (1987b) 'Horizontal Merger Policy: Problems and Changes', *Economic Perspectives*, Fall

Schumpeter, J (1947) *Capitalism, Socialism and Democracy*, Allen and Unwin

Schwartz, M (1986) 'The Nature and Scope of Contestability Theory', *Oxford Economic Papers*, Supplement 38

Stigler, G J and Sherwin, R A (1985) 'The Extent of the Market', *Journal of Law and Economics*, October

Telser, L G (1960) 'Why should manufacturers want fair trade?' *Journal of Law and Economics*

Triffin, R (1940) *Monopolistic Competition and General Equilibrium Theory*, Harvard University Press

US Department of Justice and Federal Trade Commission (1992) *Horizontal Merger Guidelines*, DOJ, Washington

Venit, J (1990–1) 'Evaluation of concentrations under the Merger Control Regulation: the Nature of the Beast', *Fordham International Law Journal*

Vickers, J and Hay, D (1987) 'The Economics of Market Dominance', in Hay, D and Vickers, J (eds), *The Economics of Market Dominance*, Blackwell, Oxford

Vogel, L (1990) *Droit de la concurrence et concentration économique*, Economica, Paris

Waelbroek, M (1977) 'Rapport Général: La notion d'entreprise(s) en position dominante et les méthodes de contrôle en droit comparé', *La réglementation du monopole en droit communautaire*, Collège d'Europe, Templehof, Bruges

Index

acquisitions, 115–16, 169
advertising, 44–6, 51, 53
Aerospatiale-Alenia/De Haviland
(EEC report), 126, 198
airlines, as example of market
contestability, 41
AKZO v ECS (EEC case), 189, 197
asset test, 165
atomistic competition, *see* perfect
competition

beer, and vertical agreements under
Article 85, 101
books, resale price maintenance, 95,
100–1, 149, 176, 177–81
brands, *inter-* and *intra-*brand
competition, 57, 102, 148,
176–7, 181
Brittan, Sir Leon, 117, 120–1

cartels, and market sharing, 96
Cellophane fallacy, 69, 71, 72, 80
Channel Tunnel, and sunk costs, 44
Chicago School, view, 20
coefficients, use of, 84, 87
collective dominance, and oligopoly,
112–14
collusion, 51, 184
collusive détente, 81
Commercial Solvents Corporation
(CJEC case), 108–10, 190–1,
197
competition policy, 11, 15, 27–62
criticism of, 19–21, 23–4
European Economic Community,
13, 87, 92–135
function and purpose, 12, 63–4, 175

and interventionist policies, 21–4
and liberalism, 24–6
market contestability, 40–7
perfect competition and
monopoly, 28–40
problems of oligopoly, 182–4
and promotion of aggregate
welfare, 194
role in market economy, 15–19
United Kingdom, and economic
market concept, 77
competition, potential, 77, 78–83,
89–90
concentration, 20, 59, 60
concentration indices, 83–8
conglomerate mergers, irrelevance,
60–1
consumers, interests, 25, 107
contestability theory, 20–1, 41–7
see also market contestability
Continental Can (CJEC case), 106,
107, 115, 192, 197
costs, implications of competition,
17–18
cross-entry, in critique of
contestability theory, 43
customers' dependence, as CJEC
criterion, 65

deadweight losses, 17, 30, 36–7
demand, elasticity, 31, 70–1, 73–4
demand curve, kinked, 47–52
demand-substitution, 69–71, 78–9
distribution, and vertical agreements,
56–8
dominance, 17, 21, 28–9, 64–78, 99,
193–4

abuse of, 187–8, 195
  United Kingdom, 150–8
assessment, 12–13, 63–4, 88–91,
      108, 111
  and EEC, 130–1, 162, 184–5
  strategies for and against, 18
dominant position
  abuse, 103–14
  defence, 42–3
  European Commission definition,
      59
  interpretation, and Merger Control
      Regulation, 127–35
  United Kingdom government
      paper, 60
duopoly, and *Nestlé/Perrier*, 133–4

economic principles, of competition
      policy, 12, 27–62
economies of scale, 37–8, 45
entry barriers, 41, 42–3, 45, 46, 182–3
Eurofix & Bauco v Hilti, see Hilti case
European Coal and Steel Community,
      92
European Commission
  and books, 100, 179
  decisions
    AKZO v ECS, 189, 197
    Italian Flat Glass, 113, 197
    Michelin Nederland, 106, 107,
        192, 197
    Tetrapak II, and price
        discrimination, 189–90, 197
  Directorate General for
      Competition (DG IV)
  analytical framework, 88–91
  and concentration, 87
  criteria and evaluation, 66, 75,
      77–8, 89–90
  and dominance, 64, 90–1, 105,
      108, 113
  evaluation of concentration
      indices, 87
  interpretation of Article 86, 104
  and market definition, 77

reports
    *Aerospatiale-Alenia/De
        Haviland*, 126, 198
    Nestlé/Perrier, 133–4, 185
    Varta/Bosch, 132–3, 185
Merger Control Regulation, 115–27,
      129–30, 134–5, 186–7, 195
  and Article 86 of Treaty of Rome,
      76, 127–8
  compared with United Kingdom
      policy, 170–4
  criteria, 119–21, 129
  decision process, 125–6
  implications, 192
  interpretation, 127–35
  openness following
      investigations, 170–1
  prohibited agreements, 13
  and reference to national
      authorities, 121–3
  statistics, 126, 129
  thresholds and ambit, 117–19
  time limits, 123, 124–5
  and United Kingdom, 137, 164,
      172–4
Report on Competition Policy
      (1988), 93
European Economic Community
  and books, 177–80
  competition policy, 13, 24, 87,
      92–135, 171–2, 194–5
  compared with United Kingdom,
      14, 107, 136–74
  competing philosophies, 92–3
Court of Justice (CJEC)
  cases, 110–12, 191, 197
    *Commercial Solvents
        Corporation*, 108–10, 190–91
    Continental Can, 115, 192
    Hilti case, 111–12, 189, 191,
        197
    Hoffmann-Laroche, 75, 192,
        197
    Hugin v Lipton, 110–11, 191,
        197

Philip Morris, 115
Publishers Association, 95,
    101, 197
*Stergios Delmitis v Henniger
    Bräu*, 101
VBBB/VBVB, 95, 100–1, 197
Woodpulp, 96, 113, 184
    and price determination, 33,
        51, 197
criteria for identifying
    dominance, 75
and dominance, 64, 65, 105–7,
    108
interpretation of Article 86, 104
and oligopoly, 112–14, 186
law, exemptions regarding vertical
    restrictions, 58
Merger Reports listed, 198
and mergers, 186–7, 195
and oligopoly, 184, 185–6
Treaty of Rome, 23, 92, 115
    Article 85, 112–14, 197
        enforcement, 96–7
        future prospects, 195
        and Merger Control
            Regulation, 118
        Paragraph 3, effects, 97–8
        prohibited agreements, 13
        restrictive agreements, 75,
            94–9, 100–3
        and United Kingdom
            legislative proposals, 136,
            148
    Article 86, 103–14, 193–4, 197
        analytical framework, 88
        and dominance, 64, 74
        inflexibility/suggested
            modifications, 160
        and Merger Control
            Regulation, 76, 118, 127–8
        and oligopoly, 184–5
        prohibited agreements, 13
        remedies, 162
        scope for extended powers,
            107

shortcomings, 114, 115, 188
United Brands, 189
and United Kingdom
    legislation, 159–63
United Kingdom response to,
    136
Article 92, prohibition of state
    aids, 93–4
exclusivity, and Article 85 of Treaty of
    Rome, 75, 76
expenditures, wasteful, and
    oligopoly, 54–5

four-firm concentration ratios, 84, 85,
    86
France, 74, 108, 123–4, 186–7
    competition law, 25–6
    and oligopoly, 185

games theory, and oligopoly, 54
gateways, use in United Kingdom
    legislation, 58
geography, 70, 75–6, 79, 81, 89, 129
Germany, 121–3, 186–7
    competition law, 25
    and oligopoly, 134–5, 184, 185
Gini coefficient, 84, 87

Herfindahl-Herschman index, 80,
    85–7, 88, 131–2, 185
    Nestlé/Perrier, 134
    Varta/Bosch, 133
Hilti case (CJEC case), 111–12, 189,
    191, 197
Hoffmann-Laroche (CJEC case), 75,
    192, 197
horizontal agreements, 56
horizontal mergers, 61
Hugin v Lipton (CJEC case), 110–11,
    191, 197

imports, restrictions on, 102
industries, restructuring, and Article
    85(3), 99

insurance industry, and dominance, clearance, 131
interchangeability, functional or reactive, 69–70
interventionist policies, and competition policy, 21–4
Italian Flat Glass (EEC case), 113, 197

Japan, and Merger Control Regulation, 118

laissez-faire economics, new, 19–21
Landes-Posner formula, 78, 79–80, 88
Lerner index, 66–7, 72, 80
liberalism, and competition policy, 24–6

marginal revenue, and profit maximisation, 36
market, structure, analysis, 89
market concentration, indices, 83–8
market contestability, 28, 40–7, 90
contestability theory, 20–1, 41–7
market definition, 76–7, 78–83
market economy, role of competition policy, 15–19
market foreclosure, 101
market power, *see* dominance
market, relevant, question of, 63
market share, 81–3, 129, 154
measures of, 74, 78–9, 84
market sharing, and cartels, 96
Merger Control Regulation, *see* European Commission
mergers, 115–16
and abuse of power, 60–1
changing United Kingdom view, 142
control of, trade-off beween market power and efficiency, 186–7, 195
and separate treatment of actual/potential competition, 82–3
United Kingdom policy, 163–74

Michelin Nederland (EEC case), 106, 107, 192, 197
Miller, JB, quoted, 74
Minor Importance, Notice on Agreements of, 98
monopoly, 14, 28–40, 58–60, 68–9, 151
and costs, 17
defined, 27, 76–7
and market share, 74
and pricing, 34, 38
in United States, 65
monopsony, 16, 68
subsumed by monopoly, 151
motor industry, 75, 130–1

Nestlé/Perrier (EEC report), 133–4, 185, 198

oligopoly, 17, 47–55, 85, 87, 181–6
advantages of United Kingdom law, 160
defined, 28
and dominance, 112–14, 188
and Merger Control Regulation, 131–5
oligopsony, subsumed by oligopoly, 151
overseas investment, and oligopoly, 53

parallel pricing, *Woodpulp*, 113
patent licensing, 75, 76
penalties, difference in emphasis between EEC and United Kingdom, 137
perfect competition, 28–47
perfect competition model, 27
Philip Morris (CJEC case), 115
policy enforcement, 83
press, bias against mergers, 166
price
determination, 29–35
discrimination, and *AKZO v ECS/Tetrapak II*, 189–90

elasticity, 31, 72–4, 78–80
stability, 50
value for money in use of
    resources, 15–16
pricing, and perfect
    competition/monopoly, 34,
    38
product bundling, and *Hilti* case, 68,
    189
product differentiation, as barrier to
    entry, 44–6
product innovation, and wasteful
    expenditure, 54
profit maximisation, and marginal
    revenue, 36
profits, as indication of market
    power, 67–8
public interest, 157–8, 169
    and Tebbitt doctrine, 168
Publishers Association (CJEC case),
    95, 101, 197

quality assurance, avoidance of
    verticial agreements, 58

railways, 52
recession, industrial restructuring and
    Article 85(3), 99
remedies, shortcomings of Article 86,
    114
resale price maintenance, 141–2,
    176–81
research, effect of perfect
    competition, 39
research and development
    and Article 85 of Treaty of Rome,
        75, 76
    and profits, 188–9
restraints of competition, freedom
    from, as CJEC criterion, 65
restrictive practices agreements, 94–9
Robinson, Joan, and market
    definition, 76–7

services, inclusion in United

Kingdom legislation, 142,
    144
Single European Market, 116, 128,
    130–1
'specialisation', and Article 85 of
    Treaty of Rome, 75, 76
statistics, 83–8
Stergios Delmitis v Henniger Bräu
    (CJEC case), 101
Stigler-Sherwin test, 70–1, 72
substitute products, availability, 89
sunk costs, 17, 41–2, 43–4, 90
supply-substitution, 71–2, 78–9, 81–3,
    155–6

Tebbit Doctrine, 168
technical support, avoidance of
    vertical agreements, 58
Tetrapak II (EEC case), and price
    discrimination, 189–90, 197
time, 81
trading partners, question of
    dominance over, 108
tyres, product improvement in
    oligopoly, 54

unemployment, question of, 22–3
United Brands (EEC case), and unjust
    pricing, 189
United Kingdom
    and books, resale price
        maintenance in EEC, 177–80
    City Code on Takeovers and
        Mergers, 166
    competition policy, 77, 88
        background, 137, 138–44
        and EEC, 14, 107, 136–74
    and control of mergers, 186–87, 195
    criteria for identifying dominance,
        74
    current position, 13–14, 150–3
    Department of Trade and Industry
        (DTI)
        1988 Green paper
        and Article 85, 148

and Article 86, 188
exemptions contained, 145–6
on mergers, 172–3
1989 White Paper, 136, 148–9
1992 Green Paper, on Abuse of
Market Power, 65, 74, 105,
114, 136, 159
1993 preferred option, 161–2
and non-collusive oligopoly, 114
Secretary of State
executive power, 153
power to refer mergers, 164,
165
law, exemptions regarding vertical
restrictions/gateways, 58
legislation
Competition Act 1980, 144, 152,
160
Fair Trading Act 1973, 64–5,
150–1, 161, 164–5
provisions and procedure,
143–4, 151–2
public interest, 157–8, 169
modification to conform with
Article 86, 159–63
Resale Prices Act 1964, effect, 177
Restrictive Trade Practices Act
1956, 141
Restrictive Trade Practices Act
1976, 145
and Merger Control Regulation, 117
mergers
policy on, 163–74
pre–1965 attitude, 23
Monopolies and Mergers
Commission (MMC), 64,
112, 152, 153–7, 199
analytical framework, 88–91,
155–7
criteria, and market definition,
77–8
evolution, 140–1, 142
investigations

Cat and Dog Foods, 155, 156,
199
Ford Motor Company, 90, 155,
156–7, 192, 194, 199
Household Detergents, 53,
182, 199
procedure, 165–6
1965–79 statistics, 143
Office of Fair Trading, 143, 146–7,
167, 191–2
and oligopoly, 132, 184, 185
restrictive agreements, 145–150
time limits, 124
United States
current practice, theoretical
background, 78–80
and Merger Control Regulation, 118
Merger Guidelines, 69, 78–80, 83,
129
and concentration indices, 86–7
and Landes-Posner formula, 88
use of Herfindahl-Hirschman
index, 131–2
new laissez-faire economics, 19–20
Sherman Antitrust Act 1890, 64
Supreme Court, monopoly,
defined, 65

Varta/Bosch (EEC report), 132–3,
185, 198
VBBB/VBVB (CJEC case), 95, 100–1,
197
vertical agreements, 56–8, 176–81
vertical independence, 77
vertical integration, 46
vertical mergers, 61

water, mineral, and *Nestlé/Perrier*,
133–4
welfare, aggregate, 180
Woodpulp (CJEC case), 96, 113, 184
and price determination, 33, 51, 197